WORDS TO GOD, WORD FROM GOD

The psalms challenge and sustain us in a number of ways, and in times of new challenges to the very fabric of the church, to its faith, and its values, we need to re-examine these ancient prayers and songs.

Words to God, Word from God explores the place and function of the psalms in Christian prayer, preaching, and worship. Examining the dual nature of the psalms as both words to God and word from God, the author brings together the historical experience of the church, biblical studies and theological reflection to focus on the application of the psalms in contemporary Christian life. A number of individual psalms are explored in terms of what they have to say about prayer or what theological issues they raise for contemporary life. This book encourages a reclamation of the psalms in the private and public prayers of the church and in the preaching of the word.

*To the memory of my father, Maurice Roy Wallace
and the grandson he never knew,
Manjit Singh*

Words to God, Word from God

The Psalms in the Prayer and Preaching of the Church

HOWARD NEIL WALLACE
Melbourne College of Divinity, Australia

ASHGATE

New Revised Standard Version Bible, copyright 1989, Division of Christian Education of the National Council of the Churches of Christ in the United States of America. Used by permission. All rights reserved.

Published by
Ashgate Publishing Limited
Gower House
Croft Road
Aldershot
Hampshire GU11 3HR
England

Ashgate Publishing Company
Suite 420
101 Cherry Street
Burlington, VT 05401-4405
USA

Ashgate website: http://www.ashgate.com

British Library Cataloguing in Publication Data
Wallace, Howard N.
  Words to God, word from God : the psalms in the prayer and preaching of the church
  1. Bible. O.T. Psalms – Criticism, interpretation, etc.
  2. Bible. O.T. Psalms – Liturgical use 3. Prayer
  I. Title
  223.2'06

Library of Congress Cataloging-in-Publication Data
Wallace, Howard N., 1948–
  Words to God, word from God : the Psalms in the prayer, and preaching of
the church / Howard N. Wallace.—1st ed.
      p. cm.
  Includes bibliographical references and index.
  ISBN 0-7546-3691-7 (hardcover : alk. paper)—ISBN 0-7546-3692-5 (pbk. : alk. paper)
  1. Bible. O.T. Psalms—Criticism, interpretation, etc. I. Title

BS1430.52.W35 2004
223'.26—dc22

2004015914

ISBN 0 7546 3691 7 HBK
ISBN 0 7546 3692 5 PBK

Printed and bound in Great Britain by TJ International Ltd, Padstow, Cornwall

Contents

Preface

The earliest experience of the psalms that I can remember was in my late teens. I had not been brought up in a church home so I was not familiar with very many Scripture passages. It was only when I became involved in a Methodist youth group, and fell under the influence of the congregation's stress on Bible study, the need for personal prayer and commitment to Christ, that Scripture, and the psalms in particular, became a part of my life.

I remember that in worship services each week a psalm portion would be read from the back of the Methodist Hymn book. The reading was done responsively. I understood little about why we read a psalm in each service, and why we read it in this funny way. My non-church background was part of the reason that I understood little about what we did. But another part of the reason was that the congregation I belonged to gave little public thought or attention to why we read the psalms in services and why we did it that way. Clearly many people in the congregation cherished the psalms and knew them well. They could respond to the reading of them in worship in a personal way. But I do not remember anything being said or done in their public reading that was meant to help the congregation speak the words of the psalm with genuine feeling, or engage the sentiments or ideas put forward, or see new meaning in them. What I remember most was the tediousness of the exercise, the monotone nature of the readings, and the lack of real engagement other than maybe at an individual, private level.

I regret that my earliest experience of the psalms was like that. As I look back from a broader Christian perspective I now understand why we read the psalms in that particular way. I also now know that the psalms have been one of the mainstays of the Church and individual Christians throughout the centuries and that they continue to offer words to sustain us in faith. My early experience did very little to help me hear the words afresh or let me engage in some significant way with them. The psalms do challenge and sustain us in a number of ways, and in times of strong and new challenges to the very fabric of the Church, to its faith and its values, we need to re-examine these ancient prayers and songs, along with other elements that have been the foundations of Christian piety and faith.

One of the ways the psalms challenge us is in terms of religious language, the way we express matters and feelings of faith. Sometimes it can be our experience that the language we use to speak to God in worship and what we are taught about faith and God is at odds with who we are as people in our experience and feelings. Yet it seems that the psalms do not participate in any charade when it comes to speaking to or about God and life experience. They challenge us to let our prayer and praise be consonant with our experience and our feelings.

The psalms also challenge us in terms of the discipline of prayer. I struggled with this issue for a long time. The congregation I was in as a teenager taught me that prayer and Bible study did indeed involve discipline, but it so easily became the case that the discipline itself was more important than the prayer or encounter with the Biblical text. It was a discipline which took little account of who I was, how I thought, or what I experienced. I learned a lot about faith within the parameters of that discipline, but it was often the case that faithfulness was expressed through discipline rather than the discipline being shaped by the faith and serving to nourish the latter.

I do not believe that the psalms would want to leave us in that quandary. Whether individually or as a collection, they draw us into a discipline that both fosters faith and prayer, and encourages their expression in all circumstances. As traditional prayers and songs of the Church, the psalms contain words that let us, as communities or individuals, express who we are before God. They keep us talking to God in the whole of our lives and about the whole of our lives. They encourage dialogue with God, especially at times when experience rubs hard up against hopes and expectations.

The psalms also challenge us in our understanding of prayer. They invite us to pray and to grow and develop in prayer. They also invite us to recognise that prayer – in the form of dialogue and meditation – is a part of life and a potentially greater part than we sometimes recognise.

I have spoken mostly about prayer to this point. The psalms are prayers and have been a core element in the prayers of Judaism and the Church for 2000 years or more and they still have a role to play in both our private and corporate prayer and spirituality, and in pastoral care as much as it involves prayer. But the psalms are also part of Scripture, part of the word of God to God's people. Their place in Scripture has always had an element of uncertainty attached to it, especially around the question of whether the psalms function in the same way as the rest of Scripture. The fact is that the psalms have always played an important theological and educative role in the life of the Church. They are prayers, but their usefulness does not stop with our praying them. They also demand from us a listening ear.

The psalms have been used in the life and worship of both Christians and Jews as far back as we are able to gauge. They have been used by countless faithful people over the centuries both as a source for their hymnody and in their conversation with God. There is something of a revival of psalm singing going on in the Church at present. That needs to be accompanied by a renewal of the study of and use of the psalms in other contexts. It is my hope that the discussion below will stimulate the reader's thoughts about the psalms and allow her or him to see the psalms in new ways as an important resource within ministry.

Let me close with some words from Psalm 102:

> [18] Let this be recorded for a generation to come,
>   so that a people yet unborn may praise the LORD:
> [19] that he looked down from his holy height,
>   from heaven the LORD looked at the earth,
> [20] to hear the groans of the prisoners,
>   to set free those who were doomed to die;
> [21] so that the name of the LORD may be declared in Zion,

and his praise in Jerusalem,
 [22] when peoples gather together,
  and kingdoms, to worship the LORD.

It remains to thank those who have contributed to this book in many different ways. A number of my colleagues have read portions of this work and given constructive criticism. They include Patrick Miller, Robert Gribben, Mark Brett, Wes Campbell, Graeme Griffin, Charles Sherlock, Chris Willcock, and my friend and golf partner Peter Blackwood. In the last case many a good conversation about the psalms has been punctuated by a bad shot from the rough. My thanks also go to my wife Bronwyn, who kindly read the whole of the manuscript and indicated where corrections were needed. Any remaining errors are my responsibility.

Abbreviations

BibBh	*Bible Bhashyam*, Kottayam, India
CBQ	*Catholic Biblical Quarterly*
DJD	Discoveries in the Judean Desert
HSS	Harvard Semitic Studies
JBCE	Joint Board of Christian Education, Melbourne
Jeev	*Jeevadhara*, Kottayam, India
JSOT	*Journal for the Study of the Old Testament*
JSOTSup	Journal for the Study of the Old Testament, Supplementary volume
LXX	Septuagint
NIBC	New International Biblical Commentary
NRSV	New Revised Standard Version
RCL	Revised Common Lectionary
REB	Revised English Bible
SAP	Sheffield Academic Press
SBLDS	Society of Biblical Literature Dissertation Series
ZAW	*Zeitschrift für die Alttestamentliche Wissenschaft*

PART I
INTRODUCTION

Chapter 1

The Dual Role of the Psalms
in the Church

This is the secret of the Psalms. Our identity is hidden in them. In them we find ourselves, and God. In these fragments He has revealed not only Himself to us but ourselves to Him.

Thomas Merton[1]

Introduction

Throughout its life the Church has maintained two equally important traditions relating to the psalms. One has to do with the use of psalms in prayer and song to God. The other concerns the use of the psalms for the instruction and guidance of the faithful. The crux at the heart of this matter is theological. Should the psalms be understood more in terms of human words to God, or as God's word to humans? Or are they both at the same time? Over the centuries this issue has been expressed in different ways, with different answers given. At times uncertainty, or even a difference of opinion, has been evident. Both consciously and unconsciously, it has affected the Church in its day-to-day life, from the construction of lectionaries for the public reading of scripture, to how individuals and communities have shaped their prayers to God.

What, then, are the origins of these two traditions and how have they developed in the Western Church? We do not need to give a full historical picture here, but by focusing on key events, individuals, and attitudes up to the time of the Reformation, we can see the particular issues involved. To extend the following survey beyond this would result in repetition of the same or similar understandings and uses of the psalms, and simply track the waxing and waning of the traditions. The survey will also show that each of the traditions has received from the Church as a whole due weight over time. Although individuals or groups at particular points in the Church's life have, from time to time and from place to place, favoured one tradition over the other, in the long term a degree of balance has been struck.

---

[1] In his diary as a young monk: Merton, T. (1956), *The Sign of Jonas*, Image Books, New York, p. 248.

The Psalms in Israel

We do not know a lot of the details of worship and liturgy in ancient Israel, let alone the way the psalms were used, but we can make some basic points. We read in the psalms: 'Worship the LORD with gladness; come into his presence with singing' (Ps 100:2) and 'Hear my prayer, O LORD; let my cry come to you' (Ps 102:1). There is mention of singing or instrumental accompaniment in some psalm headings or within the psalms themselves (e.g. Pss 6:1; 9:2; 27:6; 54:1 etc.). Some psalms could indicate different speakers uttering different sections of the psalm. Psalm 136 reads:

> [1] O give thanks to the LORD, for he is good,
>   **for his steadfast love endures forever.**
> [2] O give thanks to the God of gods,
>   **for his steadfast love endures forever.**
> [3] O give thanks to the Lord of lords,
>   **for his steadfast love endures forever;**
> [4] who alone does great wonders,
>   **for his steadfast love endures forever;**

The repetition of the second line, which runs through the whole psalm, suggests that a responsorial or antiphonal pattern might have been used for this psalm. However, beyond this sort of information we have few details in the Book of Psalms on how they were sung or prayed. The Books of Chronicles give us glimpses of post-exilic worship and indicate the use of choirs for psalm singing (1 Chron 16:7, 41-42). These choirs were groups of Levite priests serving in the temple. They were designated by their ancestral names of Asaph, Heman and Jeduthun. The first two of these are mentioned in the Book of Psalms. Psalm 150 also gives some indication of the types of instruments that may have been used to accompany psalm singing. Thus, Israel appears to have spoken or sung the psalms to God, at least as part of its worship.

As well as speaking to God in psalms, the people of Israel heard the voice of God speaking to them in various ways in those very same psalms. We can also trace this back to a time before the psalms were accepted as part of the canon of Scripture. 1 Chron 25:1-8 records the appointment of groups of Levites, whom we noted above sang psalms in worship, 'to prophesy with lyres, harps, and cymbals' (v. 1). Verse 6 makes it clear that these people served in relation to the music in the temple, but their duty is referred to as 'prophesying.' The verb that occurs here is also used for prophets elsewhere. Clearly, the task of the temple musicians was not only to offer hymns to God in temple services, but also to help in the mediation of the divine message to the people. This is further suggested by verses 7 and 8 where we find mention of both teacher and pupil casting lots for their duties, as well as references to training and discipline. In temple worship the casting of lots was associated with the determination of the divine will by the priests and Levites. The connection of divination with the role of temple musicians, as well as that of priests, indicates the importance of temple music and the need for it to be in accord with divine order. It would, therefore, seem that the psalms which the musicians sang were understood not only as offerings of prayers and songs to God, but also as words from God, and hence standing in continuity with other forms of prophecy or divinely inspired words to humans. Thus, already in their earliest use the psalms fulfilled a dual role, as both words to God and words from God; words to be said as well as words to be heard.

The Psalms in the New Testament

In the very early Church the psalms gained much more prominence in their function as words to be heard and listened to, than in their function as words to say to God. As far as we can tell from the New Testament evidence this seems to have been the case. While the psalms were part of the liturgical life of the early Church, much more weight is given in the New Testament to their role in the development of the theological thinking of the Church as it went about the task of understanding the life and work of Jesus.

Only a few New Testament passages speak of the role of psalms as words spoken or sung to God in worship. In Col 3:16-17 and Eph 5:19 there is mention of singing psalms although in both places 'psalms' are linked with 'hymns and spiritual songs'. Clearly, psalms were not the only songs offered in worship. The same situation probably holds for the mention of 'psalm' (NRSV 'hymn'; the Greek is *psalmos*) in 1 Cor 14:26. The question of which psalms or how many from the canonical collection were used is difficult to answer. It may well have been only a small number.[2] We could draw the same conclusion in relation to the use of psalms in prayer, although it is clear that some psalm forms and their words influenced the prayer of the early Church. We can see this in some New Testament writings, e.g. the Magnificat (Luke 1:46-55; cf. 1 Samuel 2 and Psalm 113), the Song of Zechariah (Luke 1:68-75), and the Song of Simeon (Luke 2:29-32).

In contrast to this situation, there is a good deal of evidence in the New Testament for the important role the psalms played in preaching and teaching. They were understood as part of the word of God in prophecy and possibly played a greater role as readings in the ministry of the word in early Christian liturgy, than they did as part of prayer or praise.[3] In over half of the citations or allusions to the psalms in the New Testament, we see them used in the context of preaching and teaching. Paul frequently made use of the psalms in his letters, either to build his arguments or to support them. For example, in Romans 3 he employed material from various psalms on seven occasions.[4] While Jesus is reported to use the psalms in his own general teaching on only a few occasions, e.g. Luke 23:46 (Ps 31:5), in

---

[2] Cf. Bradshaw, P. (1995), *Two Ways of Praying*, Abingdon, Nashville, p. 75.
[3] Bradshaw, P. (1981), *Daily Prayer in the Early Church: A Study of the Origin and Early Development of the Divine Office*, SPCK, London, p. 43.
[4] The following psalms are used in Romans 3: Pss 5:9 (v. 13); 10:7 (v. 14); 14:1-3 (vv. 10-12); 36:1 (v. 18); 51:4 (v. 4); 116:11 (v. 4); and 140:3 (v. 13).

many places he is portrayed using the words of various psalms to speak about himself.[5] It is often through such quotations or allusions that the New Testament writers interpret the life and work of Jesus. They see the psalms either as prophecy fulfilled by Jesus (e.g. Matt 13:34-35) or as texts understood fully in the sayings and events of Jesus' life (e.g. Jn 2:16-17). These instances can be summed up by the statement in Luke 24:44 'Jesus says "These are the words I spoke to you while I was yet with you, that all things must be fulfilled that are within the Law of Moses and the Prophets and the Psalms concerning me".'

New Testament writers used a number of psalms to interpret the life and work of Jesus.[6] These included some which had been interpreted by a number of 1st century CE Jewish sects as messianic, but were not limited to that group. Early Christians did not simply apply an earlier Jewish messianic interpretation of psalms to Jesus. Rather, the experience of Jesus and the events at the end of his life gave rise to Christian messianic interpretation of many psalms. The two most important psalms for the interpretation of the end of Jesus' life were Psalms 22 and 118. The former was used in particular to interpret the passion of Jesus, especially in the Gospels of Matthew and Mark,[7] while Ps 118:22-26 are quoted or alluded to in a number of places.[8]

The Psalms in the History of the Church [9]

In the centuries following the New Testament period, considerable developments in the two traditions relating to the psalms took place. Moreover, they became more intricately connected. The New Testament tradition of Christians gathering for meals and individuals singing psalms and songs continued. Until recently it had been assumed that early Christian singing of psalms continued a practice of the Jewish Synagogue. However, a 'new consensus' has emerged which argues that it was not until the fourth century, after the more official recognition of Christianity under the emperor Constantine, that the shape of daily and weekly prayer and worship stabilized with the singing of psalms holding a firm place in that. According to this 'new consensus' that there was little singing of psalms in Christian worship before the third century, with newly composed hymns being favoured. The scant New Testament evidence for psalm singing noted above would

---

[5] E.g. Matt 21:16 (Ps 8:2 LXX); 21:42 (Ps 118:22-23).

[6] E.g. Ps 2:1-2 is quoted in Acts 4:25-26; Ps 2:7 in Acts 13:32; Ps 110:1 in Matt 22:44 (= Mark 12:36, Luke 20:42-3), Heb 1:13 etc.

[7] Ps 22:1 in Matt 27:46, Mark 15:34; Ps 22:7 in Matt 27:39, Mark 15:29; Ps 22:8 in Matt 27:43; and Ps 22:19 in Matt 27:35, Mark 15:24 (cf. Luke 23:34 and John 15:24). Also cf. Ps 22:18 in John 19:24 and Ps 22:22 in Heb 2:12.

[8] Ps 118:22-23 in Matt 21:42, Acts 4:11, and 1 Pet 2:7; and Ps 118: 25-26 in Matt 21:9, Mark 11:9, Luke 19:38.

[9] For more extensive summaries of the periods to follow see Bradshaw, *Two Ways of Praying,* esp. ch. 5, 'Psalms and Prayer', pp. 73-87, and Shepherd, M.H. (1976), *The Psalms in Christian Worship: A Practical Guide,* Augsburg, Minneapolis.

seem to favour this position. Furthermore, some early Christian writers on hymnody are ambiguous to say the least in what they say. For example, in the late second or early third century Tertullian, in a statement similar to 1 Cor 14:26, speaks of Christians bringing to gatherings a 'hymn' (and the Greek is *psalmos*). This could refer to either a scriptural or non-scriptural song.[10] A major factor in bringing about a change in this position was the growing popularity of heretical hymns, especially Gnostic hymns, in the second century. In order to combat this, the singing of biblical psalms was promoted. Some modification to this 'new consensus' could be made by suggesting that, while there were many hymns composed and sung at early Christian gatherings, the singing of biblical psalms should not entirely be ruled out.

The singing of psalms became a part of 'cathedral' worship by the end of the fourth century.[11] As the daily office developed in the cathedrals, some psalms became associated with particular attitudes or times of day. For example, in many places verses from Psalm 51, especially v. 15, 'O Lord, open my lips, and my mouth will declare your praise,' were used as the opening prayer of the day, while Psalm 104 was associated with the evening because of vv. 19-23:

> [19] You have made the moon to mark the seasons;
> > the sun knows its time for setting.
> [20] You make darkness, and it is night,
> > when all the animals of the forest come creeping out.
> [21] The young lions roar for their prey,
> > seeking their food from God.
> [22] When the sun rises, they withdraw
> > and lie down in their dens.
> [23] People go out to their work
> > and to their labor until the evening.

Psalms 148-150 became the central element of the morning office everywhere. These psalms were often repeated on a daily basis as part of the prayer of the community.

The function of the psalms as words to be heard in teaching, preaching, and theology was strengthened over the first three centuries of the Christian era. Those who support the 'new consensus' mentioned above would argue that the primary role of the psalms in early Christian worship was as readings. In this context the psalms continued to play a major role in the interpretation of the person and work of Jesus, although they were also used when discussing issues such as God, the Church, and humankind. They played a part in debates about moral and social issues, and were influential in devotional and liturgical practices.

---

[10] *Apology*, ch. xxxix, in A. Roberts and J. Donaldson (n.d., reprint 1989), *The Ante-Nicene Fathers. Vol. III Latin Christianity: Its founder, Tertullian, Vol. I.* Eerdmans, Grand Rapids, p. 47.
[11] Bradshaw, *Two Ways of Praying*, p. 76.

In daily worship some psalm verses were used as a simple congregational response. P. Bradshaw argues this developed from what he has called a 'paracletic ministry of the word', by which he means the use of selected readings to meet the spiritual needs of the congregation and to encourage them in their faith.[12] Thus, we start to see an interweaving of the traditions of the psalms as words said to God, and words heard as instruction or encouragement. Bradshaw writes that in the cathedral tradition '… in spite of their role as hymns or prayers, the psalms still function in a way as God's word addressed to human beings, not just as the words of human beings addressed to God.'[13]

Many in the early Church understood the Old Testament writings in general as predictions concerning Christ. They perceived the relationship between the testaments largely in terms of prophecy and fulfilment. They dealt with the psalms in exactly the same way as they dealt with other Old Testament texts. For example, in the mid-second century Justin Martyr constructed his *Dialogue with Trypho*, a lengthy piece of Christian apologetic, as a response to Trypho, a Jew, who approaches Justin seeking his philosophy and opinion about God. Justin employs many passages from the Old Testament, treating the psalms, which are among the most frequently cited texts, in the same way as he does other texts.[14]

Later theologians continued to see the psalms as a source for Christian doctrine and theology, as in the case of Athanasius (c. 295-373 CE), especially in his *Letter to Marcellinus*, a sick friend.[15] Athanasius thought of Israel's history, as represented in the psalms, as an allegory for the Christian life. This was further interpreted in relation to Christ. Thus, he understood the psalms both in terms of prophecy relating to Christ and as words relating to the Christian life. He wrote to Marcellinus that the psalms were not like other Scripture which contained the words of others. The psalms contained prophecies about the future but they were also words that could be taken as one's own.[16] He said that in other books of the Bible, one learns what one should or should not do, about the coming saviour, and about the deeds of the kings and saints,

> But in the Book of Psalms, the one who heard, in addition to learning these things, also comprehends and is taught in it the emotions of the soul, … Therefore through hearing it, it teaches not only to disregard passion, but also how one must heal passion through speaking and acting.[17]

Allowing for Athanasius' distrust of passion and emotion, he is arguing that one not only learns of the sacred story and law in the psalms but of our response to that and how the faithful should live their life. Learning and praying, hearing and

---

[12] Bradshaw, *Daily Prayer in the Early Church*, p. 153.

[13] Bradshaw, *Two Ways of Praying*, p. 77.

[14] See Falls, T.B. (1948), *Writings of Saint Justin Martyr*, in *The Fathers of the Church: A New Translation*, Vol. 6, The Catholic University of America, Washington, pp. 147-366.

[15] Gregg, R.C. (ed.) (1980), *Athanasius: The Life of Antony and The Letter to Marcellinus*, SPCK, London, pp. 101-130.

[16] *Letter to Marcellinus*, §§ 10-11, *ibid.*, pp. 108-110.

[17] *Ibid.*, p. 108.

saying, are thus both involved in the use of the psalms. While Athanasius stressed that one of the problems with singing the psalms was that it could just be for the music, he nevertheless thought it advantageous for several reasons.[18] In his view the psalms are sung for the benefit of the believer and their belief. Thus, Athanasius has a sophisticated understanding of the psalms, as both word from God, and available for us to take up as our word to God.

As the Church's traditions developed, the performance of the psalms responsorially became more frequent. A cantor would sing each verse and the congregation respond with a refrain. The refrain was effectively the congregation's praise in response to hearing the word of the psalm. St John Chrysostom, whose life spanned the fourth and fifth centuries, stressed that the response should be made in the spirit of having genuinely heard the word sung:

> Do not think that you have come here simply to say the words, but when you make the response, consider that response to be a covenant. For when you say, 'Like the hart desires the watersprings, my soul desires you, O God', you make a covenant with God. You have signed a contract without paper or ink, you have confessed with your voice that you love him more than all, that you prefer nothing to him, and that you burn with love for him.[19]

The situation in the early monastic tradition of daily worship was a little different. Monastic prayer was intended initially to encourage spiritual growth, so the whole collection of psalms, which was interpreted in relation to Christ, was used in worship over time. This was the case both in informal worship and at regular times of prayer. During the latter, a psalm would be read or chanted by one person while others listened. After a period of silence for personal reflection, a prayer was said, followed by the Lord's Prayer or a collect. The next psalm was then read. Sometimes responsorial or antiphonal chanting would be used for the reading.[20] The prayer which followed the silence became the ancestor of the psalm-collect, a short prayer which took up a verse or phrase from the psalm and gave it a Christian interpretation.[21] The fact that monks were often required to learn the psalms by heart, and that the Book of Psalms was a focus for early commentaries, meant that they could not but help hear the words of the psalms in daily worship.

Through the middle ages, as monastic orders adopted the cathedral understanding of the offices, there was a fusing of traditions in relation to the psalms. The monastic principle of the use of the whole collection of psalms with its christological interpretation was combined with the cathedral concept of the psalms as the Church's hymns of praise. According to Bradshaw, several consequences flowed from this. He says that this fusion

---

[18] *Letter to Marcellinus*, §§ 27-29, *ibid.*, pp. 123-126.

[19] Exposition on Ps. 41:5. Quoted in Bradshaw, *Two Ways of Praying*, p. 77.

[20] *Ibid.*, pp. 78-79.

[21] This practice has recently reappeared, for example, in Theology and Worship Ministry Unit for the Presbyterian Church (U.S.A.) and the Cumberland Presbyterian Church (1993, 1995), *Book of Common Worship*, Westminster John Knox, Louisville.

... resulted in the belief that it was the chanting of the psalm itself – rather than the response made to the verses – that glorified God, so that the psalms ceased to be seen as God's word addressed to the worshippers and were viewed instead as the voice of the church to God.[22]

In addition, antiphonal psalmody changed so that it became a system of two choirs chanting alternate verses with the virtual loss of the refrain. The period for silent reflection disappeared and the *Gloria Patri* ('Glory to the Father ...') was added as a doxology at the end of the antiphonal psalm. Bradshaw concludes: 'In short, the psalms were no longer used *in* Christian prayer but *as* Christian prayer.'[23] The principle of hearing the psalms as word of God, which had been a strong part of daily prayer in the monastic tradition, but also present in the cathedral tradition, was overtaken to a large degree by an understanding of the psalms as the Church's praise. Saying the psalms in the form of hymns and prayers began to dominate western worship and spirituality.

On the other hand, the understanding of the psalms as prophecy, especially in relation to Jesus Christ, persisted through the middle ages, especially in the areas of theology and commentary. For example, Gilbert of Poitiers, the first serious scholastic commentator on psalms, writing between 1110 and 1117 C.E., was interested in developing a systematic theology out of the psalms. This contrasted with the devotional approach toward the psalms of monastic exegetes. He also saw the psalms speaking about Christ.[24] Peter Lombard, building on the work of Gilbert and others, saw David as a prophet and evangelist, inspired by the Holy Spirit and foretelling the coming of Christ and the Church. He sought to work out from the psalms an ethical and dogmatic theology on the nature of Christ, human nature, and related topics.[25]

In terms of hearing the psalms and using them in preaching and teaching, there was little change in this general position among some of the reformers. Erasmus, like the Church Fathers before him, saw each psalm as a prophecy of Christ,[26] however, John Calvin, in the introduction to his commentary on the psalms, shifted the emphasis away from this. The psalms became much more for him instruction to us on how to pray, praise God and conduct our lives.[27] He wrote eloquently on the way the psalms portray the fullness of the life of the godly

---

[22] *Two Ways of Praying*, p. 80.

[23] *Ibid.*

[24] See Colish, M.L. (1992), '*Psalterium scholasticorum*: Peter Lombard and the Emergence of Scholastic Psalms Exegesis,' *Speculum*, Vol 67/3, pp. 531-548, esp. pp. 536-538.

[25] *Ibid.*, 539-548.

[26] Heath, M.J. (1991), 'Allegory, Rhetoric and Spirituality: Erasmus's Early Psalm Commentaries,' in A. Dalzell et al. (eds), *Acta Conventus Neo-Latini Torontonensis: Proceedings of the Seventh International Congress of Neo-Latin Studies*, Medieval and Renaissance Texts and studies, Birmingham, pp. 363-370, esp. p. 369.

[27] Calvin, J. (1845-9), *Commentary on the Book of Psalms*, trans. J. Anderson, Calvin Translation Society, Edinburgh. See also Mays, J.L. (1990), 'Calvin's Commentary on the Psalms: The Preface as Introduction,' in T. George (ed.), *John Calvin and the Church: A Prism of Reform*, Westminster/John Knox, Louisville, pp. 195-204.

person. He saw the writers describing their own experiences and feelings in such a way as to draw the reader into an examination of their own circumstance. He wrote of the psalms:

> But here the Prophets themselves, seeing they are exhibited to us as speaking to God, and laying open all their inmost thoughts and affections, call, or rather draw, each of us to the examination of himself in particular, in order that none of the many infirmities to which we are subject, and of the many vices of which we abound, may remain concealed.[28]

He goes on to say that since a principal way to find safety is to call on God, and that since there can be no 'better and more unerring rule' in this than the psalms, it follows 'that in proportion to the proficiency which a man shall have attained in understanding (the psalms), will be his knowledge of the most important part of celestial doctrine.'[29] In other words, the psalms are a key to developing statements of faith. Later he speaks of an 'infallible rule' prescribed in the psalms for directing the faithful in giving praise to God.[30]

In Geneva, developments took place in the use of psalms in worship that were of great importance. These developments influenced the place of the psalms in worship and spirituality in the reformed tradition as it evolved over the following centuries, in Europe, Great Britain, North America and elsewhere. While in the medieval mass, the congregation had sung verses from the psalms at most, in Geneva the singing of whole or large portions of psalms was promoted. The gathered congregation sang and not just the choir, so there was a shift in focus back toward the congregation as the worshipping community. Moreover, the singing was in the vernacular and not Latin. An additional major change was in the use of metrical reworkings of the psalm texts rather than the psalms themselves. These changes led to an increased use of the psalms by the faithful outside of the liturgy, and a consequent blurring of the distinction between liturgy and life, worship and work. They also contributed to a spirituality of the word. The music that accompanied the psalms played the important role in opening the Scripture up to the laity. Through singing they gained an intimate knowledge of the psalms, which became a part of daily thought and prayer.[31]

While Calvin notes that the psalms are in the form of words to God, and concentrates his remarks on the potential influence of the psalms upon an individual's prayer and manner of life, his comments on the psalms portray a more complex approach. Not only are the psalms 'replete with all the precepts which serve to frame our life to every part of holiness, piety, and righteousness' but also in the psalms 'there is nothing wanting which relates to the knowledge of eternal

---

[28] Calvin, *Commentary on the Book of Psalms*, p. xxxvii.

[29] *Ibid.*

[30] *Ibid.*, p. xxxviii.

[31] Witvliet, J.D. (1998), 'Spirituality of the Psalter: Metrical Psalms and liturgy and Life in Calvin's Geneva,' in D. Foxgrover (ed.), *Calvin and Spirituality and Calvin and his Contemporaries*, Calvin Studies Society Papers, 1995, 1997, Calvin Studies Society, Grand Rapids, pp. 93-117, esp. pp. 116-117.

salvation.'[32] He speaks of them as containing an 'unerring' and 'infallible' rule, as a source for understanding 'celestial doctrine', and of their authors as 'prophets'. He describes a situation in which the psalms speak with similar authority and effect to the rest of Scripture. This view echoes in many ways the earlier view of Athanasius.

We should also note Martin Luther's assertion about the prophetic function of the Davidic psalms. Luther, like many before him, saw the psalms as prophetic texts concerning Christ.[33] He argued that, in terms of being inspired by the Holy Spirit in his prophecy regarding Christ, David even surpassed the other prophets. On the basis of David's last words in 2 Sam 23:1-4, Luther argued that David spoke with 'great presumption and unique boasting beyond all prophets'. While other prophets said 'The word of the Lord came to me', David in his last words proclaimed 'His word was spoken by me.' Luther concluded:

> With this expression he indicates some extremely intimate and friendly kind of inspiration. Other prophets confess that they spoke, but this one declares that in a unique way it was not he who spoke but the Spirit who spoke through him. Although the Spirit spoke by all the prophets, as we sing, it is not stated thus regarding him.[34]

Luther had no doubt that the psalms were the inspired word of God. Nor did he gloss over the fact that the psalms are in the form of human words to God. He sought to maintain the balance, also expressed in Athanasius and Calvin, that the psalms are both divine and human words. Luther went to great pains in one preface to his lectures on the psalms, to stress the need to 'sing the psalms with the mind' as well as with the voice.[35] So for him, and many others both before and after, the psalms were not only words for the prayers of the faithful, but were also to be understood as part of the total prophetic witness in Scripture, as God's word to the people. They were there to be heard as well as said.

Not just a Christian Issue

It has not only been Christians who have been concerned about the status and nature of the psalms. In medieval times Jews debated two questions relating to the psalms. These questions, while set in a different context, bore a close relationship to matters debated in the Church. The questions for Jews were these. First, were the psalms inspired and what was their subsequent standing in relation to *Torah*? Secondly, what was their intended use in worship? These two questions were inextricably bound together.

---

[32] *Ibid.*, p. xxxix.

[33] Luther, M. (1974), *First Lectures on the Psalms I: Psalms 1-75*, in H.C. Oswald (ed.), *Luther's Works*, Concordia Publishing House, St. Louis, Vol. X, p. 7.

[34] *Ibid.*, pp. 9-10. See also Luther, M. (1972), *Treatise on the last words of David*, in M.H. Bertram (ed.) *Luther's Works*, Concordia Publishing House, St. Louis, Vol XV, pp. 265-352.

[35] Luther, *First Lectures on the Psalms*, p. 3.

A number of influential Jewish commentators argued strongly against positions which said that the Prophets and the Writings, which formed the second and third sections in Jewish Scripture (or *TaNaK*), should be regarded as 'transmitted tradition,' and hence did not have the same status as *Torah*, the first section of *TaNaK*. The psalms were part of the Writings. These commentators argued for the inspired nature of the psalms and viewed the book in a position complementary to that of the *Torah* and the Prophets.[36] One of the more well known of these commentators, Saadiah Gaon (882-942 C.E.), saw the Book of Psalms as a kind of second *Torah* in which all the words were the Lord's. Most of his discussion was in the context of argument against the Jewish sect known as the Karaites. This sect, which arose in the eighth century and had many different sub-groups, generally gave pre-eminence to the teachings of Scripture, especially *Torah*, and downplayed the importance of the Oral Law promoted by the Rabbis. Some Karaite groups emphasized individual Bible Study.

Saadiah argued at length for the psalms to be considered as one of the 'revealed books ... intended for command and prohibition'.[37] The psalms were to be read for guidance in all matters of life, just as the *Torah* was read. However, he sought a sense of balance in his argument and stressed, as the Karaites also did, that the psalms should be read as a 'book of praises' as part of synagogue liturgy.[38] The Karaite view, expressed in one form in the introduction to a commentary by Salmon ben Yeruham (born c. 910),[39] held the Book of Psalms in high regard seeing in it many parallels to the *Torah*. However, according to Salmon, the psalms were unique, for while they were for edification and guidance, they were specifically for guidance 'in the commandments of praise and exaltation.'[40] Saadiah also argued against another Karaite view which said that the psalms consisted of human words, which could be used in one's own speech to God, but which were in no way divine speech.[41]

The renowned Jewish poet, biblical scholar, and philosopher, Abraham Ibn Ezra (1089-1164), wrote a commentary on the psalms in 1156.[42] In his commentary, Ibn Ezra addressed, among other things, the question of whether the psalms were prayers or prophecies. He argued against another Karaite writer, Moses Ibn Giqatilah (eleventh century C.E.), who saw the psalms as 'non-prophetic' prayers, that is, not inspired by the Holy Spirit. However, since men of lofty spiritual and religious standing wrote them, they were, nonetheless, to be read

---

[36] Simon, U. (1991), *Four Approaches to the Book of Psalms: From Saadiah Gaon to Abraham Ibn Ezra*, trans. L.J. Schramm, State University of New York, Albany, p. 205 and pp. 283-284, n. 134.

[37] Sokolow, M. (1984), 'Saadiah Gaon's Prolegomena to Psalms,' *Proceedings of the American Academy of Jewish Research*, Vol. 51, pp. 131-174, esp. p. 146.

[38] Simon, *Four Approaches to the Book of Psalms*, p. 27.

[39] Salmon apparently had a copy of Saadiah's commentary before him while writing the introduction to his own. *Ibid.*, p. 60.

[40] *Ibid.*, p. 61.

[41] Sokolow, 'Saadiah Gaon's Prolegomena to Psalms,' esp. pp. 131, 148.

[42] He had apparently penned at least fragments of an earlier one in c. 1140.

and heard for their spiritual value.[43] In response, Ibn Ezra developed a complex approach to the psalms. He classified them as 'prophetic prayer.' Along the way he discussed prayers found among the words of the written prophets. In developing this classification, he argued that there is abundant theological 'lore' to be found in these prophetic prayers.[44]

Psalms as Words to God and Word from God

The theological crux in the place of the psalms in the life of the Church is whether they should be understood more in terms of human words to God, or as God's word to humans, or both. The sketch above indicates that the Church has, historically at least, preferred the third option. The psalms have been understood and used both as words to offer to God, as well as words from God. While individuals such as Athanasius, Calvin, and Luther did not address the issue directly, they maintained an overall balance in their works between these two traditions. At other times, for example in the early development of practices of daily prayer in the Church, the balance was struck both over time and between different communities of faith. In that specific example it was achieved by the existence of the complementary approaches of the cathedral and monastic traditions.

Of course, there have been periods when the balance has been upset. On occasion the role of the psalms as word to God has dominated the Church's practice, if not its thought. This was especially the case in worship following the fusion of the two traditions in the daily office. It was also the case when the elaboration and development of the responses in the Sunday services reached the point where professional singers were needed. On the other hand, counter moves to this imbalance were struck. This was so not only in Protestant traditions, the beginnings of which are outlined above, but also within later Catholic traditions.

We will see later that current denominational and ecumenical lectionaries would prescribe the use of the psalms in Sunday worship primarily in the role of word to God. Over against this has been the recent scholarly treatment of psalms in which the psalms have been studied in much the same way as other books of Scripture. The same approaches have been used, especially form, literary, and traditio-historical criticism. There has been debate over the canonical shape of the entire Book of Psalms, asking whether the collection has been given its particular shape, in whole or in part, either to address certain historical problems or to help shape the life of one who prays the psalms. As much as this scholarly endeavour helps shape the life of the Church, it reinforces the role of the psalms as Scripture or a word from God to be heard by the community of faith. So the interplay of the two traditions goes on.

---

[43] Simon, *Four Approaches to the Book of Psalms*, pp. 126-128.
[44] *Ibid.*, pp. 189-216.

This interplay echoes the incarnational nature of God's word as proclaimed in both Jesus Christ and in Scripture – divine word enfleshed in human form, which in its human form returns to God. In the psalms this takes the specific form of human word said to God being recognized as a word to be heard from God, that it in turn might become again a human word to God. It is in this final guise that the psalms can be distinguished from other Scripture. We witness the divine grace in God's gift of words through which we might in turn speak back to God. But these same words were once those our forebears in the faith spoke to God. Part of the sustenance needed for our life in faith is found in this intimate conversation. Nevertheless, while the psalms can be distinguished from other Scripture in this way, they are also consistent with its sentiments. Isaiah states (Isa 55:10-11):

> [10] For as the rain and the snow come down from heaven,
>> and do not return there until they have watered the earth,
> making it bring forth and sprout,
>> giving seed to the sower and bread to the eater,
> [11] so shall my word be that goes out from my mouth;
>> it shall not return to me empty,
> but it shall accomplish that which I purpose,
>> and succeed in the thing for which I sent it.

The same sentiment is expressed in relation to Jesus Christ in the hymn in Phil 2:6-11:

> [6] who, though he was in the form of God,
>> did not regard equality with God
>> as something to be exploited,
> [7] but emptied himself,
>> taking the form of a slave,
>> being born in human likeness.
> And being found in human form,
> [8] he humbled himself
>> and became obedient to the point of death –
>> even death on a cross.
> [9] Therefore God also highly exalted him
>> and gave him the name
>> that is above every name,
> [10] so that at the name of Jesus
>> every knee should bend,
>> in heaven and on earth and under the earth,
> [11] and every tongue should confess
>> that Jesus Christ is Lord,
>> to the glory of God the Father.

The Apostle Paul sees the same principle embodied in the life of the Church through the work of the Spirit: 'And because you are children, God has sent the Spirit of his Son into our hearts, crying, "Abba! Father!"' (Gal 4:6)

Further questions and issues arise in light of this discussion. For example, we note that many points above turn on a hermeneutic that sees the psalms as prophecy, literally foretelling of Christ in various ways. Such a hermeneutic would not be widely accepted today. Thus, we need to consider once again how these ancient Israelite psalms relate to our Christian faith, and especially our devotion to Jesus. To address this and other matters requires further historical investigation and theological reflection. It is best to do this in the context of developing the discussion on the two traditions of the psalms in the following chapters. What I have said above clearly indicates that each of the traditions relating to the psalms has its place in the life of the Church. We need now to look in a more detailed way at the psalms as words said to God and words heard from God, and to ask how we can continue to appropriate them within the contemporary Church.

PART II
THE PSALMS AS WORDS TO GOD

Chapter 2

The Psalms as Prayers

The Psalms are given to us to this end, that we may learn to pray them in the name of Jesus Christ.

Dietrich Bonhoeffer[1]

We can use the psalms as words to God *in prayer*, be it in private prayer, public worship, or in pastoral care when we pray for or with others. But the Book of Psalms is more than just a collection of prayers. It is not just another resource for prayer to be left on the shelf until we have run out of our own words and are in need of some inspiration. As soon as we engage with this book we find ourselves not only with some words we can use to pray, but being encouraged, even invited, to be actively involved in prayer. Through the language of individual psalms, their content, their use, and in a number of other ways, we are invited to join countless faithful people in speaking to God in prayer. Regardless of the situation, be it in times of trouble, doubt, thankfulness, or joy, the psalmists invite us to: 'wait for the LORD; be strong, and let your heart take courage' (Ps 27:14); 'commit your way to the LORD; trust in him' (Ps 37:5); 'give thanks to the LORD' (Ps 106:1); 'rejoice in the LORD' (Ps 33:1); and 'sing praises to God, sing praises' (Ps 47:6).

The invitation to pray is not only given by the psalmists but is also put into the mouth of God. '"Call on me in the day of trouble", the Lord says, "I will deliver you, and you shall glorify me"' (Ps 50:15). In Ps 91:14-15 we read:

> [14] Those who love me, I will deliver;
>   I will protect those who know my name.
> [15] When they call to me, I will answer them;
>   I will be with them in trouble,
>   I will rescue them and honor them.

On occasion, the psalmists give their own response to these invitations. It is positive and involves the whole of life. In response to the call 'Praise the Lord, O my soul!' the psalmist answers in Ps 146:2 'I will praise the LORD as long as I live; I will sing praises to my God all my life long.' And in Ps 122:1 the psalmist proclaims: 'I was glad when they said to me, 'Let us go to the house of the LORD!''

---

[1] Bonhoeffer, D. (1970), *The Psalms: The Prayer Book of the Bible*, trans. J.H. Burtness, Augsburg, Minneapolis, p. 15.

But we can go one step further. The Book of Psalms not only offers words to pray, and even an invitation to pray, it teaches us how to pray. Prayer involves more than words or even a willingness to participate. Prayer, and especially the discipline of regular prayer, does not come naturally to us. We need to learn how to pray as Dietrich Bonhoeffer argued in his book, *The Psalms: The Prayer Book of the Bible*.[2] He began there by recalling the disciples' request that Jesus teach them how to pray. In response, Jesus taught them the Lord's Prayer (Luke 11:1; cf. Matt 6:5-13). Bonhoeffer stressed that it is a dangerous error to assume that the 'heart can pray by itself', for that can lead to a confusion between our feelings, wishes, sighs etc. and prayer. He said: 'Prayer does not mean simply to pour out one's heart. It means rather to find the way to God and to speak with him, whether the heart is full or empty.'[3]

The psalms take us into a world of prayer and seek to help us find our way in that world. They set before us a particular way of praying and understanding prayer. They teach us how to pray as well as offer words with which to pray. Of course, the words of prayer and the way of praying cannot be separated. The psalms are not simply a handy source of 'prayer texts', either to support our own feelings, sighs etc., or to fill our mouths with acceptable words. They have their own way of speaking to God and about God, their own shape and discipline. If we accept the psalmist's invitation to pray, we also accept an invitation to explore the riches of a particular way of praying. Our own prayer can then become richer. 'The richness of the Word of God', Bonhoeffer remarked, 'ought to determine our prayer, not the poverty of our hearts' and for him this related particularly to the words of the psalms.[4] The psalms, of course, are not the only resource for prayer. Nor is their way of praying the only way. But over two millennia of Christian tradition, they have been the life-long guide and companion in prayer to countless people of faith. They have become the backbone of the Church's prayer life. Rediscovering their usefulness, especially in church circles where they have been lost or neglected as a resource for prayer, can strengthen our prayer life greatly.

---

[2] *Ibid.* Similar remarks have been made by Guiver, G. (1988), *Company of Voices: Daily Prayer and the People of God*, SPCK, London, p. 3; and Barth, K. (1985), *Prayer*, 2nd ed., trans. S.F. Terrien, Westminster, Philadelphia, p. 26.
[3] Bonhoeffer, *Psalms*, pp. 9-10.
[4] *Ibid.*, pp. 13-16, esp. 15.

Chapter 3

The World of Prayer in the Psalms

A World of Conversations

Many Conversation Partners

What kind of world of prayer is set forth in the psalms? The first thing we can say about it is that it is a world full of conversations. Most of the psalms contain direct speech. They are 'dialogue-poems'[1] in which the psalmist is constantly speaking with another in relationship. This might not surprise us, especially if we think of prayer as speaking to God. However, if we examine the psalms carefully we discover that the conversations do not always involve the same parties nor are they on the same topic. Many different conversations are taking place and there are many participants in these conversations.

Of course, the psalmist and God are the main parties involved in these psalm conversations. In just less than half of the psalms, the psalmist addresses God directly.[2] In another major group the psalmist speaks to another party as well as to God.[3] Lament psalms, in which the psalmist or his/her community is in some difficulty, make up the greater portion of psalms in these two groups. In a third major group of psalms, which comprises almost a quarter of the collection, the psalmist speaks to parties other than God for all or the greater part of the psalm.[4] By way of contrast to the first two groups, the majority of the psalms in this third group are either hymns of praise or thanksgiving psalms. In almost all of these the

---

[1] To use a phrase of Fisch, H. (1988), *Poetry with a Purpose: Biblical Poetics and Interpretation*, Indiana Univ., Bloomington, p. 108. Similar points are made by Brueggemann, W. (1974), 'From Hurt to Joy, from Death to Life', *Interpretation*, (1974) Vol. XXVIII, pp. 3-19, esp. p. 4-5, and Balentine, S.E. (1993), *Prayer in the Hebrew Bible: The Drama of Divine-Human Dialogue*, Fortress, Minneapolis, pp. 9, 261-4.

[2] In this group of psalms the psalmist speaks either for him or herself or on behalf of the community, as indicated by use of the pronouns 'I' or 'we', 'me' or 'my'. Frequently the psalmist addresses God with 'you' or 'your' but in a number of these psalms, either in part or whole, the psalmist speaks of God in the third person (e.g. Pss 16; 18; 19, 23 etc.).

[3] The other party varies from psalm to psalm. It can be 'the enemies' (e.g. Pss 4; 6), the congregation (e.g. Pss 9-10; 46), the king (e.g. Psalm 21), the faithful (e.g. Pss 30; 31), or Israel (e.g. Psalm 131). The psalm can even include a soliloquy by the psalmist (e.g. Psalms 42-43).

[4] E.g. Pss 20; 34; 37; 47 etc. God is addressed directly in only a few hymns (Pss 8; 65; 76; 84; 104; and 145).

psalmist calls upon others to trust in God, to praise or give thanks, or debates with them about God's faithfulness etc.[5] For example, in Ps 47:5-7 we read:

[5] God has gone up with a shout,
> the LORD with the sound of a trumpet.
[6] Sing praises to God, sing praises;
> sing praises to our King, sing praises.
[7] For God is the king of all the earth;
> sing praises with a psalm.

However, even in this group, the relationship between the psalmist and God remains central. It is the key relationship within a network of relationships. Thus, in the psalms, prayer arising out of pain and distress is more often expressed in direct conversation with God. Praise of God more often has its place in the wider conversation of the community. While pain and distress require direct response, praise is more likely found in the context of public proclamation.[6]

Maintaining the Conversation

In each of these groups of psalms, the psalmist takes the responsibility for maintaining the conversation. Of course, the psalmist's words dominate the conversation, but in many psalms there is a strong sense of speech coming toward the psalmist as well as going out from him/her. That is, the psalms are fully a two-way (or multi-way) communication. This is especially the case where the words of God are quoted, sometimes at length. However, it is important to see just how the psalmist experiences this conversation. In Psalm 75 we can plot the speeches by the psalmist and God as follows:

Psalmist:
[1] We give thanks to you, O God;
> we give thanks; your name is near.
> People tell of your wondrous deeds.

God:
[2] 'At the set time that I appoint
> I will judge with equity.
[3] When the earth totters, with all its inhabitants,
> it is I who keep its pillars steady.
[4] I say to the boastful, "Do not boast,"
> and to the wicked, "Do not lift up your horn;

---

[5] The only exception is Psalm 133 in which the psalmist delights in kindred living together. Even here it is clear that faith in the Lord undergirds the psalmist's sentiment.

[6] A few psalms do not fit neatly into the three major groups. These consist either of a monologue by the psalmist (Psalm 73), or psalms in which the audience is unclear (Pss 1; 15; 111; 114; 120; and 122). Psalm 121 is unusual in being addressed mostly to the psalmist.

[5] do not lift up your horn on high,
    or speak with insolent neck.'"

Psalmist:
[6] For not from the east or from the west
    and not from the wilderness comes lifting up;
[7] but it is God who executes judgment,
    putting down one and lifting up another.
[8] For in the hand of the LORD there is a cup
    with foaming wine, well mixed;
 he will pour a draught from it,
    and all the wicked of the earth
    shall drain it down to the dregs.
[9] But I will rejoice forever;
    I will sing praises to the God of Jacob.

God:
[10] 'All the horns of the wicked I will cut off,
    but the horns of the righteous shall be exalted.'

The psalmist initiates the exchange with a proclamation of thanks to God. When God speaks, it is not in direct response to that, but rather to assert the right to declare the time of judgment of the earth. The foundation for this is God's role as creator and sustainer of the earth. None can boast before God. The psalmist's response (vv. 6-9) clearly picks up on God's statements about 'lifting up', that is exaltation, and executing judgment. When God returns to speak in v. 10, it is not in response to the psalmist, but to develop further God's own point in vv. 4-5 about the 'horn' as a sign of exaltation. In other words, the conversation is two-way but God's participation shows an independence that is not there for the psalmist. Moreover, God's word in the conversation is a proclamation of God's own sovereignty.

In other psalms where God is quoted at length the word 'spoken' by God can be a reaffirmation of God as the one who brings justice for the poor and needy (Ps 12:5-6), the declaration of God as one bound to the people by covenant (Ps 50:5) and hence justified in judgment of the people (vv. 7-23), a recall of events from Israel's past (Pss 81:6-16; 95:8-11), or some promise from the past relevant to the current situation (Pss 60:6-8 = 108:7-9; 68:22-23). Psalm 132 is a clear example where the promise has been made to the Davidic dynasty:

[11] The LORD swore to David a sure oath
    from which he will not turn back:
 'One of the sons of your body
    I will set on your throne.
[12] If your sons keep my covenant
    and my decrees that I shall teach them,
 their sons also, forevermore,

shall sit on your throne.'
[13] For the LORD has chosen Zion;
 he has desired it for his habitation:
[14] 'This is my resting place forever;
 here I will reside, for I have desired it.
[15] I will abundantly bless its provisions;
 I will satisfy its poor with bread.
[16] Its priests I will clothe with salvation,
 and its faithful will shout for joy.
[17] There I will cause a horn to sprout up for David;
 I have prepared a lamp for my anointed one.
[18] His enemies I will clothe with disgrace,
 but on him, his crown will gleam.'

The psalmist thus hears God's voice in the conversation in terms of promises made in the past, in events from the past when God has acted for the people, or in terms of basic understandings of who God is in relation to the people or to creation as a whole. The conversation is a genuine dialogue, although each conversation partner speaks in a different way.

Difficulty arises, however, when the psalmist is acutely aware that the conversation has become thoroughly one-sided, and senses not just a lack of response from God, but total silence. The psalmist may see this as an expression of God's anger (e.g. Ps 89:46). In several cases, he/she sees it as an unjust act on God's part. For example in Psalm 44 we read:

[8] In God we have boasted continually,
 and we will give thanks to your name forever.
[9] Yet you have rejected us and abased us,
 and have not gone out with our armies.
[10] You made us turn back from the foe,
 and our enemies have gotten spoil.
[11] You have made us like sheep for slaughter,
 and have scattered us among the nations.
[12] You have sold your people for a trifle,
 demanding no high price for them.
 ...
[17] All this has come upon us,
 yet we have not forgotten you,
 or been false to your covenant.
[18] Our heart has not turned back,
 nor have our steps departed from your way,
[19] yet you have broken us in the haunt of jackals,
 and covered us with deep darkness.
[20] If we had forgotten the name of our God,
 or spread out our hands to a strange god,
[21] would not God discover this?

> For he knows the secrets of the heart.
> [22] Because of you we are being killed all day long,
>> and accounted as sheep for the slaughter.

A similar situation exists in Psalm 89. God has made a promise to King David and his descendants. The following extract begins near the end of a long quotation of God's promise. However, in v. 38 the psalmist turns to the actual experience of the kings.

> [35] 'Once and for all I have sworn by my holiness;
>> I will not lie to David.
> [36] His line shall continue forever,
>> and his throne endure before me like the sun.
> [37] It shall be established forever like the moon,
>> an enduring witness in the skies.'
> [38] But now you have spurned and rejected him;
>> you are full of wrath against your anointed.
> [39] You have renounced the covenant with your servant;
>> you have defiled his crown in the dust.
> [40] You have broken through all his walls;
>> you have laid his strongholds in ruins.
> [41] All who pass by plunder him;
>> he has become the scorn of his neighbors.

In these circumstances the psalmist demands that there be some response on the basis of a presumed relationship. The psalmist will not let the conversation lapse for reason of silence by God, especially where some injustice on God's part is perceived. To do so would be to toy with idolatry, that is to settle for some 'god' who is less than the one in covenant with Israel, or even to move toward a kind of atheism believing God to be totally ineffectual. It could also imply that the psalmist is party to the injustice.[7] The demands of the psalmist keep God alive and part of the conversation. This is especially the case in lament psalms, of which Psalm 44 and the end of Psalm 89 are examples. But the psalmist does not just lament the situation. He/she demands that God respond to their cry. In Psalm 44, a community lament which was possibly said after defeat in battle, the psalmist cries in desperation at the end of the psalm:

> [23] Rouse yourself! Why do you sleep, O Lord?
>> Awake, do not cast us off forever!
> [24] Why do you hide your face?
>> Why do you forget our affliction and oppression?
> [25] For we sink down to the dust;
>> our bodies cling to the ground.

---

[7] Brueggemann, W. (1989), 'The Psalms as Prayer', *Reformed Liturgy & Music*, Vol. XXIII, pp. 13-26, esp. p. 22.

²⁶ Rise up, come to our help.
    Redeem us for the sake of your steadfast love.

There are many other references to God hiding his face in the lament psalms. The psalmist uses this expression to describe the silence and/or distance of God as Ps 69:17-18 clearly show:

¹⁷ Do not hide your face from your servant,
    for I am in distress -- make haste to answer me.
¹⁸ Draw near to me, redeem me,
    set me free because of my enemies.

Pss 55:1 and 102:2 express the same sentiment. This experience of God's face being hidden can be equated with death (Pss 30:7; 55:1; 88:14), judgment (Ps 89:46), or oppression by enemies (Pss 10:1; 13:1). In these cases God appears not to be involved or active in the psalmist's life. This is inexplicable to the psalmist, who is uncertain and asks open-ended questions of 'why?' and 'how long?' The experience of God's presence in the past gives some hope for the future, but the psalmist is continually frustrated by the silence and/or distance of God in the present circumstances. Before any further praise can be given to God, some attention needs to be given to the difficulties of life as it is presently experienced. There must be some word on God's part.

The form of the lament psalms gives the psalmist the opportunity to articulate the experience of God's silence. One element of the form in particular gives the psalmist the explicit chance of arguing his/her case. It has been called the 'motivational clause'. This is a specific statement within the lament psalm wherein the psalmist either urges God or seeks to persuade God to act for him/her. The psalmist can use a variety of arguments. Frequently God is urged to act 'for the sake of (God's) steadfast love' (e.g. Pss 6:4; 44:26; 69:16; 115:1 etc.), or for the sake of God's own name or glory (e.g. Pss 25:11; 79:9; 143:11 etc.). The psalmist can promise that those whom God delivers will give thanks and recount God's praise (e.g. Ps 79:13), or using the reverse argument, remind God that the dead cannot praise (Pss 6:5; 115:17). In some psalms, the whole psalm becomes an argument for God to act for the psalmist or the community. For example, in Psalm 74, where the psalmist laments the sacking of the Jerusalem temple, several interrelated arguments are used. It begins:

¹ O God, why do you cast us off forever?
    Why does your anger smoke against the sheep of your pasture?
² Remember your congregation, which you acquired long ago,
    which you redeemed to be the tribe of your heritage.
    Remember Mount Zion, where you came to dwell.
³ Direct your steps to the perpetual ruins;
    the enemy has destroyed everything in the sanctuary.
⁴ Your foes have roared within your holy place;
    they set up their emblems there.

The psalmist calls God to remember the congregation acquired long ago (v. 2). There is a plea to the past acts of God, specifically to the Exodus and conquest. There is also a reference to the time of the establishment of the people as those in covenant with God, and of the selection of Mount Zion as the place of God's presence. The centre of the psalm recalls the past acts of God:

> ¹² Yet God my King is from of old,
>   working salvation in the earth.
> ¹³ You divided the sea by your might;
>   you broke the heads of the dragons in the waters.
> ¹⁴ You crushed the heads of Leviathan;
>   you gave him as food for the creatures of the wilderness.
> ¹⁵ You cut openings for springs and torrents;
>   you dried up ever-flowing streams.
> ¹⁶ Yours is the day, yours also the night;
>   you established the luminaries and the sun.
> ¹⁷ You have fixed all the bounds of the earth;
>   you made summer and winter.

Here the psalmist remembers the act of creation itself and God's sovereignty over all aspects of creation. These past events, which stand before all else, are in sharp contrast to the present where the psalmist proclaims God's absence (vv. 9-11). Inherent in the psalmist's words is a plea that God should act in the present in a way consistent with actions in the past.

The psalmist goes on to describe the actions of the enemy as not only against Israel but also against God. As the psalmist addresses God, he/she describes the enemy as '*your* foes', they have roared in '*your* holy place', set '*your* sanctuary' on fire, 'desecrated the dwelling place of *your* name', and 'burned the meeting places of God' (vv. 4-8). Later the enemy is said to scoff and 'revile *your* name' (v. 16). Thus, the psalmist makes Israel's problem God's problem too. God is asked not only to act out of compassion for the people, out of a sense of justice for the poor, or even out of a sense of loyalty and commitment to God's people 'of old', but also for God's own sake and for God's praise:

> ¹⁹ Do not deliver the soul of your dove to the wild animals;
>   do not forget the life of your poor forever.
> ²⁰ Have regard for your covenant,
>   for the dark places of the land are full of the haunts of violence.
> ²¹ Do not let the downtrodden be put to shame;
>   let the poor and needy praise your name.
> ²² Rise up, O God, plead your cause;
>   remember how the impious scoff at you all day long.
> ²³ Do not forget the clamor of your foes,
>   the uproar of your adversaries that goes up continually.

The issue at the heart of all of this is whether God will act as God, the one who is sovereign of all creation as vv. 12-17 proclaim. The enemy is reported as proclaiming boldly 'We will utterly subdue them' (v. 8) speaking about defeating Israel. The parallel line in that verse, however, proclaims that 'they have burned all the meeting places of God in the land'. This is not just an attack on the people of God but is a direct attack on the very power and being of God. At least this is how the psalmist sees it and how he/she puts the case to God for God to intervene. God's reputation and character are as much at stake in the present crisis as is the future of the community.[8] A similar point is made in Psalm 115 where the issue is the efficacy of the people's trust in God. After the nations say 'Where is their God?' the psalmist proclaims:

> [3] Our God is in the heavens;
>> he does whatever he pleases.
> [4] Their idols are silver and gold,
>> the work of human hands.
>
>   …
> [8] Those who make them are like them;
>> so are all who trust in them.
>
> [9] O Israel, trust in the LORD!
>> He is their help and their shield.

While the psalmist employs a number of arguments to urge God into action, the fundamental assumption is that God can act for the psalmist and can be persuaded to do so.[9] The psalmist maintains the conversation with God, even though the latter has fallen silent, believing that things can change, even God's mind. The cry is not simply for the deliverance of the psalmist and/or the community, but for God to act as God has done before, in accord with the just, righteous, and compassionate nature of God, and in keeping with the existing relationship with the psalmist or the people. It is commonplace in some circles today to see prayer as an activity which is primarily about changing the pray-er, either realigning his/her perspective on the world, so it is more in tune with God's, or stirring him/herself into action in relation to their own prayer. But this is not what the psalmists are about in their prayers. In many psalms the future of the relationship that is the basis of the conversation has become the topic of conversation and the psalmist uses a number of arguments and points around this issue to keep the relationship alive and persuade God to act.

---

[8] See also Balentine, S.E. (1983), *The Hidden God: The Hiding of the Face of God in the Old Testament*, OUP, Oxford, esp. pp. 164-176.
[9] See also Miller, P.D. (1994), *They Cried to the LORD: The Form and Theology of Biblical Prayer*, Fortress, Minneapolis, pp. 114-127.

God's Silent Presence

The fact that the psalmist's words dominate some psalms does not suggest that the earlier statement that the psalms are essentially 'dialogue-poems' is wrong and they are after all monologues, and worst of all monologues in vain. God is silent in many psalms, yet the psalmist believes that can be changed and feels justified in trusting that the Lord will, or should, answer his/her prayer. In many psalms we see that such trust is neither out of order nor a waste of time.[10]

In some psalms, the psalmist even proclaims that he/she has been answered. This is particularly true in individual lament psalms. Psalm 6 is a case in point. It begins with a desperate cry to the Lord in the face of opposition, described as the threat of death.

> [1] O LORD, do not rebuke me in your anger,
>   or discipline me in your wrath.
> [2] Be gracious to me, O LORD, for I am languishing;
>   O LORD, heal me, for my bones are shaking with terror.
> [3] My soul also is struck with terror,
>   while you, O LORD – how long?
>   ...
> [5] For in death there is no remembrance of you;
>   in Sheol who can give you praise?
> [6] I am weary with my moaning;
>   every night I flood my bed with tears;
>   I drench my couch with my weeping.
> [7] My eyes waste away because of grief;
>   they grow weak because of all my foes.

In the midst of this the psalmist petitions God:

> [4] Turn, O LORD, save my life;
>   deliver me for the sake of your steadfast love.

The mood of the psalm changes in v. 8.[11] The psalmist declares confidently that the Lord has accepted his/her prayer.

> [8] Depart from me, all you workers of evil,
>   for the LORD has heard the sound of my weeping.
> [9] The LORD has heard my supplication;
>   the LORD accepts my prayer.

---

[10] Fløysvik, I. (1977), *When God becomes an Enemy: The Theology of the Complaint Psalms*, Concordia Academic Press, St. Louis, pp. 154-175.

[11] The reason for this mood change in nearly all the lament psalms is not clear. We discuss this below in more detail in the section 'The extremes of life in the psalms' and note the reference in n. 38.

In some psalms the straightforward movement toward confidence is less clear than it is in Psalm 6. For example, in Psalm 27, which will be discussed further below, there is a constant tension between petition and trust. The psalmist knows the agony of waiting in the face of disaster.

> [3] Though an army encamp against me,
>> my heart shall not fear;
>> though war rise up against me,
>>> yet I will be confident.
>
> ...
>
> [11] Teach me your way, O LORD,
>> and lead me on a level path because of my enemies.
> [12] Do not give me up to the will of my adversaries,
>> for false witnesses have risen against me,
>> and they are breathing out violence.
> [13] I believe that I shall see the goodness of the LORD
>> in the land of the living.
> [14] Wait for the LORD;
>> be strong, and let your heart take courage;
>> wait for the LORD!

In both Psalms 12 and 91 the promises of God are quoted as a way of furthering trust that God will answer prayer. In Psalm 91 the psalmist encourages those who 'live in the shelter of the Most High' to feel assured about their security. The psalm ends with a quotation of God's words:

> [14] Those who love me, I will deliver;
>> I will protect those who know my name.
> [15] When they call to me, I will answer them;
>> I will be with them in trouble,
>> I will rescue them and honor them.
> [16] With long life I will satisfy them,
>> and show them my salvation.

The psalmist states confidently in Psalm 65 that the Lord is the one who hears prayer and answers his people with acts of deliverance:

> [1] Praise is due to you,
>> God, in Zion;
>> and to you shall vows be performed,
> [2] O you who answer prayer!
>> To you all flesh shall come.
>
> ...
>
> [5] By awesome deeds you answer us with deliverance,
>> O God of our salvation;
>> you are the hope of all the ends of the earth

and of the farthest seas.[12]

In some psalms, such as in Psalm 6 above, the answer to prayer has apparently already been received, either in personal terms as in Psalm 138:

[3]On the day I called, you answered me,
    you increased my strength of soul.

or in terms of the heroes of the past who now become an example, as in Psalm 99:

[6] Moses and Aaron were among his priests,
    Samuel also was among those who called on his name.
  They cried to the LORD, and he answered them.
[7] He spoke to them in the pillar of cloud;
    they kept his decrees,
    and the statutes that he gave them.
[8] O LORD our God, you answered them;
    you were a forgiving God to them,
    but an avenger of their wrongdoings.

While these examples demonstrate the confidence of the psalmist in God answering prayer, they also indicate that the answer to prayer is not part of the psalm itself. It is clear from the psalms that do speak of an answer having been received, that the response of the Lord to the psalmist comes in its own time and in ways that do not necessarily involve words. The Lord's response to the psalmist's petition can be seen variously in victory in battle (Ps 20:6, 9), relief from fear (34:4), a humbling of enemies (55:19), rescue from danger (60:5; 91:15; 108:6), material events (65:5), freedom from the taunts of enemies (6:8; 69:13; 120:1), Israel's experience in the exodus through the wilderness (81:7), preserving life (86:1), or in security of some kind (118:5) etc. Thus, while the psalmist speaks in the psalms within a relationship and expects some response, he/she recognizes that the response by the Lord cannot be controlled. Psalm 69 expresses this well. The psalmist asks the Lord to answer at an 'acceptable time'. At the same time the psalmist expresses urgency in relation to the response.

[13] But as for me, my prayer is to you, O LORD.
        At an acceptable time, O God,
        in the abundance of your steadfast love, answer me.
      With your faithful help [14] rescue me
        from sinking in the mire;
      let me be delivered from my enemies
        and from the deep waters.
[15] Do not let the flood sweep over me,
        or the deep swallow me up,

---

[12] Other examples are Pss 38:15; 143:1, 7 etc.

> or the Pit close its mouth over me.
> [16] Answer me, O LORD, for your steadfast love is good;
>   according to your abundant mercy, turn to me.

So while God is silent in some psalms, the psalmist still presumes that a relationship exists, and that he/she can engage God in conversation. He/she demands to be heard, and in many cases, has confidence that his/her words will be, or even have been, heeded. As one writer has remarked, the psalms of lament are 'prayers of faith, not protests of unbelief'.[13] The psalmist will not let the experience of God's silence or absence govern his/her view of the world. The psalmist knows of other possibilities and his/her prayers are a way of ensuring that God has some space within which to respond to the pray-er.[14]

Our Conversations with God and Others

The idea of prayer as conversation raises issues for consideration in our own prayer life. Some might have difficulties in seeing prayer as conversation or of seeing conversation - at least some forms of it - as prayerful. Few prayers in public worship are genuinely conversational. Some of them, especially intercessory prayers, fall into the trap of becoming a list of wants or needs that we expect God to fill. Other prayers become sermons in another guise, reminding the congregation of the way of God in the world and of the proper response to that way.[15] Of course, expressing wants or needs to God can be a genuine and worthy thing, especially when they are said for others or the pray-er is in genuine need. It is also important that the construction of prayers be accompanied by deep theological reflection. It ought not to be underestimated how much both pray-ers and those led in prayer can learn about God and discipleship in the act of prayer. However, the dominant model of prayer in the psalms is that of conversation. The psalms invite us to explore that model and use it, and, in the process, discover new aspects of our relationship with God and of the practice of our faith.

When we speak of prayer in the psalms in terms of conversation, we are, of course, using a metaphor. Metaphors involve the interaction of two concepts or thoughts, which in this case are 'prayer' and 'conversation'. What we know about one of these helps us organize our thinking or reorganize it in relation to the other.[16] Thus thinking about 'conversation' helps stimulate thinking about the

---

[13] Fløysvik, *When God becomes an Enemy*, p. 162.

[14] For a helpful discussion on this in the Old Testament in general see Fretheim, T. (1988), 'Prayer in the Old Testament: creating space in the world for God', in P.R. Sponheim (ed.) *A Primer on Prayer*, Fortress, Philadelphia, pp. 51-62.

[15] Brueggemann, 'From Hurt to Joy', p. 5.

[16] On metaphors in general see Black, M. (1962), *Models and Metaphors: Studies in Language and Philosophy*, Cornell University, Ithaca, pp. 19-43, esp. pp. 38-43; Newsom, C.A. (1987), 'A Maker of Metaphors: Ezekiel's Oracles against Tyre', in J.L. Mays and P.J. Achtemeier (eds.) *Interpreting the Prophets*, Fortress, Philadelphia, pp. 188-199, esp. p. 189; and Stienstra, N. (1993), *YHWH is the Husband of his People: Analysis of a Biblical Metaphor with Special Reference to Translation*, Kok Pharos, Kampen, pp. 17-40.

nature of prayer and vice versa. In this process we must not only give careful attention to all aspects of the metaphor, but also to the limits within which it operates. We can enhance our understanding of prayer through study of this metaphor but if it is pushed beyond its limits it can become distorted and destructive.

In human terms, 'conversation' implies among other things, that the parties involved have a relationship. The identity and self-understanding of each of the parties is, in one way or another, dependent on that relationship. Each party is in a real sense constituted by the conversation with the other.[17] Both the conversation itself and the other partner help shape the identity of the person who enters into conversation. The relationship develops, provided each party is ready to speak and listen to the other when they meet. This implies that the pray-er is reconstituted in part, or has his/her identity reshaped, in the act of prayer. Who we are is determined, at least in part, by our prayers, their content, and their form. It also implies that in prayer the pray-er should be genuinely involved in the conversation and both free, and having the responsibility, to bring the full range of human experience to bear in prayer. God, as our conversation partner, does not want our polite expression or timid submission.[18]

At this point I could ask: 'Is God also constituted through prayer?' This question raises both the matters of the limits of the metaphor of prayer as conversation, and of the limits of our thinking about God. When we think of God's part in prayer we cannot consider God simply in the way we would any human conversational partner. Some qualification is needed. After all, God is not bound by the limits of space and time, as are all forms of human conversation. Moreover, God is understood as omniscient, not one who necessarily needs to be informed in any way. The psalmists understood that God knows us better than we know ourselves and nothing is hidden from God. In Psalm 139 the psalmist says:

[1]Lord, you have searched me and known me.
[2]You know when I sit down and when I rise up;
     you discern my thoughts from far away.
[3]You search out my path and my lying down,
     and are acquainted with all my ways.
[4]Even before a word is on my tongue,
     O Lord, you know it completely.

So God in this psalm is not like any ordinary, human conversation partner. To treat God as such would be to distort God's nature.

On the other hand, to define God simply in terms of omniscience (or even in terms of omnipotence or omnipresence) can be equally a distortion. It is easy to assume in many of our prayers, at least as it is reflected in our words if not in our hearts, that God either sits back patiently (or even condescendingly?) hearing our

---

[17] See on this Fisch, *Poetry with a Purpose*, p. 109. Cf. also Brueggemann, 'From Hurt to Joy', pp. 4-5, and Balentine, *Prayer in the Hebrew Bible*, pp. 9, 261-4.
[18] So also Balentine, *Prayer in the Hebrew Bible*, p. 263.

requests or problems, or inertly accepts our praise or thanks. As such, prayer can simply become mechanistic, a form of appeasement with a sense of duty attached and with its own polite and proper language. This can lead to subtle forms of either atheism or idolatry. The same danger exists here as with the sense of God's silence in prayer. We might not really expect anything to come from our prayers because the God to whom we pray is not actively engaged with the world, either through lack of power or lack of interest.[19] Alternatively, we might simply expect God to hand out what we desire.

The psalmist challenges us in this regard. He/she assumes that the God to whom we pray is indeed actively engaged with the world or, at least, is expected to be so; that a genuine conversation can take place. This is all the more important when God might appear from time to time to be silent or unresponsive to our prayers. The psalms constantly remind us of the conversational nature of prayer and that one can have both trust in and expectation of God as a conversation partner. The covenant relationship between Israel and the Lord, which stands behind this prayer, is itself dialogical in nature.[20]

But the psalmist challenges us not only in terms of assuming that God is or should be actively engaged in the world; they challenge us in terms of how we think our prayers relate to that engagement. In other words, is the point of at least some of our prayers to influence or change God's action in the world in some way? While we might privately assume that an omniscient and omnipotent God doesn't need reminding about what is happening on earth and how God should respond, the psalmist publicly contests that view. He/she seeks some response from God asking 'how long?' The psalmist believes God can be persuaded. His/her prayers are not mechanistic or offered simply to appease God in some way. Nor does God act mechanistically. Rather, the psalmist engages God in matters that are important to him/her and God alike. He/she prays that God would act as they have come to understand God's action and will, namely in terms of righteousness and justice, but particularly in terms of mercy and compassion.[21] As Balentine explains, this does not assume that God was acting prior to a particular prayer in ways contrary to God's nature.

> The Hebrew Bible never promotes prayer as a means to manipulate or to control God. When God changes, God acts in ways that are consonant with the divine nature. God does not act *before* prayer out of character, then *after* prayer more in character. Instead God changes *as God*, not as the creatures, hence God always acts in ways that are consistent with divine purposes.[22]

A similar situation exists in relation to other prayers in Scripture. When God hears the prayers of Moses or the prophets on behalf of the people, and heeds them, this suggests a change of mind on God's part. But this is not to be confused

---

[19] See Brueggemann, 'The Psalms as Prayer', p. 22.

[20] So also Balentine, *Prayer in the Hebrew Bible*, p. 262.

[21] Miller, P.D. (1993), 'Prayer as Persuasion: The Rhetoric and Intention of Prayer', *Word & World*, Vol. 13, pp. 356-62.

[22] Balentine, *Prayer in the Hebrew Bible*, p. 270.

with what we might regard as arbitrary action or divine inconsistency. Rather, it is part of a picture of God who is continually moved toward exercising mercy, compassion, and justice in relation with humankind. It is a picture consistent with God's action in Jesus Christ. As we pray for God to act in a particular situation, to answer our prayer, or to change in some way, we know that God has already acted for the world in Jesus Christ. He is the exemplar of God changing as God. That does not mean that our prayers now are useless. On the contrary, we are aware that in Jesus God is responding to our prayers, is answering them, and is changing as God in response to them, regardless of whether we pray before or after his response.

When we deny the possibility of God genuinely responding to and engaging us in our prayers, we remove God just that bit further from any real empathy with the human condition. We effectively keep God out of the life of the community of faith. We distort the nature of God. The incarnation of God in Jesus Christ constitutes a deep conversation between God and humanity. If we discount God's active part in our prayer we break the connection between God's presence and work in Jesus Christ and the work of God in our present world. To maintain the metaphor of prayer as conversation and of God as 'conversation partner' keeps us aware of that connection and a sense of God as actively pursuing the divine will in the world. The role of the Church in prayer has been described as being '*to keep the community and the world in God*; and ... *to keep God in the community and in the world.*'[23]

In regard to our own part in prayer, if we neglect the conversational aspect of prayer we run the risk of denying a good deal that is at stake for us in our relationship with God. We deny ourselves a way of raising matters of doubt or uncertainty in relation to our faith. We can end up praying to an image of God, which is too well formed and inflexible, and to whose will all our words must conform. We can also finish up having no real way of joining our prayers in genuine heart felt sympathy to the voices of those who suffer needlessly or as a result of injustice in the world. At most we might politely seek clarification from God on what God is up to. At worst, we run the risk of manipulating the relationship by keeping it comfortable but ineffectual. In the psalms Israel did not settle for that. Brueggemann suggests that Israel stubbornly stays in the conversation with the Lord (Yahweh) 'not because there are no alternatives, but because *Israel will not concede that the conversation of prayer belongs wholly to Yahweh* or *happens wholly on Yahweh's terms.*' Israel has a stake in the conversation and is 'part-owner' of the process of prayer.[24]

The psalms encourage us to perceive prayer as our conversation with God and in doing so to (re)discover some of the depths of our relationship with God. If we take the psalms as our guide for prayer, or even as our prayers, then they bring about conversation with God. As we read the psalms we cannot escape the dialogue that is there. We get caught up in it. This is partly because of the

---

[23] *Ibid.*, ch. 11.
[24] Brueggemann, 'The Psalms as Prayer', p. 21. Also in Brueggemann, W. (1995), *The Psalms and the Life of Faith*, Fortress, Minneapolis, pp. 56-57.

undefined subjects of 'I' or 'we' in many psalms. We can easily assume the role of the speaker when there is no clear indication of whose words these might be. We speak to God as 'you'. In many of the psalms addressed to Israel or the assembled worshippers we find ourselves part of the audience and the objects of various imperatives or invocations. We hear ourselves called on to sing a new song, praise the Lord, or give thanks to God. The very language of the psalms invites us to move into their context with relative ease. It also allows, in many cases, for the psalm to come into our world with almost equal ease. The psalms not only offer an invitation to think about prayer in a particular way, but constitute *an invitation to pray*.

There is no doubt that a rediscovery of prayer has been taking place in recent decades. The burgeoning interest in spirituality testifies to this. The recapturing of the need to address spiritual questions evident in the wider society is part of this shift. In this context the psalms invite us to rethink our understanding of prayer and to see ourselves more involved in prayer than we might think we are already. Conversation is a part of our daily lives. We engage in it with many different people and in many different contexts. To capture a sense of prayer as conversation might be to realize that the means for prayer and the opportunity for prayer are more readily available to us than we may have thought.

Many of us already engage in conversations about our lives, experiences, hopes and frustrations. These conversations can be with close friends, family, strangers, or even ourselves. Some will be private and personal. Some, especially ones we might have with ourselves, will concern the sort of things that we do not even let our most intimate friends and family in on. Some conversations will be specifically with God. In any case, God is privy to them all. The invitation of the psalms to consider prayer as conservation is also an invitation to re-conceptualize more of our life in terms of prayer. But, as we noted above, Bonhoeffer argued that prayer is not just a pouring out of the heart. It requires discipline and learning. So, while the psalms invite us to see more of our life in terms of prayer, there is also an invitation to discipline more of our life and its conversations by prayer, not in terms of a public display of piety but in terms of a greater awareness of God's presence and engagement with us.

A World Embracing Every Experience

The Extremes of Life in the Psalms

If the psalms are full of conversations, then they are conversations about real-life experiences. They invite us to see prayer in relation to *all* of life's experiences. They incorporate a broad array of human emotions and responses. Throughout Christian history many who have studied the psalms have recognized this. As early as the fourth century C.E., St. Athanasius expressed this sentiment:

For I believe that the whole of human existence, both the dispositions of the soul and the movements of the thoughts, have been measured out and encompassed in those very words of the Psalter. And nothing beyond these is found among men.[25]

Others have made similar statements, e.g. St. Chrysostom and St. Basil of Cappadocia, both also of the fourth century.[26] John Calvin spoke of the openness of the psalms to the range of human emotions. He referred to them as 'an anatomy of all parts of the soul', and with arguments similar to those of St. Athanasius, writes:

... for there is not an emotion of which anyone can be conscious that is not here represented as in a mirror. ... The other parts of Scripture contain the commandments which God enjoined his servants to announce to us. But here the prophets themselves, seeing they are exhibited to us as speaking to God, and laying open all their inmost thoughts and affections, call, or rather draw, each of us to the examination of himself in particular, in order that none of the many infirmities to which we are subject, and the many vices with which we abound, may remain concealed.[27]

In a similar fashion, but more succinctly, Martin Luther wrote in his preface to the Psalter:

Where does one find finer words of joy than in the psalms of praise and thanksgiving? There you look into the hearts of all saints, as into fair and pleasant gardens, yes, as into heaven itself. ... On the other hand, where do you find deeper, more sorrowful, more pitiful words of sadness than in the psalms of lamentation? There again you look into the hearts of all the saints, as into death, yes, as into hell itself.[28]

And a little later in the same document he says:

Hence it is that the Psalter is the book of all saints; and everyone, in whatever situation he may be, finds in that situation psalms and words that fit his case, that suit him as if they were put there just for his sake, so that he could not put it better himself, or find or wish for anything better.[29]

Throughout Christian history the connection of psalms to the entire spectrum of human experience has been acknowledged.

Critical studies of the psalms in recent decades have also focused on this aspect. Many scholars have attempted to classify the psalms into a number of types. The German scholar Hermann Gunkel (1862-1932) was a pioneer in this

---

[25] *Letter to Marcellinus*, par. 30, in Gregg, R.C. (ed.) (1980) *Athanasius: The Life of Antony and The Letter to Marcellinus*, SPCK, London, p. 126.

[26] Quoted in Kirkpatrick, A.F. (1902), *The Book of Psalms*, CUP, Cambridge, pp. c and ciii-civ.

[27] Calvin, *Commentary on the Book of Psalms*, Vol. 1, p. xxxvii.

[28] Martin Luther, (1960), *Luther's Works, Vol. 35: Word and Sacrament I*, Muhlenberg, Philadelphia, pp. 255-56.

[29] *Ibid.*, p. 256.

endeavour. He tried to establish a correlation between the types of psalms and the different worship contexts in which they might have been used in ancient Israel.[30] In his analysis the psalms ranged from laments sung in situations in which the well-being of the community as a whole was threatened, or an individual was in personal distress, through to songs of thanksgiving for deliverance from distress. These two types stood as the extremes. He stated: 'In the alternation between lament and song of thanks there unrolls the whole life of the pious'.[31] He echoes the words of both Calvin and Luther.

Claus Westermann attempted to refine Gunkel's analysis. Westermann spoke of the extremes of praise and lament, however, he noted that most laments end in at least a vow of praise, especially the individual laments.[32] Thus, while praise and lament are the dominant categories in the psalms, all others being included within them, and while they are the two poles of human address to God, there is continuity between them. This sense of continuity means that not only do psalms offer a range of prayers for the extreme and intermediate situations in life, they help the pray-er make the transition from one situation to another.

An example of this movement can be found in Psalm 28. It begins:

> [1] To you, O Lord, I call;
>> my rock, do not refuse to hear me,
>> for if you are silent to me,
>> I shall be like those who go down to the Pit.

After further supplications to the Lord the psalm shifts quite suddenly in vv 6-7 to:

> [6] Blessed be the Lord,
>> for he has heard the sound of my pleadings.
> [7] The Lord is my strength and my shield;
>> in him my heart trusts;
>> so I am helped, and my heart exults,
>> and with my song I give thanks to him.

Another example of this often sudden transformation is found in Psalm 22. It begins with a cry of desolation to God and goes on metaphorically to describe the pitiful state of the psalmist in terms of being beset by ravenous creatures. At the conclusion of the description of the psalmist's troubles we read:

> [19] But you, O Lord, do not be far away!
>> my help, come quickly to my aid!

---

[30] Gunkel, H. (1967), *The Psalms: A Form-Critical Introduction*, Fortress, Philadelphia.

[31] Quoted in Westermann, C. (1965), *The Praise of God in the Psalms*, John Knox, Richmond, p. 24.

[32] Westermann, *The Praise of God in the Psalms*, pp. 52-81, esp. pp. 70-81. For laments ending in a vow of praise see e.g. Pss 3; 6; 10; 13; 22; 28; 31; 54; 56 etc. See *ibid.*, p. 80 for Westermann's full list of examples.

²⁰ Deliver my soul from the sword,
>   my life from the power of the dog!
²¹ Save me from the mouth of the lion!

>   From the horns of the wild oxen you have rescued me[33]
²² I will tell of your name to my brothers and sisters;
>   in the midst of the congregation I will praise you ...

There is a sudden movement from complaint and plea to praise in the psalm. How and why this movement takes place is not clear. Scholars have suggested a range of hypotheses to explain this change. When considering the original context of the psalms, some have suggested that a third party, possibly a priest, uttered a 'salvation oracle' or conducted some ritual at the point of transition. This is not recorded in any of the lament psalms but, it is presumed, was sufficient to bring about a change in the psalmist. Alternatively, the announcement of praise itself might have been considered a guarantee of divine intervention for the psalmist, thus inducing a change in perspective. It might even be the case that the clause beginning 'but...' in Ps 22:19 (and in other psalms, e.g. Ps 13:5) indicates that the complaint itself already held within it an element of trust or turning to the Lord.[34] Whatever it might be that brings about the transformation, it is clear that it does take place in these psalms. We should also note in passing that this transformation in lament psalms is not always in the same direction, from lament to praise. It can sometimes go the other way, as for example in Psalm 85 or Psalms 9-10, which have often been seen as one psalm. Psalm 88 is the only psalm that does not encapsulate the movement noted here. It consists entirely of complaint and plea. While it is a single example, it does allow the possibility of prayer without the hope of transformation.

Westermann called for the inclusion of both the language of lamentation as well as praise, of suffering as well as joy, within our worship. They are both equally part of our being. He argued that something is amiss in our worship 'if praise of God has a place in Christian worship but lamentation does not. Praise can retain its authenticity and naturalness only in polarity with lamentation'.[35]

Another contributor to this discussion has been Walter Brueggemann. He draws on the work of Paul Ricoeur who sees the dynamics of life as a movement between times of disorientation and times of reorientation.[36] Brueggemann adds a

---

[33] The verb rendered in the NRSV as 'you have rescued me' reads in the Hebrew 'you have answered me'. One could read Ps 22:21 as:
>   Save me from the mouth of the lion;
>   From the horns of the wild oxen!
>   You have answered me. ...

[34] See Brueggemann, 'From hurt to joy', pp. 8-10 for a summary of proposals to that date.

[35] Westermann, C. (1974), 'The Role of the Lament in the Theology of the Old Testament', *Interpretation*, Vol. 28, pp. 20-38, esp. p. 27.

[36] Brueggemann, W. (1980), 'Psalms and the Life of Faith: A Suggested Typology of Function', *JSOT*, Vol. 17, pp. 3-32 and also Brueggemann, W. (1984), *The Message of the Psalms*, Augsburg, Minneapolis, pp.15-25. See also Goldingay, J. (1981), 'The Dynamic

further category, 'times of orientation' in which an individual feels a 'sense of holistic orientation, of being "at home"'.[37] Brueggemann associates various types of psalms with these three times in our lives. He sees greater movement in the psalms than Westermann did. That movement is connected to the shape of the life of faith of the pray-er. Following Westermann's analysis of the laments, Brueggemann notes that the lament expresses in 'microcosm' the movement that is seen in larger terms in the psalms. The plea element in the laments looks back to times of orientation while the praise element looks forward in hope.[38]

Finally, we should note the work on lament psalms by C.C. Broyles. [39] He sees an inner distinction in lament psalms between 'psalms of plea' or 'non-God-lament psalms', and 'psalms of complaint' or 'God-lament psalms'. In the non-God-lament psalms, the psalmist pleads with or invokes God to deliver him/her or the people from some situation of distress. Either circumstances or some 'enemy' has caused the situation. This is by far the most common form of lament. An example is Psalm 31:

> [14] But I trust in you, O LORD;
>   I say, 'You are my God.'
> [15] My times are in your hand;
>   deliver me from the hand of my enemies and persecutors.
> [16] Let your face shine upon your servant;
>   save me in your steadfast love.
> [17] Do not let me be put to shame, O LORD,
>   for I call on you;
>   let the wicked be put to shame;
>   let them go dumbfounded to Sheol.
> [18] Let the lying lips be stilled
>   that speak insolently against the righteous
>   with pride and contempt.

The God-lament is quite different. In this type of psalm the psalmist argues with or complains to God. He/she believes God has not acted on his/her behalf when God should have, or God has acted in some way against the psalmist. In the absence of such action or in the face of hostile action, the psalmist feels he/she has a right to complain.[40] The Lord has either been negligent or God's power to act is

---

Cycle of Praise and Prayer in the Psalms', *JSOT*, Vol. 20, pp. 85-90 which seeks to refine and slightly correct Brueggemann's 'Psalms and the Life of Faith'. Brueggemann replies briefly to Goldingay in 'Response to John Goldingay's 'Dynamic Cycle of Praise and Prayer' (*JSOT* 20 [1981] 85-90)', *JSOT*, Vol. 22, (1982), pp. 141-2.

[37] Brueggemann, 'Psalms and the Life of Faith', p. 5.

[38] *Ibid.*, p. 16.

[39] Broyles, C.C. (1989), *The Conflict of Faith and Experience in the Psalms: A Form-Critical and Theological Study*, Sheffield Academic Press, Sheffield.

[40] *Ibid.*, p. 221. Broyles classifies the following as psalms of complaint: community complaints, Pss 9-10, 44, 60, 74, 77, 79, 80, 85, 89, 90, and 108; and individual complaints,

questionable. The psalmist's problem is not only his/her own. God's own character is at stake. An example is Psalm 102:

[1] Hear my prayer, O LORD;
   let my cry come to you.
[2] Do not hide your face from me in the day of my distress.
   Incline your ear to me; answer me speedily in the day when I call.
   . . .
[8] All day long my enemies taunt me;
   those who deride me use my name for a curse.
[9] For I eat ashes like bread,
   and mingle tears with my drink,
[10] because of your indignation and anger;
   for you have lifted me up and thrown me aside.

Gunkel, Westermann and others have listed praise and lament as the extremes in psalm types. Broyles, on the other hand, sees the extremes as praise and *complaint*. This puts another slant on the life experiences addressed in the psalms. If the extremes are praise and lament in general, then there is a presumption that the relationship between the psalmist and God remains essentially the same in all circumstances. The psalmist's situation may change but he/she can always turn to God, who is in relationship with them, either to give praise or to ask for help. The situation is much more complex if the extremes are praise and complaint. Not only do the psalms portray address to a God who is in relationship with the psalmist and who can help or who deserves praise, but he/she also suggests that a pray-er can address God directly about the very state of their relationship. The psalmist can even complain that God has not been faithful to the relationship and has let them down in some respect. In this Broyles touches on the issue of God's silence in psalm conversation, a point we considered above. We have already noted that, regardless of other ills and oppressions, the psalmists are not reluctant to name God's silence or absence as a problem that needs to be addressed. I cited several examples above but Ps 35:22-25 will suffice to illustrate the matter again. The urgency of this situation and the desperation of the psalmist need to be heard in these demands. After outlining his/her plight, the psalmist says to the Lord:

[22] You have seen, O LORD; do not be silent!
   O Lord, do not be far from me!
[23] Wake up! Bestir yourself for my defense,
   for my cause, my God and my Lord!
[24] Vindicate me, O LORD, my God,
   according to your righteousness,
and do not let them rejoice over me.

Pss 6, 13, 22, 35, 39, 42-43, 88, and 102. The more radical complaint psalms arise from near death situations or national disasters.

²⁵ Do not let them say to themselves,
   'Aha, we have our heart's desire.'
Do not let them say, 'We have swallowed you up.'

But this bold address does not signal that the relationship with God is irretrievably broken. The address itself holds within it the possibility of redress of any difficulty.[41]

Thus, the psalms are prayers that not only praise God or call upon God in times of distress. They boldly address questions of God's faithfulness, commitment and fulfilment of promises as well as questions of the psalmist's own faithfulness etc. The invitation of the psalms to pray is thus an invitation to enter a world, which for many Christians is not only uncharted territory but possibly risky territory. It is to enter a world where the conversation is not constantly governed by codes of politeness and reserve, but is honest when it needs to be, and brutally so at times.[42] It is a world in which the pray-er has permission to speak with God about any experience, even ones which call for confronting God.

In the psalms it is permissible to speak honestly with God about the times of despair, doubt, and hopelessness. However, this may require a lot of us if we pray such prayers. It can require us to be honest about the circumstances of our own lives. It can also require that we reshape our understanding of God. Often we build up a picture of God dominated by thoughts of either gentle love or powerful control. When things go wrong it is so easy to see it as a result of our own sinfulness, or as part of some greater plan of God about which we know little. Some may even feel that complaining about God is being unfaithful. The psalmist recognizes his/her own sinfulness as well as God's rule over all things. Above all he/she recognizes the importance of honest speech in a relationship. It can be extremely uncomfortable. It can also be a risky thing. It makes both parties vulnerable and puts the relationship to the test.[43] Nevertheless, it is a point at which hope is realized. The psalmist sets before us the challenge of taking up these risky but hopeful words when needed.

Strong Words and Violent Thoughts

But what level of honesty can a relationship bear? Speaking about the risk of honest speech in prayer raises the question of what we do with that group of psalms that seek retribution, often in what seem the most violent terms. Toward the end of Psalm 139 we find one such passage:

¹⁹ O that you would kill the wicked, O God,
   and that the bloodthirsty would depart from me –

---

[41] *Ibid.*, pp. 224-5. Cf. also Onunwa, U. (1988), 'Individual Laments in Hebrew Poetry: A Positive Response to the Problem of Suffering', *Jeev*, Vol. 17, pp. 101-111.

[42] In relation to the Lutheran context see Meyer, L. (1993), 'A Lack of Laments in the Church's use of the Psalter', *Lutheran quarterly*, Vol. ns. 7, pp. 67-78.

[43] Broyles, *The Conflict of Faith and Experience*, pp. 51-52.

[20] those who speak of you maliciously,
    and lift themselves up against you for evil!
[21] Do I not hate those who hate you, O LORD?
    And do I not loathe those who rise up against you?
[22] I hate them with perfect hatred;
    I count them my enemies.

Other passages include Pss 69:22-28; 109:6-20; and 137:7-9, the last one well known for the brutality wished upon the children of the psalmist's enemies. In referring to these passages C.S. Lewis has remarked that: 'In some of the psalms the spirit of hatred which strikes us in the face is like the heat from a furnace mouth'.[44] Many Christians protest that they do not like the psalms because of passages like these. At the very least, those who do use the psalms in prayer find these words of retribution difficult. The sentiments in these psalms seem to stand in stark contrast to the Christian teaching of loving one's enemies and praying for them (Matt 5:44; Luke 6:27-28). Does not praying these words of retribution simply turn God into a God of vengeance fashioned after our most base feelings?

The problem centres on how we perceive the presence of such words in the Bible, and their usefulness for our prayers. A key point is to recognize that the feelings of anger, hatred, and revenge expressed in these psalms are common human feelings. We have all had them at one time or another. We may not like having such feelings and we try not to let them rule our lives. Nevertheless, we do know these feelings and occasionally can harbour them in extremely subtle ways. This is especially so when we feel threatened. In a book devoted to this topic, the psalms scholar E. Zenger cites the German political psychoanalyst, Thea Bauriedl, who argues that images of enemies are common to all people and arise '*out of necessity*, as soon as our anxiety in interpersonal conflicts becomes too strong'.[45] In cases where a person is the victim of violence, injustice, or some other strife, these feelings can be particularly strong. C.M. Cherion has remarked that the problem many people have with the description of 'enemies' in the psalms is a 'Christian problem'. It stems from an inability to fathom the depths of human feelings. He goes on to say that it is a pseudo-Christian

> continuation of the disastrous anaemic sentimentalism that does not want to look beyond the pallid range of experience of bourgeois decency, and refuses to look squarely at a world ruled by violence, strife, injustice, anguish.[46]

Some might feel as though they want to question the strength of this statement at the very least. However, it raises the question of whether there is something active in our Christian response to the command of Jesus to love our

---

[44] Lewis, C.S. (1977), *Reflections on the Psalms*, Fount, London, p. 23.
[45] See Zenger, E. (1996), *A God of Vengeance? Understanding the Psalms of Divine Wrath*, trans. L.M. Maloney; Westminster/John Knox, Louisville, p. viii.
[46] Cherion, C.M. (1982), 'Attitude to Enemies in the Psalms', *BibBh*, Vol. 8, pp. 104-117.

enemies that prevents us from dealing with our feelings of vengeance.[47] Maybe it is an overriding sense of guilt? Cherion is suggesting at least that we can deny our own feelings of enmity and hatred at the same time as we sentimentalize the command to love our enemies. The result is that we avoid the issue of justice in a world in which violence is a daily occurrence. I could also add, that in an effort to deal with issues of justice, as individuals or as society, we often let our feelings of enmity and hatred rule. In the political arena, issues of law and order are often couched solely in terms of retribution, e.g. in harsher gaol penalties for offenders. In either case, there is no reconciliation between the issue of justice, the depth of human feelings, and the biblical command to love one's enemies.

Zenger argues that the so-called 'psalms of vengeance' are founded on the view of God as a God of justice. These psalms are in fact a cry for justice in a world for which God is supposed to care. They presume that God, who created the world for all creatures for life, must act justly and ensure that justice is done.[48] The sufferer in these psalms is often seen as righteous, either innocent or confessing trust in God's *hesed* ('covenant loyalty' or 'faithfulness'). These so-called 'psalms of vengeance' have the same characteristics as other laments, which operate from the assumption that the oppression by the enemies is unjust.[49] Psalm 7 is a good example:

> [1] O LORD my God, in you I take refuge;
>   save me from all my pursuers, and deliver me,
>   ...
>
> [3] O LORD my God, if I have done this,
>   if there is wrong in my hands,
> [4] if I have repaid my ally with harm
>   or plundered my foe without cause,
> [5] then let the enemy pursue and overtake me,
>   trample my life to the ground,
>   and lay my soul in the dust.
>
> [6] Rise up, O LORD, in your anger;
>   lift yourself up against the fury of my enemies;
>   awake, O my God; you have appointed a judgment.
> [7] Let the assembly of the peoples be gathered around you,
>   and over it take your seat on high.
> [8] The LORD judges the peoples;
>   judge me, O LORD, according to my righteousness

---

[47] Caldwell, C.F. (1990), 'A Pastoral Perspective on the Psalms', in J. Knight and L.A. Sinclair (eds), *The Psalms and Other Studies on the Old Testament*, Nashotah House Seminary, Nashotah, pp. 86-95, esp. p. 89, suggests that the Psalms can invite us to look into our own souls and see what is there.

[48] Zenger, *A God of Vengeance?* pp. 63-69.

[49] Dearman, J.A. (1985), 'The Psalms as Prayers', *Austin Seminary Bulletin*, Vol. 101, pp. 25-30, esp. p. 29.

and according to the integrity that is in me.
⁹ O let the evil of the wicked come to an end,
>   but establish the righteous,
>   you who test the minds and hearts, O righteous God.
¹⁰ God is my shield,
>   who saves the upright in heart.
¹¹ God is a righteous judge,
>   and a God who has indignation every day.

The enemy of the psalmist is also the enemy of God. The psalmist expects God to carry out justice, as I noted above, and urges God to do so. I mentioned earlier that the suffering of the psalmist is a threat to the sovereignty of God. God must be seen to uphold justice with the vindication of his faithful. I noted a number of arguments the psalmist uses to get God to act. Psalm 94 provides the clearest expression of God as the avenger of the righteous. It begins:

¹ O LORD, you God of vengeance,
>   you God of vengeance, shine forth!
² Rise up, O judge of the earth;
>   give to the proud what they deserve!

Zenger asks whether Ps 94:1-2 does indeed portray God as a God of vengeance. He argues that this is a problem of language. The word translated 'vengeance' in most Christian works and Bibles is misleading. It is the Hebrew word *neqomot*, a plural noun form. The word speaks of punishment and justice, not acts of retribution outside the legal system. The fact that it is plural is a reference to acts of justice. He states:

> It is thus not a matter of making a statement about the nature of God, but about God's way of acting (which Luther also tries to retain with the translation 'to whom vengeance belongs').[50]

He continues:

> The analogue in the background here is precisely not uncontrolled or secret vengeance, but the public intervention of a legitimate, constituted authority that makes its decisions according to legal principles and whose intention is to protect and advance the common good through a legitimate imposition of punishment.[51]

Thus the 'vengeance' in the psalms is principally a concern for justice. Those innocently oppressed by others cry out for God to see that justice is done.

There are some who, while accepting some or all of the points above, would argue that these psalms can be part of the Christian's prayer only in some eschatological sense. That is, they ought not be used against our human 'enemies'

---

[50] Zenger, *A God of Vengeance?* p. 70.

[51] *Ibid.*, p. 71.

but apply only to God's ultimate victory over evil.[52] However, I think that in the terms set out above we can view expressions of so-called 'vengeance' in the psalms in new ways. One way, which I will take up in more detail later, is in terms of prayers of intercession. These psalms are the words of those who have suffered innocently, and who cry out to God for justice. We can use them as prayers on behalf of those in our own world who suffer in similar fashion. We may not feel the way the psalmist does, and we might resist seeing our own acquaintances as 'enemies'. However, there are those for whom we care and pray who are oppressed and who do have feelings of hatred against the perpetrators of violence, strife, and injustice. We can bring those people and their feelings before the God who seeks justice in the world.

But there is another way in which we can employ these so-called psalms of 'vengeance'. If we are honest with ourselves, there are times when we feel angry, threatened, vulnerable, or anxious, and we might want to utter words as dark as those in these psalms. I noted above that Bauriedl remarked that when feelings of anxiety become too strong for us, we can create our own images of enemies. It is a way of dealing with our anxiety. In such situations, the psalms offer us words to express these feelings. We may feel as though our prayers are not the place for such words or feelings. But the psalms suggest otherwise. They do not hide who we are and the feelings we have, even of anger, hatred, or vengeance. They have been spoken out of every human experience. Prayer is the place where those experiences are voiced.[53] What is important is that in the case of laments, those experiences are voiced in conversation with God. These psalms involve us in a conversation with God about our 'enemies' and our feelings of oppression, anxiety, anger, and even hatred. We lay such feelings before the one who is judge of all and who seeks justice for all, even our enemies. These feelings are not left to rage unattended, nor do they issue in personal vengeance. They are brought into the presence of God for attention and action as needed. And as I noted above, God's answer or response in the conversation, will not always be what we expect, nor come when we want.

Such feelings are to be no less a part of our prayer when they arise directly in our relationship with God. This is the point Broyles makes in his description of the God-lament psalms. If there are feelings of oppression, anxiety, anger, or even hatred in our relation with God, then these need to be expressed within that relationship. Failure to take such opportunities will lead at least to shallowness of relationship, or more seriously to alienation. One writer has commented, 'there is

---

[52] Sheppard, J. (1997), 'The Place of the Imprecatory Psalms in the Canon of Scripture', part I in *Churchman*, Vol. 111/1, pp. 27-47, and part II in *Churchman*, Vol. 111/2, pp. 110-126.

[53] In a similar vein see Kaniarakath, G. (1989), 'Praying the Psalms as an Experience of Prophetic Solidarity', *Jeev*, Vol. 19, pp. 105-117; Carney, S. (1983), 'God Damn God: A Reflection on Expressing Anger in Prayer', *Biblical Theology Bulletin*, Vol. 13, pp. 116-120; and Zub, D.J.C. (1992), 'God as the Object of Anger in the Psalms', in F. Tebbe (ed.), *Church Divinity 1991–1992*, Graduate Theological Foundation, Donaldson, IN, pp. 47-63.

no Biblical foundation for the conception of an emotionless God worshipped by emotionless people'.[54]

The psalms encourage us to bring all our experiences before God. They teach us that nothing is inadmissible in God's presence in our understanding of prayer as a genuine conversation with God. The lament psalms especially show us that God takes the conversation seriously and honours the combination of honesty and dialogue.[55] Our reluctance to move into this area, either in the formal liturgy of the community, or in personal prayer, could arise from a number of matters. We may not want to acknowledge the disorientation, confusion, or anger in our lives. We may not want to speak about these things publicly. It may be that our habit of polite and ordered words in God's presence is so strong that we cannot or do not want to venture into the risky area of honest words about how life really is at times. The psalms would draw us into that risky domain. Of course, there are matters of sensitivity to consider. A community of faith may need to be led carefully into such a domain. It may not be appropriate to speak of all private hurts etc. in the public context. Such things may have to be taken into account, but to enter this risky domain, which is related to the way of the cross, may ultimately be for the health of the community and of the individual pray-er.[56]

In all of this the issue of forgiveness should not be forgotten. And this is not just a Christian issue. Forgiveness of one's 'enemies' or at least compassion toward them was an issue in late Old Testament texts: Lev 19:17, 18; Prov 24:17, 25:21. The matter of 'vengeance' in the psalms cannot be dismissed as simply an issue of the old dispensation, which has been replaced by the new, or of the Old Testament superseded by the New Testament. It is not a matter of a Jewish-Christian division. The psalms have something to offer us by way of instruction as to who we are as Christian pray-ers. As we use the psalms in our prayers with the commands of Jesus to forgive embedded in our Christian conscience (Matt 18:21-35; Mark 11:25; Luke 6:37; 17:3-4; John 20:23), forgiveness is brought together with honesty and dialogue. The former shapes the dialogue and gives purpose to honest speech. It moves honesty and dialogue beyond catharsis. On the other hand, honesty and dialogue help prevent forgiveness from becoming an empty pious act. After all, genuine forgiveness presumes both honesty and open communication.

Prayer and the Whole Book of Psalms

Each psalm has a place in a total life of faith. Each invites us to pray and to shape our prayer in a certain way according to experience. However, it is not only through individual psalms that we learn about prayer. The grouping of small numbers of psalms, and even the organization of the whole Book of Psalms, can suggest ways in which we might discipline our prayer life. Whether such groupings

---

[54] Carney, 'God Damn God', p. 117; see also Zub, 'God as the Object of Anger in the Psalms', esp. pp. 56-59; and Nowell, I. (1994), 'The "Cursing" Psalms', *The Bible Today*, Vol. 32/4, pp. 218-222.

[55] Brueggemann, 'From Hurt to Joy', p. 5.

[56] Brueggemann, *Message of the Psalms*, pp. 51-53.

or overall organization were intentional on the part of the ancient editors of the Book of Psalms is not our direct interest here, nor is it crucial for our reading and praying of the psalms. The scholars will continue to debate the issue. What is important for our purpose is that as we pray the psalms, whether in their canonical order or not, we remain open to detecting connections between various psalms, across small collections, and even over the whole book.

In terms of small groupings of psalms, we find that in the early parts of the collection especially, certain groups of psalms fit the pattern: statements of lament and doubt followed by restatements of God's rule over the nations. For example, Psalm 42-43 (an individual lament) is followed by Psalm 44 (a community lament over defeat in battle), which is in turn followed by Psalms 46-48 emphasizing God's victory over the nations. Pss 38, 39 and 40:1-10 also fit this sequence, as possibly do other groups such as Pss 11-16; 17-18; 20-21; 22-24; 31-34.[57]

In terms of the total collection of psalms, there has been wide recognition of a movement in the Book of Psalms from a predominance of lament psalms at the beginning, especially in Book I (Psalms 1-41), to a predominance of psalms of praise toward the end of the collection.[58] The book ends with a great cacophony of praise in Psalms 146-150. The final Hebrew word in the book is *hallelujah*, 'Praise the Lord'. The movement is by no means a smooth one but overall we can see a trend.[59] While we might argue that the final declaration of praise has both theological and eschatological dimensions, in that the end of all creation is to proclaim God in all glory, it has implications for the life of the pray-er as well.[60] If the pray-er prays through the psalms in their canonical order, then he/she is caught up in the movement toward a point where all creation gives exuberant praise to God. This suggests that the goal of the life of faith is to be lost in the praise of God. The psalms as our prayers direct us in that way. It also implies that even the thoughts and expressions in some psalms of 'vengeance' seeking justice will ultimately be overwhelmed by praise. Ps 150:6 with its bold call: 'Let everything that breathes praise the LORD! Praise the LORD!' anticipates a time when even the enemies with their cruel taunts, so often mentioned in the psalms, will ultimately be overwhelmed by praise. Lament as prayer to God in time of pain,

---

[57] For a study in this general area see Miller, P.D. (1994), 'Kingship, Torah Obedience, and Prayer: The Theology of Psalms 15-24', in K. Seybold and E. Zenger (eds), *Neue Wege der Psalmenforschung für Walter Beyerlin*, Herder, Freiburg, pp. 127-142.

[58] For example, Westermann, C. (1981), *Praise and Lament in the Psalms*, John Knox, Atlanta, pp. 250-258; Miller, P.D. (1986), *Interpreting the Psalms*, Fortress, Philadelphia, p. 67.

[59] In Book I there are hymns of praise and expressions of trust in Pss 8, 19, 29, and 33. Note also the laments in Book V, namely Pss 109, 120, 123, 126, 130, and 140-143.

[60] See Miller, *Interpreting the Psalms*, p. 67. Note Childs, B.S. (1979), *Introduction to the Old Testament as Scripture*, Fortress, Philadelphia, p. 518 who says: '...the final form of the Psalter is highly eschatological in nature. It looks forward to the future and passionately yearns for its arrival.' Cf. also Wilson, G.H. (1992), 'The Shape of the Book of Psalms', *Interpretation*, Vol XLVI/2, pp. 129-142, esp. pp. 138-139. Cf. also Brueggemann, W. (1991), 'Bounded by Obedience and Praise: The Psalms as Canon', *JSOT*, Vol. 50, pp. 63-92.

hurt, and alienation, will give way to the praise of God in the joy of the community of all creation.

As I mentioned briefly above, the movement from lament to praise is not simply a one-way journey, ever seeming to come closer to its goal. Rather, it is a journey with interruptions and constant movements back and forth. It is neither a smooth journey nor an easy one. Nevertheless, it is there. Therefore, to accept the invitation to pray with the psalms is to accept an invitation not only to be transformed within individual experiences, but also to move towards a life lost in the praise of God. This requires commitment as well as acceptance. It involves obedience,[61] or discipleship in the Christian parlance. It is to see praise as the goal of our lives, our end. The thought of being lost in praise helps sustain us along the way. Here is an invitation to lose our life in the praise of God and to realize that in that our life finds its fulfilment.[62]

Along with this movement from lament to praise in the collection of psalms, one could note a movement from a situation where individual psalms predominate to one in which community psalms are more frequent. This might be expected if we remember that psalms of praise belong to the group in which the psalmist speaks mainly to parties other than God. Again, this is not a steady or consistent movement. Nevertheless, it can be noted and helps shape the identity of the pray-er of the psalms as one who ultimately belongs to a greater community of pray-ers.

If we accept the invitation in the psalms to discipline our life in the way of prayer, we are not only offered words of conversation that fit our experiences, and which, by their shape, help us in the transformation from one experience to another. We are offered a picture of a larger movement in life, a larger set of conversations that move inextricably toward the praise of God. Within this context we are called to see and understand our individual experiences and to shape our lives and prayer not only in terms of those experiences but of the whole movement of our life.

A World with its Own Language

The psalms are poems. As the psalms invite us to enter their world of prayer, they also invite us into the world of poetry, a world rich in metaphor, symbol, imagery, and rhythm. Of course, the psalms are not the only poems in the Old Testament. The prophetic writings use poetry extensively. Nor are all prayers in the Old

---

[61] Wilson, 'The Shape of the Book of Psalms', pp. 136-7. Wilson argues that the movement toward praise and life takes place through obedience. He understands Psalm 1, which notes obedience to *torah* (NRSV 'law') as the mark of the righteous person (v. 2), as a guide to how the psalms that follow are to be read, namely as *torah*. There are other ways to relate the mention of *torah* in Psalm 1 to the whole collection of psalms without denying the movement in the collection nor for the need of obedience.

[62] There is a twist here on the well-known saying of Jesus in Matt 10:39 and parallels. While the saying of Jesus is about the acceptance of the way of the cross, there is also a sense in which we will gain our life as we lose it in the unhindered praise of God.

Testament poems. There are many prose prayers in the prophets or narrative books.[63] However, the Book of Psalms consistently presents its prayers in poetic form and the impact and importance of this should not be overlooked.

Poetry and prayer belong together. Poetic forms are not only useful in the formation of prayers, but they assist in the greater aim of prayer. Poetry and prayer are similar in nature. Poetry aims to go beyond the ordinary. Prose, especially discursive prose that argues a case, often seeks to convey information within a specific historical, syntactical, and logical framework. Poetry transcends the bounds of this framework in order to explore more deeply the nature of reality itself. One writer has put it that in discursive prose words 'embrace meaning', while in poetry 'they explode meaning'.[64] Others would go even further and argue that poetry also has a creative function and seeks to bring into reality what is not.[65] This transcending of boundaries within the language of poetry happens in two directions. First, it is a transcending of outer boundaries, those which mark the limits of what we know, perceive, or experience. Secondly, it is a transcending of our inner boundaries, those which determine how we see ourselves in relation to the world and God. G. Hughes, in a brief but helpful discussion on prayer, argues that prayer is a *kind* of poetry in that it both speaks 'at the 'frontier' of what we can know or achieve' and yet is not content with describing things as they are or stating the familiar. Rather, prayer as a *kind* of poetry should have a capacity 'to pluck at the awareness of worshippers', to elicit surprise or reawaken wonder in God's presence.[66]

Another aspect of poetry relevant to our consideration of prayer concerns the words, phrases, and expressions used. As I noted above, poetry employs language richer in metaphor, symbol, and imagery than prose. It does not try to express wholeness by describing something completely or exhaustively. It seeks to be succinct, employing a minimum of words, to expose and explore the heart of things. Unlike prose, where we strive for a logical, sequential relationship between clauses, sentences, and paragraphs, poetry operates much more on the aesthetic level. There is, of course, logic in the argument within many poems which must be noted. However, the techniques for developing that logic are not the same as those used within prose. An appreciation of both the aesthetics of a poem, as well as the interplay between poetic form, imagery, rhythm etc., is necessary for the 'logic' of the poem to be understood. This is true both at the level of individual lines and at the levels of the stanza or whole poem.

When we speak about the language of poetry and its relation to the language of prayer, we are getting to the heart of the language of faith according to the Catholic theologian K. Rahner. He says that the capacity and practice of perceiving and understanding the poetic word is actually a prerequisite of the life of faith. He remarks:

---

[63] For an introduction to the prayers of the Old Testament see Miller, *They Cried to the Lord*, and Balentine, *Prayer in the Hebrew Bible*.
[64] Broyles, *Faith and Experience*, p. 30.
[65] Brueggemann, 'Psalms and the Life of Faith', p. 17.
[66] Hughes, G. (1992), *Leading in Prayer*, JBCE, Melbourne, pp. 9-11.

And so it is true that the capacity and practice of perceiving the poetic word is a presupposition of hearing the word of God.... the poetic word and the poetic ear are so much part of man that if this essential power were really lost to the heart, man could no longer hear the word of God in the word of man. In its inmost essence, the poetic is a prerequisite for Christianity.[67]

This connection of poetry to matters of faith was recognized long ago. Jewish writers, in a ninth century C.E. Midrash, imagined God musing on the importance of poetry and song:

Were it not for the poetry and song that they [all flesh and blood] recite before me daily, I would not have created the world; and whence do we know that the Holy One, blessed be he, only created the world on account of poetry and song? From the verse which says (Psalm 96:6), 'honor and majesty are before him, strength and beauty are in his sanctuary.' That is to say, honor and majesty are before him in heaven, but strength and beauty arise from his sanctuary on earth.... And whence do we know that the Holy One, blessed be he, created the heavens for the matter of poetry? From the verse which says (Psalm 19:1), 'The heavens declare the glory of God...' And whence do we know that Adam opened his mouth in a song of praise? From the verse which says 'A Psalm, a poem for the Sabbath day. It is good to give thanks to the Lord, and to sing praise to thy name, O most high!' (Psalm 92:1).'[68]

If we accept what Rahner says about the close connection between poetry and faith and apply it to the psalms, then we see that it is neither an accidental nor an arbitrary choice on the part of the psalmists, that the psalms are poems. There is a natural coherence between these prayers and songs and their poetic form. If we then take the psalms as our prayers or use them in our praying we are invited into the world of poetic speech. This gives us all the advantages that poetic language has over prose. It allows us to speak at the boundaries of our existence, and to go beyond our own knowledge and experience, both externally and internally. It allows us to transcend the limits of our own words, to give expression to what we feel, hope for, or lament over, without the boundaries of our speech limiting our part in the conversation. Brueggemann notes this freedom inherent in the poetic language of the psalms when he remarks: 'This kind of speech resists discipline, shuns precision, delights in ambiguity, is profoundly creative, and is itself an exercise in freedom.'[69]

There certainly is freedom in this language but we should be careful how we understand this resistance to discipline. Brueggemann speaks of it in the context of the danger of reading even the poetic language of the psalms in a descriptive fashion. This lends itself to management, control, and powerlessness rather than to surprise and creativity. While we acknowledge this possibility, we ought not to imagine his words to be an invitation to equate freedom with a total

---

[67] Rahner, K. (1966), *More Recent Writings*, Theological Investigations, Vol 4, Helicon, Baltimore, p. 363.

[68] *Midrash Otiyyot Derabbi Akiba*, ch. 1, Wertheimer, S.A (ed.) (1914), Jerusalem, pp. 1-2, quoted in Fisch, *Poetry with a Purpose*, p.119.

[69] Brueggemann, W. (1982), *Praying the Psalms*, St. Mary's, Winona, p. 28.

lack of discipline in prayer. I would understand the resistance to discipline, about which Brueggemann speaks, to be a resistance to the sort of discipline that restricts and prescribes our response. However, a discipline is needed if we are to appreciate the poetic language of the psalms let alone be shaped by that language in our prayer life. This is a discipline of learning (as much as we are capable), of time and of submission to guidance. What I am talking about here is akin to the point Bonhoeffer makes about prayer in general, namely that we have to learn how to pray. If prayer and poetry are similar in nature, and we are to take the psalms as our guides in prayer, then we need to attend to their poetic language.

What I have said so far about prayer and poetry may lead some to think that we must be poets in order to pray. This is not the case, at least not in terms of becoming accomplished poets. It is the case that we can learn more about how to pray if we give some attention to the poetic language of the psalms and other prayers, even in a limited way. This is especially the case when considering prayers composed for public worship, but can be equally applicable in our private prayers. We live in a world where the imaginative use of words is not always cherished and where we want words to mean what they say.[70] But the poetic world of the psalms is one where there is a multiplicity of images, often piled one on top of the other. For example note Ps 22:12-18:

> [12] Many bulls encircle me,
>   strong bulls of Bashan surround me;
> [13] they open wide their mouths at me,
>   like a ravening and roaring lion.
>
> [14] I am poured out like water,
>   and all my bones are out of joint;
> my heart is like wax;
>   it is melted within my breast;
> [15] my mouth is dried up like a potsherd,
>   and my tongue sticks to my jaws;
> you lay me in the dust of death.
>
> [16] For dogs are all around me;
>   a company of evildoers encircles me.
> My hands and feet have shriveled;
> [17] I can count all my bones.
>   They stare and gloat over me;
> [18] they divide my clothes among themselves,
>   and for my clothing they cast lots.

To understand the poem we must be ready to let these many images spark our imagination and feelings. This section begins (vv. 13-14) with images of wild or

---

[70] Brueggemann, W. (1989), *Finally comes the poet*, Fortress Press, Minneapolis, p. 1, where he speaks of 'poetry in a prose-flattened world'.

dangerous animals, strong bulls and lions, the latter of which did roam wild in and around ancient Israel. The psalmist paints a picture of being surrounded by such creatures. The images spark fear in us all. However, immediately the psalmist has generated a sense of fear, the images shift to ones of poured out water and melted wax, things that can run everywhere and be difficult to control (v. 14). The psalmist's imagery takes another sudden turn in the very next verse to one of a dryness of mouth, like one would experience in a dry and dusty place. The mention of the potsherd reinforces the imagery at this point. A potsherd is a piece of broken pottery, dry and baked hard by the furnace of the potter, but which because of its broken state has been discarded. The image of the dry and dusty place subtly, but naturally, shifts to become the 'dust of death' at the end of the verse. Verse 16 returns to the picture of being surrounded by ravenous beasts, this time dogs. It recalls the threat and fear of vv. 13-14. But also, in Old Testament terms, it plays on the idea of death with dogs being described as the scavengers who devour discarded bodies in several texts (e.g. Exod 22:31; 1 Kgs 14:11; 16:4; Isa 56:11; Jer 15:13; Pss 59:6, 14; 68:23 etc.). The image of the enemies gloating recalls other statements about the enemy reviling the psalmist (e.g. Pss 13:2,4; 42:9; 44:16; 55:3; 143:3).

The imagery leads us to the point where the psalmist feels death is near. Along the way feelings are evoked of fear, helplessness, of dying of thirst, and of scavengers and taunters waiting for the psalmist's death, or being impatient even for that. There is a confusion of images in this part of the psalm and that too contributes to the feeling the psalmist conveys. We have an appreciation of the sheer terror and confusion of this experience. The imagery does not just help us in understanding the psalm; it bears a large part of the meaning. An appreciation of this helps in generating our own prayers in relation to this psalm.

It might be helpful at this stage to outline some of the features of Hebrew poetry. Most of us are familiar with such things as the use of metaphor, imagery, symbolism, various 'sound effects', and word plays within English language poetry. Hebrew poets also employed these devices. However, there are other aspects of Hebrew poetry that might be less familiar.[71]

An important element in Hebrew poetry is the paralleling of words or ideas within consecutive lines, or half lines of a poem. This feature is widespread in ancient Semitic poetry, of which Hebrew poetry is but one strand. In parallelism, it is usually the case that the second element in a parallel pair develops or explores the first element in some way.[72] The elements within a parallel pair can be similar in some way, as for example in Psalm 117:

[1] Praise the Lord, all you nations!

---

[71] For a good general introduction to Hebrew poetry see Petersen D.L. and Richards, K.H. (1992), *Interpreting Hebrew Poetry*, Fortress, Minneapolis.

[72] See especially the works by Alter, R. (1985), *The Art of Biblical Poetry*, T. & T. Clark, Edinburgh, esp. pp. 3-26, and (1986) 'The Psalms: Beauty Heightened through Poetic Structure', *Bible Review*, Vol. Fall, pp. 29-41; and Kugel, J.L. (1981), *The Idea of Biblical Poetry: Parallelism and its History*, Yale University, New Haven, esp. pp. 1-58.

Extol him, all you peoples!

Or in Psalm 114:

> [1] When Israel went out of Egypt,
>   the house of Jacob from a people of strange language,
> [2] Judah became his[73] sanctuary,
>   Israel his dominion.

In both of these cases the parallel elements are fairly close. The parallelism has been created simply by using synonyms in the respective lines. In other verses, a similar idea might be expressed but the two parallel lines give different nuances to the overall idea. For example, in Ps 117:2a we read:

> For great is his steadfast love toward us,
>   and the faithfulness of the Lord endures forever.

Here the two lines complement each other, each adding a slightly different point to the overall impact. The concepts of 'steadfast love' and 'faithfulness' are essentially synonyms in the Hebrew, but in the second line the word 'Lord' makes specific the pronoun 'his' in the first line. Moreover, the first line stresses that the Lord's steadfast love is directed 'toward us' while the second line speaks of the eternal nature of the Lord's faithfulness. Thus, the parallelism functions in such a way that the lines not only reinforce each other but contribute slightly different aspects to the overall concept. Together the lines say that not only is the Lord's love eternal but that it is directed 'toward us' thereby specifying the beneficiaries of the faithfulness and the endurance of the love 'toward us'.

Parallelism can also be achieved by juxtaposing opposing ideas or antonyms within as many lines or half lines. An oft quoted example is found in Ps 1:6 where we read:

> For the Lord knows the way of the righteous,
>   but the way of the wicked perishes.

In this verse, the way of the righteous and the way of the wicked stand in contrast to each other. The statement that qualifies each highlights this. The way of the wicked perishes but the Lord knows the way of the righteous. The verse gives the added sense that the Lord's knowing something (or someone) means life for that thing or person.

Another feature used occasionally within Hebrew poetry is repetition of structure. This can occur within the stanzas of a poem, for example in Psalm 107, which I will discuss below, or over the whole poem itself. An example of the latter

---

[73] The Hebrew text reads 'his'. Note the NRSV inserts the word 'God's' to make it clear whose sanctuary is referred to. The Hebrew text, however, maintains an element of mystery early in the psalm. The identity of the unspecified 'his' is only revealed in v. 7.

is Psalm 114, which recalls the exodus from Egypt. The two central stanzas repeat a number of elements but in the first of these stanzas they are set in the form of a statement. In the second they appear as an extended question.

³ The sea looked and fled;
    Jordan turned back.
⁴ The mountains skipped like rams,
    the hills like lambs.

⁵ Why is it, O sea, that you flee?
    O Jordan, that you turn back?
⁶ O mountains, that you skip like rams?
    O hills, like lambs?

Surrounding this sequence are the first and last stanzas of the psalm, vv. 1-2 and 7-8 respectively. Each of these has reference to the exodus. The paralleling structure of the whole poem focuses on the transforming power of Israel's God, who not only causes the sea and the Jordan river to flee, but brings water from flinty rock and even makes a vulnerable people into his sanctuary and dominion.

Psalm 22 presents another structure altogether. It begins with a statement of the psalmist's lament (vv. 1-2). The psalmist next recalls the holiness of God in relation to the faith of the ancestors (vv. 3-5). Then there is a return to the present lament (vv. 6-8) only to be followed by recollection of the psalmist's own past experience of trust in God even from his/her birth (vv. 9-11). The lament then returns in longer form (vv. 12-21a) to be followed by the extended praise of God (vv. 21b- 31). Thus, lament, which increases in length as the psalm moves on, alternates with recollections of faithfulness, both nationally and personally. The mood changes of a person in deep distress, who feels all the fear, helplessness, confusion, and terror of imminent death, are portrayed vividly in the structure of the psalm. As we read the psalm we trace the psalmist's shifts between feeling utterly oppressed and ashamed, even to the point of death, and asserting or claiming trust in God. From the low points we are taken to heights of trust, only to come back down to the point of dismay and feeling undone. These ups and downs, and back and forth movements reflect the human movement in suffering. But at the end of the psalm the lengthy section of praise counters even the longest of the lament sections. In this psalm, the continued presence of the lament is felt deeper and deeper and past recollections of God's presence do not reduce its severity. In fact, the juxtaposition of lament and recollection only serves to strengthen the lament. However, given even the severity of the lament, the psalm finally testifies to the view that praise will prevail.

Psalm 23

We will look at Psalm 23 as an example of how poetic language relates to the meaning of the psalm. This psalm is one of the best known and most widely used of all psalms. Nothing in the psalm indicates what the psalmist's situation might have been. The psalm is, thus, best understood by attending to the way the psalmist has expressed his/her ideas, that is, by giving attention to its poetic form.

Metaphors convey meaning in Psalm 23. Two metaphors dominate the verses of the psalm, that of the shepherd (vv. 1-3) and that of the banquet table (v. 5).[74] Many scholars break the psalm into two sections based on these metaphors. However, the poem is complicated by an overlapping structure marked by the way the Lord is addressed. The name 'Lord' appears only in vv. 1 and 6. In these same sections (vv. 1-3 and 6) the Lord is referred to in the third person, 'he.' But in vv. 4-5 the Lord is addressed directly as 'you.' Thus, the sections of the psalm marked off by the two metaphors cross over the sections marked off by the pronouns used to address the Lord. Other scholars have divided the psalm into yet more sections based on proposed metrical and syntactic structures.[75]

The psalm is clearly written from the point of view of the 'sheep' or the 'guest' at the banquet. The metaphors convey a sense of complete provision and protection by the Lord. The parallelism in vv. 2-3a develops the point made about the Lord's provision:

> [2] He makes me lie down in green pastures;
> > he leads me beside still waters;
> [3] he restores my soul.

The parallel lines in v. 2, which imply lush pastures and placid waters, refer to both food and drink in abundance and goodness, while the third line (v. 3a), which could be translated 'he restores my life', encapsulates the entire sentiment. The sense of provision and abundance is conveyed in the banquet metaphor both by the banquet itself and by the overflowing cup (v. 5). The idea of protection is covered by the image of the rod and staff protecting the psalmist in the darkest of circumstances (v. 4), and by the table being set in the presence of enemies in v. 5.

The parallelism in vv. 2-3 functions not only at the level of meaning of words and images created. The two lines in v. 2 are parallel also in their grammatical construction. In Hebrew the word order of the lines is:

> in pastures of green - he makes me lie down;
> > beside waters of stillness - he leads me;

However, when we get to v. 3b, the word order in the Hebrew is reversed. It reads:

---

[74] It could be argued that the shepherd metaphor of vv. 1-3 continues in v. 4, and the banquet metaphor in v. 6. The case of v. 4 is ambiguous as v. 3 concludes with a reason for the statements in vv. 1-3. Verse 6 begins with an initial particle in Hebrew, indicating an independent statement.

[75] See the study by Freedman, D.N. (1980), *Pottery, Poetry, and Prophecy: Studies in Early Hebrew Poetry*, Eisenbrauns, Winona Lake, pp. 275-302, originally published in Orlin, L.L. et al., (eds) (1976), *Michigan Oriental Studies in Honor of George C. Cameron*, Dept. of Near Eastern Studies, University of Michigan, Ann Arbor, pp. 139-166.

he leads me - in paths of right(ness)

Thus, a contrast is set up in the order of the words and how the reader encounters them, thereby interrupting the previous pattern and causing the reader to pause before he/she reads the short and stark statement: 'for the sake of his name'. Thus the reader's focus at the end of this section is brought back to the Lord, where it all began: 'The Lord is my shepherd'. While the greater portion of vv. 1b-3 stress the provision and abundance experienced by the psalmist (as the sheep), surrounding the section are references to the Lord and his name. There is no confusion as to who is responsible for the abundant provision, and who is the ultimate focus for the psalmist.

The metaphors of the psalm do not just function at the literal level of real shepherds and sheep or banquets, giving a sense of abundant provision and protection. Both the main metaphors allude to other matters thereby suggesting many layers of meaning. The images of shepherd and banquet can both be associated with kings and gods in Israel and the ancient Near East. The epithet of shepherd for God is found in Gen 49:24; Isa 40:11; Ezek 34:11-16 (cf. Pss 80:1; 95:7; and 100:3). It is found elsewhere in the ancient Near East, for example in relation to the sun-god Shamash,[76] or in relation to the ideal picture of the Pharaoh of Egypt, of whom it is said:

> He is the shepherd of all people, evil is not in his heart. Though his herds may be small, he has spent the day caring for them.[77]

The presence of enemies in v. 5 could allude to their defeat and humiliation and maybe a royal victory celebration. As a parallel to this, in an ancient letter from the city of Irqata in Lebanon the local king seeks the support of the Egyptian Pharaoh in defeating the local opposition. He says in part:

> May the king, our lord, heed the words of his loyal servants. May he grant a gift to his servant(s) so our enemies will see this and eat dirt.[78]

On the other hand, Ps 23:5 could simply underline the sense of protection even in the presence of enemies.

Allusions to the story of the Israel's exodus out of Egypt can also be seen in the psalm. The image of the Lord leading his people like a shepherd is found in relation to the exodus story in Pss 77:20; 80:1 and in Ezek 34:11-24; Isa 40:11; and 49:10 in the context of the second exodus from Babylon to Jerusalem after the exile. The Hebrew expression for 'I shall not want' occurs elsewhere in the Old Testament only in Neh 9:21, where it refers to the Lord's provision for his people in the wilderness. The sense of Israel 'lacking nothing' during the exodus is also

---

[76] Pritchard, J. (ed.) (1969), *Ancient Near Eastern Texts Relating to the Old Testament*, 3rd ed., Princeton University Press, p. 387.

[77] *Ibid.*, p. 443.

[78] EA 100 in Moran, W.L. (ed. and trans.) (1992), *The Amarna Letters*, Johns Hopkins University, Baltimore, p. 173.

present in Deut 2:7. In terms of the banquet metaphor, we note the reference in Ps 78:19 where, in the midst of a recall of Israel's wandering in the wilderness, the people grumble and ask, 'Can God spread a table in the wilderness?' While the presence of the enemies mentioned in Psalm 23 is lacking in Psalm 78, the allusion to God's provision in times of hardship is clear.

Multiple meanings are evident also in some individual expressions in Psalm 23. The phrase in v. 3, translated variously as 'paths of righteousness' (RSV) or 'right paths' (NRSV) is ambiguous even in the Hebrew. Does it mean that the Lord leads the psalmist in ways of righteousness wherein the psalmist exercises justice and truth? If so, this would support a 'royal' interpretation of the psalm. Or does it mean that the Lord leads the psalmist in the right paths, namely ones that do not present the psalmist with obstacles or threats to his or her well-being? The second meaning fits well the sense of provision and protection in the rest of the psalm.

Meaning is also conveyed in the psalm by way of its overall structure. The name of the Lord is only found in vv. 1 and 6 as I noted above. These references surround everything else in the psalm and further the sense of the Lord's protection of the psalmist. This is a poetic device pointing us to the fact that the Lord is the beginning and the end of our trust. The Lord protects the psalmist by his goodness, mercy, and provision. This protection is there even in times of danger. In vv. 1-3 the psalmist's relation with the Lord is developed. In v. 4 the intimacy of the relationship is revealed by stating the psalmist's lack of fear, and the closeness and comfort of the Lord in the most threatening of places, 'the darkest valley' or 'the valley of the shadow of death.' It is at this point, where the closeness of the Lord is stated, that there is the shift to the more intimate second person pronoun 'you' when referring to the Lord. Thus, even the places of danger are enveloped within the circle of the Lord's care. The structure of the poem underlines that. Moreover, it concludes with two lines ending in the words 'all the days of my life' and 'my whole life long.' The protection and provision of the Lord will never cease. Such is the sheer confidence and trust of the psalmist. Praying the words of this psalm is not just a matter of uttering words of comfort. It is an engagement with a level of reality that goes beyond the level of any threat to our well-being.

This is something that only poetic language can attempt to convey adequately. It is a reminder that in prayer we are engaging in an exercise that transcends our everyday living. It will require structures and expressions that take us beyond the normal into that world.

Giving some attention to the poetic language in the psalms can enhance and deepen our own prayers. Of course, in our prayers we are not creating poems for their own sake, nor for some ostentatious reason. We are not promoting ourselves before others or God. When we give attention to the poetry of the psalms and emulate some of its features in our own prayers we are seeking to find new ways of strengthening and deepening our prayer life. Finally, some further words from G. Hughes are appropriate at this point. He says:

> 'Our prayers are not meant to be poems, then. But because language is the medium of prayer, and because for several reasons poetic language speaks to and from deeper places within us, the prayers we pray in public (that is, prayers which expect

to gather other people's consciousness up into them) do need to be a *kind* of poetry.'[79]

While he says this in relation to contemporary prayers composed for worship, it relates to the use of psalms in public and private prayer. They are already poems, breaking the boundaries of our experience. As such they readily lend themselves to becoming our prayers.

A World in which we are Not Alone

Another aspect of the world of prayer in the psalms is that it is a world in which the pray-er is never alone. This is expressed within the psalms themselves. It is patently clear in the hymns of praise or thanksgiving psalms, which constitute the majority in the third major group of psalms mentioned earlier. In these the psalmist speaks to parties other than God for all or the greater part of the psalm. The psalmist is firmly situated within the community of God's people and seeks to embrace others in his/her joy and praise. However, it is in the other two major groups of psalms that the threat of undesired solitude is strongest. In these psalms, the psalmist either addresses God alone, or speaks to one other party as well as to God. As I noted lament psalms form the greater portion of these groups. Thus, it is in the context of lament when the psalmist suffers pain, rejection, illness, or some other form of distress, and when he/she needs the comfort of others and companionship most, that the threat of solitude and abandonment is greatest. The psalmist never desires solitude, but in his/her prayers arising out of hurt and distress, feels it acutely. For example in Ps 31:10-13 we read:

> [10] For my life is spent with sorrow,
>   and my years with sighing;
>   my strength fails because of my misery,
>   and my bones waste away.
> [11] I am the scorn of all my adversaries,
>   a horror to my neighbors,
>   an object of dread to my acquaintances;
>   those who see me in the street flee from me.
> [12] I have passed out of mind like one who is dead;
>   I have become like a broken vessel.
> [13] For I hear the whispering of many – terror all around! –
>   as they scheme together against me,
>   as they plot to take my life.

Not only does the psalmist face adversaries in v. 11, but he/she has also become a horror to neighbours, an object of dread to acquaintances, and a cause for flight for the passer by. Friend and foe, familiar and stranger, all abandon the psalmist in

---

[79] Hughes, *Leading in Prayer*, p. 19.

his/her plight. They plot together as it were (v. 13) even though their motive and intent may not be the same. The psalmist has become like one who has died, is forgotten and cast aside. The feeling of utter abandonment of the psalmist by friends is also expressed clearly in Ps 38:11-14. The psalmist feels like one who has no way of communication with the world. He/she is totally alone.

> [11] My friends and companions stand aloof from my affliction,
>   and my neighbors stand far off.
> [12] Those who seek my life lay their snares;
>   those who seek to hurt me speak of ruin,
>   and meditate treachery all day long.
> [13] But I am like the deaf, I do not hear;
>   like the mute, who cannot speak.
> [14] Truly, I am like one who does not hear,
>   and in whose mouth is no retort.

The extreme statement of this feeling occurs in Psalm 88, the one lament in which there is no stated movement to praise. It begins with a long statement comparing the psalmist's present situation with death, where neither God's hand (i.e. power) nor God's memory (i.e. consideration) reaches:

> [3] For my soul is full of troubles,
>   and my life draws near to Sheol.
> [4] I am counted among those who go down to the Pit;
>   I am like those who have no help,
> [5] like those forsaken among the dead,
>   like the slain that lie in the grave,
>   like those whom you remember no more,
>   for they are cut off from your hand.
> [6] You have put me in the depths of the Pit,
>   in the regions dark and deep.
> [7] Your wrath lies heavy upon me,
>   and you overwhelm me with all your waves.

The psalmist then declares that those close to the psalmist have shunned him/her 'You have caused my companions to shun me; you have made me a thing of horror to them' (v. 8). The same points are made again in slightly different order and ways in vv. 9b-18. The psalmist calls to God continually but then asks through a series of rhetorical questions whether God's work and steadfast love are effective in the realm of the dead (vv. 10-12). The psalmist asks again why the Lord's face is hidden, and likens his/her situation to death (vv. 14-16). Finally, he/she expresses feelings of being abandoned by human as well as God, although at the heart of it, it is all the work of God: 'You have caused friend and neighbor to shun me; my companions are in darkness' (v. 18).

Even when the psalmist feels alone in prayer, he/she still longs for the community of God's people and counts him/herself among the people of God or 'the poor.' This is the case clearly in Psalms 12 and 14. In both cases the psalmist states that there is no longer anyone who is 'godly' or 'wise'. A sense of desolation on the part of the psalmist is engendered at the start of each Psalm:

Psalm 12

¹ Help, O LORD, for there is no longer anyone who is godly;
　　the faithful have disappeared from humankind.
² They utter lies to each other;
　　with flattering lips and a double heart they speak.

Psalm 14

¹ Fools say in their hearts, 'There is no God.'
　　They are corrupt, they do abominable deeds;
　　there is no one who does good.
² The LORD looks down from heaven on humankind
　　to see if there are any who are wise,
　　who seek after God.
³ They have all gone astray, they are all alike perverse;
　　there is no one who does good, no, not one.

However, at later points in each of these psalms the perspective changes. The psalmist either quotes words from the Lord, which indicate an intention to act because the 'poor' are despoiled (12:5), or the psalmist proclaims that the Lord is the refuge of the 'poor' and will confound the plans of the evildoers (14:6). Even when the psalmist feels abandoned by God, he/she has a sense of identity with the community of God's people over time. While this makes the psalmist's plight more acute, it also serves as a strong argument for persuading God to act on the psalmist's behalf. We could compare Ps 22:1-5:

¹ My God, my God, why have you forsaken me?
　　Why are you so far from helping me,
　　from the words of my groaning?
² O my God, I cry by day, but you do not answer;
　　and by night, but find no rest.
³ Yet you are holy, enthroned on the praises of Israel.
⁴ In you our ancestors trusted;
　　they trusted, and you delivered them.
⁵ To you they cried, and were saved;
　　in you they trusted, and were not put to shame.

A similar situation can apply to a community of God's people. It can, on a particular occasion, see itself in association with the much larger community of God's people, extending over a greater period of time. This is evident in Psalm 74, which, as I noted earlier, was written after the Babylonians sacked the Jerusalem temple in 587 B.C.E. Psalm 74 is full of words relating to time.[80] Within the psalm a conflict is evident focussed on the relation of past, present, and future. The fact that the city and temple presently lie in ruins, together with God's apparent absence and forgetfulness of the people, raises questions about the future of the community. How long will this present situation go on? Will God ever act to restore God's own reputation and deliver the people?

> [1] O God, why do you cast us off forever?
>> Why does your anger smoke against the sheep of your pasture?
> [2] Remember your congregation, which you acquired long ago,
>> which you redeemed to be the tribe of your heritage.
> Remember Mount Zion, where you came to dwell.

Part of the difficulty for the psalmist is that the present time stands in sharp contrast to the past. I mentioned above that in vv. 12-17, in the midst of the lament over the people's present experience, the psalmist recalls a time of old, namely the time of creation. This was in part to persuade God to act and not remain silent. But also the time of creation was a time especially associated with the idea of the Lord as ruler of the entire world. The present time with its disastrous events seems to deny all that the past has proclaimed. If the Babylonians, following their god, have destroyed the Lord's own temple and captured the Lord's people, then how can the Lord be ruler? How can God not remember the people God 'acquired long ago'? The present, with its ruined temple declaring the powerlessness of Israel's God, is thus at odds with the past, when creation heralded the Lord's rule. Because of this, the psalmist sees the future in jeopardy. All that has been of importance to date now seems to be of no avail. So the people send up a cry for the Lord to remember, to act and have regard for the covenant (v. 20).[81] The psalmist sees his/her present plight as a concern for the community of God's people over time. While the ruined temple is clearly a problem for the psalmist's own generation and maybe for future generations, it is also a problem that concerns the past. If the temple stands in ruins it raises a question of the efficacy of the Lord's work in the past. The psalmist sees himself or herself intimately connected to past and future generations. He/she does not pray alone and does not pray for him/herself alone.

Not only is there a sense of belonging to a community in some individual psalms, but that same sense is also conveyed in the way the collection of psalms has taken shape. Psalms from both the private and public spheres of Israelite piety have been brought together in the Book of Psalms. Two foci have thus been created: the joys and crises of everyday life, and the great moments of public religion. The psalms touch on both of these. There is no separation between the two. In fact, in the process of collection and canonization of the psalms, a dynamic

---

[80] See vv. 1, 2, 3, 9, 10, 12, 19, 22, and 23.

[81] Cf. Also the remarks of Fisch, *Poetry with a Purpose*, esp. ch. 7, 'Psalms: The Limits of Subjectivity', pp. 104-135 and esp. pp. 112-118.

interaction has been created between private piety and public devotion.[82] This has meant that in the later use of the collection, further integration is achieved. The individual can now take up prayers from the great moments of public religion, just as the community can employ individual prayers. In this context, the individual pray-er is constantly related to the larger context of the community and vice-versa.

Another aspect of not being alone in praying the psalms can be tied to the association of the psalms with David. This tradition had its origins in Judaism before New Testament times (cf. Ecclus 47:8-10). As well as attributing existing psalms to David, new psalms were written around events in David's life, for example Psalm 151 from the Apocrypha. One manuscript from the Dead Sea Scrolls attributes 1050 psalms to him plus songs.[83] The tradition continued to develop over a long period and more and more psalms were attributed to David. It was well established by the first century C.E. and was assumed by New Testament writers (e.g. Mark 12:35-37 and parallels; Acts 1:16-20; Heb 4:7 etc.) and other early Christian writers. At one level, this had to do with the matter of authority and inspiration as David was seen as the author of the psalms. This was especially the case in those psalms where a brief reference to some event in David's life was added as a heading (e.g. Pss 3, 18, 34, 51 etc.).

Recently, some scholars have asked whether this growing attribution of the psalms to David was simply an historical claim of authorship, or whether more was involved. They have suggested that it might have had something to do with the interpretation of the psalms as Scripture or in liturgy.[84] That is, the attribution of psalms to David does not simply indicate the belief of earlier editors that David was the author of the psalms. Rather, it stamps the psalm with authority and provides a context within which the psalms are to be interpreted by later generations. In other words, the attribution of psalms to David does not simply seek to provide historical information such as who wrote the psalms.[85] What it does do is give the person of faith a context within which he/she can seek to understand the psalms. It provides a background against which the psalms can be interpreted. In short, it gives a life context, namely that of David, in which the faithful person can see the psalms functioning as prayers or hymns in all their different ways. This aspect of the process of attribution can be traced back into the biblical material

---

[82] See Butler, T.C. (1984), 'Piety in the Psalms', *Review and Expositor*, Vol. 81, pp. 385-394, esp. p. 391.

[83] 11QPs[a] DavComp. See Sanders, J.A. (1965), *The Psalms Scroll of Qumran Cave 11 (11QPs[a])*, DJD IV, Clarendon, Oxford, pp. 91-92.

[84] See Cooper, A.M. (1983), 'The Life and Times of King David according to the Book of Psalms', in R.E. Friedman (ed.), *The Poet and the Historian: Essays in Literary and Historical Biblical Criticism*, HSS 26; Chico CA: Scholars, pp. 117-131; Mays, J.L. (1986), 'The David of the Psalms', *Interpretation*, Vol. 40, pp. 143-155; and Allen, L.C. (1986), 'David as Exemplar of Spirituality: The Redactional Function of Psalm 19', *Biblica*, Vol. 67, pp. 544-6.

[85] While the ancient editors might have intended primarily to indicate Davidic authorship, many scholars today would argue against that assumption or conclude the historical information is insubstantial at best. For a general discussion see e.g. Craigie, P.C. (1983), *Psalms 1-50*, Word, Waco, TX, pp. 33-35.

itself. It could be present in the addition of titles to the psalms. Most of these titles, such as that found at the beginning of Psalm 3, 'A Psalm of David, when he fled from his son Absalom', associate the psalm with an episode in David's life. However, the episode seems to be chosen not simply in relation to David as king, but rather to highlight the human expression in the psalm. David, the king, is thus seen as a representative human.[86] The association of psalms with David in the Books of Chronicles also plays a role in this.[87] One writer suggests that David could have become '...a standard of spirituality for each generation of God's people...' from whom those who used the psalms were invited to learn.[88] If we accept this suggestion, and think of the psalms related to David in this way, then the user of the psalms has a sense that he/she is taking the words of the great king of Judah, the pray-er and singer of the psalms, as their own. His/her own supplication and praise is joined to David's, and the user's words receive acceptance in that. The user of the psalms is joined not only to the community of God's people at large but to a great pray-er of that community.

We could make a similar statement in relation to the psalms and Jesus. As we pray the psalms we pray the prayers Jesus prayed, although this should not be understood in a simple historical fashion. There is no evidence that in the Judaism of Jesus' day the psalms *as a whole* were used in worship, although there is evidence that certain psalms were used regularly in the twice daily *tamid* service at the Jerusalem Temple.[89] On the other hand, it is clear in parts of the New Testament, especially in the Epistle to the Hebrews, that the words of David in the psalms were already being appropriated as the words of Jesus in a way that set up models of prayer and faith for his followers. This is the case, for example, in Heb 10:5-10 where it is written Jesus 'said' the words of Ps 40:6-8. The writer of Hebrews applies this to an understanding of sanctification, but the saying operates at several levels. Jesus' prayer is exemplary and as such models the fidelity the Christian should exhibit.[90] One could say something similar in relation to Heb 2:10-18 with the quote from Ps 22:22. Heb 13:15 takes the issue one step further: 'Through him, then, let us continually offer a sacrifice of praise to God, that is, the fruit of lips that confess his name.' The writer of Hebrews alludes to Ps 50:14: 'Offer to God a sacrifice of thanksgiving, and pay your vows to the Most High' but sees the fulfillment of these words in the confession of Jesus' name. In other words, the psalms find their fulfilment in Jesus and in faith in him.

---

[86] See Childs, *Introduction to the Old Testament as Scripture*, pp. 520-2.

[87] See Wallace, H.N. (1999), 'What Chronicles has to Say about Psalms', in M.P. Graham and S.L. McKenzie (eds) *The Chronicles as Author: Studies in Text and Texture*, JSOTSup 263, Sheffield Academic Press, Sheffield, pp. 267-291.

[88] Allen, L.C. (1987), *Psalms*, Biblical Word Themes, Word, Waco, TX, p. 124.

[89] Trudinger, P.L. (2001), *Psalms of the Tamid Service*, PhD. Thesis, Emory University, pp. 46-62. The psalms used at these services from Sunday to Saturday were Pss 24, 48, 82, 94, 81, 93, and 92 respectively.

[90] Attridge, H. in a lecture 'Giving Voice to Jesus: Psalmodic Personification in Early Christian Literature' delivered January 22, 2001 at the conference *Up with a Shout: The Psalms in Jewish and Christian Religious, Artistic and Intellectual Traditions*, presented by The Yale Institute of Sacred Music, New Haven, Jan. 19-23, 2001.

The association of the psalms with Jesus developed over time within the life of the Church. St. Augustine (354-430 C.E.) is reported to have called Jesus 'the singer of the psalms.'[91] He and other Church Fathers interpreted the psalms in terms of hearing the voice of Christ speaking either in his own name or in ours.[92] Thus, the one who was God and human took up these human prayers and hymns as his own. Those who pray these psalms now, not only use words uttered by ancient Israelites and enter their prayer world, but also speak the language of prayer and enter the prayer world of Jesus himself. Our world of prayer is now shaped by Jesus' own language, his crucifixion, and resurrection.[93] Christ is the one who not only hears our prayers, but also has prayed them with us.[94]

The aim of this association of the psalms with David and Jesus was not to turn the psalms into some sort of magical formula, as if the repetition of words used by David or Jesus had some special significance. The point was that the one who prays with the psalms prays the prayers that the tradition associates with the great figures of prayer in the faith.[95] In Jesus' case that pray-er is God in our midst. In light of this tradition, as we pray the psalms we figuratively join with David and Jesus in our prayers, using words that are themselves regarded as given by God. This is necessarily an exercise in imagination, but it is one that can be constructive in proper circumstances. As we pray the psalms, the God to whom we pray is the same as the God to whom Israel prayed, David prayed, Jesus prayed and the Church prayed.[96] The prayers we use are those used by Israel, David, Jesus, and the Church.

When we pray using the psalms we are thus drawn into the larger community of prayer in a number of ways. Several advantages flow from this. First, the subjectivity of our prayers in spiritual and theological terms is challenged. The faith that we profess comes to us from the community of faith in

---

[91] Sabourin, L. (1974), *The Psalms: Their Origin and Meaning*, Alba House, New York, p. 171.

[92] For a full discussion see Rotelle, J.E. (2000), *The Works of St. Augustine: A Translation for the 21st Century. Part III, vol. 15: Expositions of the Psalms 1-32*, New City, New York, pp. 50-55.

[93] Cf. Kraus, H.-J. (1986), *Theology of the Psalms*, Augsburg, Minneapolis, p. 189.

[94] See below the section 'Praying in Christ' and especially the remarks on Dietrich Bonhoeffer.

[95] The association of the psalms with both David and Jesus, and sometimes with both at the same time, can be further seen in the illuminations in many medieval manuscripts of the Book of Psalms. The letter 'B', which is the first letter of the first word (*beatus*, 'blessed') in Psalm 1 in Latin, was often illuminated with scenes from the life of David. Sometimes this 'B' was doubled with 'parallel' scenes from the lives of David and Jesus, or the scribes illuminated the initial letter of Psalm 1 with scenes from David's life and the initial letter of Psalm 2 with scenes from the life of Jesus. Further illustrations of either David or Jesus could occur throughout the rest of a Psalter. See for example Alexander, J.J.G. (1978), *The Decorated Letter*, Thames and Hudson, London, p. 15 or Oliver, J. (1993), 'Devotional Images and Pious Practices in a Psalter from Liege', *Latrobe Library Journal*, Vol. 13, pp. 24-31, esp. pp. 25-26.

[96] Cf. Worden, T. (1962), *The Psalms are Christian Prayer*, Chapman, London, p. 4.

its historic as well as its synchronic dimensions. In professing that faith we are disciplined by that community and the traditions of that community. In praying the prayers of the faith, of which the psalms are a major collection, we submit ourselves to the spiritual and theological discipline of the community. In this, the words of our prayers are not limited by our imagination or experience. Nor is their theological content limited. We can even be challenged to new understandings of God and of ourselves before God. Secondly, the subjectivity of our prayers in political and historical terms is challenged. As we use the psalms in prayer we are drawn into political and historical realms related to the composition of the psalms, but with which we might be unfamiliar, or which we do not experience first hand. We can be thrust into the world of the powerful and the poor, the pious (in the positive sense of the term) and their opponents. This can prevent our prayers from being caught in a realm isolated from all else. Thirdly, in using the psalms we are not only given words but the forms of words with which to pray. The use of a common language is not only a mark of a community but one of the ways the community is constituted. It is also involved in the way the community passes on its collective experience. Thus the pray-er recognizes that he/she belongs to and draw on a long community tradition of speaking with God. He/she has available a way of speaking of hurt and pain before God that is both faithful to the tradition and has been shaped by the experience of the community over many generations. The same is true for prayers of praise. The formulaic nature of much of the language in the psalms ties the psalmist to this larger, historic community.[97]

Thus, as we pray using the psalms and join in the prayer of the whole community of God's people, we are not left to lament or praise alone or even believe that we are alone. As we use the psalms in prayer we join our prayers to those of countless others in the larger community of God's faithful people. We literally join the communion of saints in speaking to God, both in the way we pray and in what we pray. All of these points raise questions about our western values and indeed confront the tendency of our western culture to leave people to face the world in a degree of isolation, with either little accountability or support, and with a diminishing circle of human experience to draw on in spite of the wonders of modern communications technology.

An Evolving Conversation

The invitation of the psalms to enter into prayer is an invitation to enter into a conversation that is continually evolving. In the discussion above on the relation of the psalms to human experience, it could be understood that each psalm has some fixed context or situation to which it is connected. This is not the case. While the words of a psalm are fixed, the contexts within which we use them, and hence what we understand them to mean, are not. The psalms are continually being reinterpreted within new contexts.

---

[97] Fisch, *Poetry with a Purpose*, esp. pp. 112-119.

First, we should note that the process of reinterpretation is not new. Indeed, it is going on already within the Book of Psalms as it is elsewhere within Scripture. A clear example concerns Psalms 29 and 96. Psalm 29 begins:

> [1]Ascribe to the LORD, O heavenly beings,
>> ascribe to the LORD glory and strength.
> [2]Ascribe to the LORD the glory of his name;
>> worship the LORD in holy splendor.

These verses, which are addressed to the gods in the context of the heavenly court, are quoted in Ps 96:7-9. However, with some changes they are given a new context:

> [7] Ascribe to the LORD, O families of the peoples,
>> ascribe to the LORD glory and strength.
> [8] Ascribe to the LORD the glory due his name;
>> bring an offering, and come into his courts.
> [9] Worship the LORD in holy splendor;
>> tremble before him, all the earth.

Here they are addressed to the nations of the earth and set in the context of worship. What was once set in a mythic context is now firmly associated with the world of politics and temple worship.

Many scholars would see the ending of Psalm 51 as another example. Ps 51:1-17 are highly individualistic in tone and confessional in nature. Verses 16-17 express what sounds like an anti-sacrificial sentiment:

> [16] For you have no delight in sacrifice;
>> if I were to give a burnt offering, you would not be pleased.
> [17] The sacrifice acceptable to God is a broken spirit;
>> a broken and contrite heart, O God, you will not despise.

However, in vv. 18-19 the psalmist goes on to request God's blessing on Zion, and speaks of the possible reinstitution of sacrifices:

> [18] Do good to Zion in your good pleasure;
>> rebuild the walls of Jerusalem,
> [19] then you will delight in right sacrifices,
>> in burnt offerings and whole burnt offerings;
>> then bulls will be offered on your altar.

These last two verses have often been seen as a post-exilic reinterpretation of the psalm, possibly as an effort to 'correct' the view expressed in vv. 16-17. While other explanations are possible, as I will discuss in a more detailed treatment of Psalm 51 later in the chapter, the suggestion that a late addition has been made to the psalm is plausible.

In other psalms, we can surmise that a kind of 'silent' form of reinterpretation takes place as later readers take up the text. For example, those psalms which speak about the king, such as Pss 2, 72, 89, 110 etc., while initially referring to the kings of Judah would have been understood eschatologically in the days after the demise of the Judean monarchy. Even later some have been understood messianically in relation to Jesus (e.g. Pss 2, 110).

Secondly, the process of reinterpretation continues after a text has been established as part of the canon of Scripture. This can be illustrated by the way various writers have understood Psalm 23. St. Augustine understood the psalm as an allegory for the Church addressing Christ, wherein the waters in v. 2 were the waters of baptism, and the 'house of the Lord' (v. 6) represented the heavenly goal of the Christian life.[98] Later, Martin Luther in the sixteenth century saw the psalm in relation to the comfort of the individual Christian who hears and understands the Word of God as Scripture. Many of the elements in the psalm became metaphors for Scripture and the enemies became either the Papal forces or the Turks who, in Luther's view, robbed Christians of the Word.[99] Reinterpretation could thus work both positively, allowing old texts to take on new and constructive meanings in new contexts, or negatively, being used to support sometimes old prejudices in new circumstances.

Thirdly, the nature of the language of the psalms themselves invites reinterpretation. There is a lack of specificity in many psalms. The identification of the person who utters a psalm, often referred to by the pronoun 'I', the 'enemies' mentioned, as well as the audience, are frequently unclear. In most cases, little is stated expressly about the situation in which a psalm might have been used in ancient Israel.[100] Because the psalms are not fixed to any particular historical situation they are open to interpretation in many different historical situations, as the case of Psalm 23 above shows. If the Book of Psalms was a collection of hymns and prayers for both early Judaism and Christianity, then it was never seen in some antiquarian fashion. It became a resource for the ongoing understanding of the respective faiths and the worship of God, for better or worse as I noted above. Because the psalms are not fixed to the experience of any one individual or group, they are available to all to help give expression to experience. This was recognized long ago, as can be seen by referring to St. Athanasius again. While other biblical books give instruction of all sorts and guide one in both behaviour and belief, he says of the psalms:

> ... the one who hears is deeply moved, as though he himself were speaking, and is affected by the words of the songs, as if they were his own words.[101]

---

[98] See Rotelle, *The Works of St. Augustine*, pp. 244-5.

[99] Pelikan, J. (ed.) (1955), *Luther's Works. Volume 12. Selected Psalms I*, Concordia Publishing House, St. Louis, pp. 148-179.

[100] See Miller, 'Trouble and Woe: Interpreting Biblical Laments', in *Interpreting the Psalms*, pp. 48-63. Cf. also Fisch, *Poetry with a Purpose*, pp. 117-118.

[101] *Letter to Marcellinus*, par. 11, in Gregg, *Athanasius*, p. 109.

Thus, while the stereotypical and anonymous nature of the language of the psalms prevents us from investigating them in their historical context, on a more positive note it does help us relate more readily to the sentiments and experiences alluded to in the psalms, more so than is the case in other biblical books.

In the process of interpretation of a text, there is an interaction between the interpreter and the text. The interpreter asks questions of the text, the answers to which are influenced by both the question itself and the text. In a constructive context this leads to further questions and further answers etc.[102] What is applicable to interpretation in a general sense would seem equally applicable in the matter of using the psalms in prayer. The act of praying a psalm involves a level of interpretation. On the one hand, if we select a particular psalm to help us in our prayer, we usually do so because we see in the psalm something that relates to our own situation. We have interpreted the psalm sufficiently to judge that this is the case. On the other hand, if we pray the psalms according to some pattern which does not relate directly to our own situation, say in sequence or according to a regular office, then we still bring our own understanding, imagination, and context to the psalm as we pray it either for ourselves or on behalf of another. As we use the psalms in prayer we begin a process of interpretation of the psalm and some new meaning, here in the context of prayer, is generated. The psalms do not, therefore, have a singular and predictable meaning. Like any biblical text, they have multiple meanings, and the context within which we pray them and our intention in praying both open up new meanings and prohibit others.[103] The meaning(s) of a psalm in a particular context is/are not simply dependent on the pray-er's context and intention. As we bring our own situation to the psalm, or that of some other person, the psalm itself sits before us with its own pattern of words, reflecting in various ways its own ancient context and history. We enter into a cycle of interpretation and reinterpretation.[104] The psalm and our experience meet in prayer, playing with each other, informing each other, questioning each other, and illuminating each other.[105]

This alerts us to an important difference between composing prayers of our own and using the psalms, or even other texts, for our prayers. When composing our own prayers, either extemporary or ones prepared ahead for a particular occasion, we use words that in some way convey our feelings, our ideas etc., however inadequately. The conversation with God, for the most part, is one directional. That is not to say that a pray-er might not expect some answer or that the prayer might not be part of a larger healing process. In general, however, the prayer is one-way traffic. But when we pray using the psalms, the conversation is less controlled from our side because we use words penned by another. As we pray the psalms, we engage in a process of interpretation as I have noted. Thus, prayer

---

[102] See Goldingay, 'The Dynamic Cycle', pp. 88-89 in his discussion of Brueggemann's psalms of orientation.

[103] Brueggemann, 'Response to John Goldingay', p. 141.

[104] Cunningham, L.S. (1989), 'Praying the Psalms', *Theology Today*, Vol. 46, pp. 39-44, esp. pp. 42-43.

[105] Brueggemann, *Praying the Psalms*, p. 27.

in this instance is not just an expression of feelings etc. by us, but a struggle with a text through which we are speaking with God. Because the text of the psalm has its own shape and history, our prayer will in the end be something toward which both the psalm and we have contributed. It could become an occasion for discovery with some new insight or understanding. Alternatively, it could be a time of challenge or argument if the psalm contains ideas with which we struggle or even strongly disagree. That is not to say that the prayers we compose ourselves cannot be occasions for insight or challenge. It is just that in using the psalms, our prayers take shape in the process of engagement with another word.

The cycle of interpretation, about which I have been speaking, is itself a form of conversation. We enter into dialogue with the psalm in order to understand it. Both in terms of content and of the need for interpretation we are invited back into the area of conversation as we use the psalms in prayer. If we understand the text of the psalms as part of the word of God, then the dialogue invoked by the psalms is not just between ourselves and a text, but between ourselves and the one to whom we pray, who is also the one who has given us the words in the psalm with which to pray. The process of determining the meaning of the text of the psalm in the context of our prayer becomes part of our conversational prayer with God.

Being Moulded in Character

At the start of this chapter I recalled Bonhoeffer's statement: 'Prayer does not mean simply to pour out one's heart. It means rather to find the way to God and to speak with him, whether the heart is full or empty.'[106] The psalms help us in this endeavour in a number of ways. In the words they offer us for our prayers, and in the invitation they issue to be involved in prayer, they open for us a way to speak to God. But they do more than that. As we enter their world, we enter a *world of prayer* and are shaped in our prayers by that world. We learn a discipline of prayer so that no longer do our hearts pray by themselves, with the consequent confusion between our feelings, sighs and wishes etc. and prayer. Rather, we find ourselves able to speak with God 'whether the heart is full or empty'. If we follow the prayer discipline of the psalms, we find ourselves moulded in character as pray-ers.

This has been recognized not only by Bonhoeffer but by a host of ancient and modern readers and pray-ers of the psalms. I could cite once again St. Athanasius who says that the Book of Psalms:

> contains even the emotions of each soul, and it has the changes and rectifications of these delineated and regulated in itself. Therefore anyone who wishes boundlessly to receive and understand from it, so as to mold himself, it is written there.[107]

---

[106] Bonhoeffer, *Psalms*, pp. 9-10.
[107] *Letter to Marcellinus*, par. 10, in Gregg, *Athanasius*, p. 108.

He goes on to explain this in that the Book of Psalms, like other biblical books, teaches and guides but goes beyond this in teaching also 'the emotions of the soul' thereby affecting and constraining the reader so that they 'possess the image deriving from the words.' The reader or pray-er becomes the speaker of the psalm and not only hears a call for repentance or obedience, for example, but is given the words of repentance or obedience to speak. I alluded to this above when speaking about the openness of the language of the psalms and their propensity to be reinterpreted within the life of the pray-er. St. Athanasius goes on to say that in other books of Scripture, the reader hears the words as written about others. He/she may then imitate their deeds and desire to emulate them, but in the psalms the one who hears:

> ... is deeply moved, as though he himself were speaking, and is affected by the words of the songs, as if they were his own songs.[108]

The words of the psalm are thereby realized in a fuller way in the life of the reader or pray-er than is the case with other Scripture. The pray-er is moulded by the world of prayer in the psalms.

More recent scholars have argued in a related vein.[109] One writer has spoken of 'the sacramental function of the psalms'.[110] While one might be cautious about the use of the word 'sacramental' he rightly recognizes what he calls 'the distinctive power' or 'special power' of the psalms in comparison with other biblical books.[111] Brueggemann also speaks of the praise of God, within which many psalms are included, as not just a responsive activity but a constitutive one. It creates a 'life-world' through an imaginative act of speech and gesture, and, in ancient Israel, he argues it evoked 'genuine covenanted persons'.[112]

If the psalms mould us and shape us as certain kinds of pray-ers, then what does this mean? On the basis of what I have discussed so far, it might mean that we become more involved in and learn more about the conversational mode of prayer. It might also mean that we incorporate lamentation more deliberately into our prayers, both privately and publicly. Or it could mean that we begin to see our prayers in the larger context of a life movement toward the unhindered praise of God. It might mean disciplining our prayers so that there is a closer connection between particular situations and the content of our prayers, or taking up the words of psalms with which we feel uncomfortable either as our own prayers or prayers on behalf of others. It might mean being sufficiently open, honest, and trusting in

---

[108] *Ibid.*, par. 11, p. 109.

[109] Cf. also Mays, J.L. (1994), 'Means of Grace: The Benefits of Psalmic Prayer', in *The Lord Reigns: A Theological Handbook to the Psalms*, Westminster John Knox, Louisville, pp. 40-45, esp. pp. 40-41.

[110] Nasuti, H.P. (2001), 'The Sacramental Function of the Psalms in Contemporary Scholarship and Liturgical Practice', in S.B. Reid (ed.), *Psalms and Practice: Worship, Virtue, and Authority*, Liturgical Press, Collegeville, pp. 78-89.

[111] *Ibid.*, pp. 78-79.

[112] Brueggemann, W. (1988), *Israel's praise: doxology against idolatry and ideology*, Fortress, Philadelphia, p. 159.

prayer that we are ready to struggle with the words of these less acceptable prayers in conversation with God in order to learn more of who we are, be able to accept ourselves as we are, accept the need to change ourselves, or be ready when appropriate to forgive ourselves as well as ask for God's forgiveness. It might mean also beginning to understand in a deeper way who others are in their suffering or joy. It could mean being bold enough to propose that God might need to change in his dealings with the world. This can be a risky business because in the process our present character comes under scrutiny as we are exposed to the investigation and critique of the very words we use in our prayers. But then, that is the risk of prayer - to be in honest conversation with the one who knows us intimately, according to Psalm 139 as I noted above.

The prayers we pray can be consistent or inconsistent with our 'true' nature. There is always the temptation to use prayers written by others in order to clothe ourselves with a certain piety. That form of piety may, however, have little to do with who we are or how we feel or think. This is even a danger with extemporary prayers where we can easily employ language and forms of prayer that we deem acceptable to God or the community. This is not to say that prayer clothed in a certain language that is not our normal way of speaking, or which employs certain 'religious' forms cannot be meaningful for others or us. It certainly can. What I am speaking about here is when language and form are expected to carry the whole burden of meaning and cease to be intimately associated with the expression of what is innermost for us. Jesus is said to have spoken on hypocrisy in prayer in the parable of the two men praying in Luke 18:9-14, and in his teaching in Matt 6:5-8. Integrity, growth and discipline within prayer are what are at stake here. A balance needs to be struck when using the words of others for our prayers. It is a balance between using words that have meaning for us and come genuinely from the heart, so that we avoid the trap of an inauthentic piety, and using words that will help us grow in faith and prayer, and not leave us to wallow in the things that have become so familiar to us that they become meaningless.

Words of Prayer with Authority

St. Athanasius goes on to conclude the section of his *Letter to Marcellinus* I have been discussing with the following:

> And it seems to me that these words become like a mirror to the person singing them, so that he might perceive himself and the emotions of his own soul, and thus affected, he might recite them. For in fact he who hears the one reading receives the song as being about him...And so on the whole, each psalm is both spoken and composed by the Spirit so that in these same words, as was said earlier, the stirrings of our souls might be grasped, and all of them be said as concerning us, and the same issue from us as our own words, for a remembrance of the emotions in us, and a chastening of our life.[113]

---

[113] *Letter to Marcellinus*, par. 12, in Gregg, *Athanasius*, p. 111.

This raises a final matter for consideration. It concerns the dual traditions regarding the psalms which I discussed in chapter 1 and how that impacts on the place of the psalms as prayers of the Church. In particular, I wish to focus on the authority given these prayers, if they are considered both word from God and word to God. This involves the relation between the voice of the psalmist and the voice of God in the psalms. St Athanasius puts it in the quote above in terms of the psalms being 'both spoken and composed by the Spirit' and both 'said as concerning us' and 'from us as our own words'.

We noted earlier in this chapter that conversation was a major aspect of the psalms as prayer. While God is presumed to be one of the major conversation partners in most psalms, there are some in which God is quoted, either directly or indirectly.[114] In discussions of modern novels, some writers have referred to the concept of the 'authoritative word', which is the central word in the process of dialogue within the novel.[115] In the dialogue within the psalms this 'authoritative word' often appears as the word of God. Herbert Levine, whom I mentioned above in relation to the psalms as dialogue poems, considers these psalms in which the words of God are quoted. He argues that in the psalms the 'authoritative word' is fused with the words of the psalmist around it. He quotes Ps 81:5-6, 15-16 as an example:[116]

> [5] He made it a decree in Joseph,
>> when he went out over the land of Egypt.
>
> I hear a voice I had not known:
> [6] 'I relieved your shoulder of the burden;
>> your hands were freed from the basket.
>
> . . .
> [15] Those who hate the LORD would cringe before him,
>> and their doom would last forever.
> [16] I would feed you with the finest of the wheat,
>> and with honey from the rock I would satisfy you.'

In each set of verses there is free movement between the psalmist speaking about God and the direct quotation of God's words without indication of the change. This is in contrast to other literatures where the 'authoritative word' is set apart from the rest of the dialogue in order to maintain its authoritative and timeless nature. The blurring of the edges in the psalms between what the psalmist says and what God says thus gives authority to the psalmist's dialogue. Levine

---

[114] See Pss 2, 12, 35, 46, 50, 68, 75, 81, 82, 89, 90, 91, 95, 105, 110, and 132.

[115] Levine, H. (1992), 'The Dialogic Discourse of Psalms', in A. Loades and M. McLain (eds.), *Hermeneutics, The Bible and Literary Criticism*, Macmillan, Basingstoke, pp. 145-161. Levine quotes Mikhail Bakhtin and his study of European novels.

[116] Levine gives his own translation to these verses and uses Hebrew verse numbers, i.e. Ps 81:6-7, 16-17. We have quoted the NRSV version of the psalm. The slight differences in translation do not affect the argument.

concludes that in the psalms 'divine authority is completely vested in the vehicle that delivers God's word'.[117] In other words, the divine voice is seen as an extension of the psalmist's voice, and vice-versa.

Levine assumes, with reason, that the psalmists were likely members of the temple priesthood. Their position 'allowed for the blurring of boundaries' between the psalmist's words and God's.[118] This reduced the distance between the psalmist's words and the 'authoritative word' of God. In the case of later users of the psalms, the situation would not have changed very much. Although the psalms were dislodged from their temple context in much of Judaism and in Christianity, at the same time the association of the psalms with David, or in Christian communities, of the psalms with David and/or Jesus, would have provided a new authoritative aspect to the words of the psalm, replacing that previously supplied by the institutional role of the priestly psalmist. In this context, the blurred distinction between the psalmist's word and God's word would continue. Or to use St. Athanasius' words, the words of the psalms 'spoken and composed by the Spirit' also come 'from us as our own words'.

As we take up the psalms as prayers we enter this arena of 'blurred boundaries'. We can pray with the psalmist, but the psalmist's words are blurred with God's words. Our words become blurred with the psalmist's and with God's. This gives the psalms as prayers an authority not experienced in other prayers. The pray-er takes up the words of God to pray to God. In the Christian context, it is thus easy for the pray-er to enter imaginatively into these prayers as the prayers of Christ; to be able to pray them because Christ prays them and because they have been given to us to pray. We are disciplined in our prayer by the prayers of Christ.

Praying in Christ

This leads us to the matter of praying in Christ. For many centuries, Christian people or groups understood the psalms, like the rest of the Old Testament, as prophecies relating to Jesus Christ. Often interpreters simply read Jesus Christ back into Old Testament passages, so that the texts became literal prophecies foretelling the events of Jesus. These views, and the assumptions behind them, are today no longer tenable for many Christians. However, the issue of how we read the ancient Israelite psalms as *Christian* prayer still needs to be addressed.

When I discussed above the idea that when we pray the psalms, we are not praying alone, I noted that even within the New Testament, and in the Letter to the Hebrews in particular, the text of psalms was put into the mouth of Jesus. He became the speaker of the psalms as David's voice became that of Jesus. Elsewhere, psalms and other Old Testament passages were seen as fulfilled in the events of Jesus' life. This understanding continued in the work of the Church Fathers. While they respected the literal sense of the text, they also reread the psalms in the light of Christ, recognising in them not only the God whom Jesus

---

[117] *Ibid.*, p. 149.
[118] *Ibid.*

called his heavenly Father, but Christ himself. This was not only the case for psalms considered as 'messianic', but for others as well. One writer expresses this sense of Christ present for the Church Fathers in every way in the Psalms:

> Christ was the one who speaks in the psalms as the true David, as the just one who is persecuted and saved, but Christ was also the one who is spoken about in the psalms, even Christ as the one who may be spoken to in the psalms.[119]

We could also ask why these pre-Christian prayers became so central to the Church, especially in the liturgies of both daily prayer and Sunday services. B. Fischer goes so far as to say that without the Christian appropriation of the psalms, the things that mattered most to Christians, namely their baptism and the Eucharist, would not have been recalled in daily prayer. The only explanation for the role of the psalms in Christian worship is that those who introduced them did in fact read them in the light of Christ, not as a forced exercise, but in light of their Christian experience.[120] That is, the psalms were quite naturally read in the light of what was central in the Christian faith. The anonymity of the psalms, and the fact that they speak to a broad range of human experiences and issues, is involved here.[121]

Another important distinction ought to be made when thinking of the psalms as Christian prayer. It is possible to have a Christian interpretation of the psalms without interpreting them christologically. That is, we can read and pray the psalms as Christians without seeing direct or even sometimes indirect references to Jesus Christ in them. In this way we read the psalms literally, aware that an individual or community who sought God's help or wanted to praise God wrote them long ago before the time of Christ. But even so we understand that the God to whom the psalmist prayed and to whom we now pray, or the God whom the psalmist and we praise, is the one whom Jesus called Father. That is a first step toward christianisation of the psalms and one many Christians would make without too much thought.[122]

The christological interpretation of the psalms in the works of the Church Fathers, wherein they saw in the psalms words spoken by, to, or about Jesus Christ, worked on two levels. We can speak of christological interpretations 'from below' and 'from above'.[123] The former sees Christ not only as the pray-er of the psalms but the one in whose crucifixion, resurrection and ascension, the lamentations and jubilation of the psalmist are fulfilled. This type of christological interpretation began in the New Testament itself, as I have already noted. The Gospel and other New Testament writers put the words of the psalms into the mouth of Jesus, or saw them fulfilled in events of his life, death and resurrection. In this way, the suffering

---

[119] Fischer, B. (1990), 'Christological Interpretation of the Psalms seen in the Mirror of the Liturgy', in L. Leijssen (ed.), *Les psaumes: priéres de l'humanité, d'Israël, de l'Église. Hommage à Jos Luyten*. Abdij Keizersberg, Leuven, pp. 77-85, esp. p. 78.

[120] *Ibid.*, p. 79

[121] Fischer suggests something similar. He asks whether this christological interpretation of the psalms is not because the Book of Psalms is a 'deeply human book'. *Ibid.*, p. 78.

[122] *Ibid.*, p. 79.

[123] *Ibid.*, pp. 80-84.

and exaltation of Jesus was connected to that of the psalmist as an ordinary human experiencing the extremes and the in-betweens of life. It also allowed the prayers of the psalmists as ordinary people of faith to find their place in the larger working out of God's plan of salvation. However, the difficulty with this approach is in seeing some of the statements of the psalmist as those Jesus might have uttered. For example, the psalmist utters words of deep confession: 'Indeed, I was born guilty, a sinner when my mother conceived me' (Ps 51:5); and others of deep hatred: 'Pour out your indignation upon them, and let your burning anger overtake them' (Ps 69:24). Can we compare these to the idea of Christ's sinless nature (2 Cor 5:21), or to his words from the cross as recorded in Luke 23:34, 'Father, forgive them; for they do not know what they are doing'?

The second way the psalms were understood christologically, that is 'from above', was to interpret words that were originally said about or addressed to God in the psalms, as about or addressed to Christ. For example, Ps 83:19, which reads 'Let them know that you alone, whose name is the LORD, are the Most High over all the earth', became the textual basis for part of the Gloria in the liturgy of the Church:

> (Lord Jesus Christ), you are seated at the right hand of God the Father,
> for you alone are the Holy One. [124]

The former christological interpretation is the one that concerns us most in relation to prayer. How can we understand the words of the psalms becoming the prayer of Christ? Dietrich Bonhoeffer is again helpful in this. He asks the same question in at least two of his works. He says in *Psalms: the prayer book of the Bible*:

> How is it possible for a man and Jesus Christ to pray the Psalter together? It is the incarnate Son of God, who has born every human weakness in his own flesh, who here pours out the heart of all humanity before God and who stands in our place and prays for us. He has known torment and pain, guilt and death more deeply than we. Therefore, it is the prayer of the human nature assumed by him which comes here before God. It is really our prayer, but since he knows us better than we know ourselves and since he was truly man for our sakes, it is also really his prayer, and it can become our prayer only because it was his prayer. [125]

In his work *Life Together* he says that when we pray the psalms we come across parts that we may feel we cannot pray ourselves, and yet these words are part of scripture. These situations are:

> a hint to us that here Someone else is praying, not we; that the One who is here protesting his innocence, who is invoking God's judgment, who has come to such

---

[124] *Ibid.*, pp. 81-83 for further examples.

[125] Bonhoeffer, *Psalms*, pp. 20-21. Cf. also his (1954), *Life Together*. SCM, London, pp. 30-35.

infinite depths of suffering, is none other than Jesus Christ himself. He it is who is praying here, and not only here but in the whole Psalter.[126]

The Church and the New Testament writers, Bonhoeffer argues, have always recognized this. It was the point of the New Testament writers in having Jesus speak as if the words of the psalms were his own words. But Jesus continues to pray the psalms, Bonhoeffer asserts, and so becomes an intercessor for his people. Believers who pray the psalms do so as part of the body of Christ. Verses in the psalms may not, on occasion, be the immediate prayer of one part of the body. Even so they can be the prayer of other parts. In this way, the words of God become our words to God and God hears God's people when they pray the psalms, praying in the words of Jesus, the Word of God.[127] Augustine used the two phrases *psalmus vox Christi* and *psalmus vox ecclesiae* to speak of the psalms. As we grow into maturity in our faith we take our baptismal identity with Christ more seriously and grow in our understanding of it. We discover that our faith, and our prayer, is a meeting, or conversation between two persons, our Lord and ourselves. This meeting of two persons in prayer takes place in the psalms as they are prayed and read.[128]

---

[126] *Life together*, p. 31.

[127] Note also Kelly, G.B. (1991), 'The Prayerbook of the Bible: Dietrich Bonhoeffer's Introduction to the Psalms', *Weavings*, Vol. 6, pp. 36-41 on Bonhoeffer's interpretation of the psalms.

[128] See Bolz, P. (1972), 'Praying the Psalms', *Worship*, Vol. 46, pp. 204-213, esp. p. 211.

Chapter 4

What Individual Psalms Say about Prayer

Psalms 13 and 90 – Praying Laments

Psalm 13

Psalm 13 begins:

> [1] How long, O LORD? Will you forget me forever?
>> How long will you hide your face from me?
> [2] How long must I bear pain in my soul,
>> and have sorrow in my heart all day long?
> How long shall my enemy be exalted over me?
> [3] Consider and answer me, O LORD my God!
>> Give light to my eyes, or I will sleep the sleep of death,
> [4] and my enemy will say, 'I have prevailed';
>> my foes will rejoice because I am shaken.

The psalmist addresses a series of questions to God regarding his/her situation. These questions carry the burden of the psalmist's complaint, which is primarily against God (v. 1). God's apparent disregard for the psalmist's plight undergirds the pain, sorrow, and humiliation, which the psalmist bears before the 'enemy' (v. 2). The repetition of 'how long?' intensifies the complaint and underlines the depth of the psalmist's pain.

In this prayer there is the assumption that God is powerful enough to effect some change in the psalmist's plight. It is the way of God to effect transformation in life. Not even the psalmist's sinfulness will negate the transformative activity of God (cf. Ps 69:5). On the other hand, the psalmist has freedom to question God when it seems God has not used that power. The sense of urgency generated in Ps 13:1-2 is maintained in v. 3 by the use of the abrupt imperatives 'consider and answer'. The psalmist demands an answer from God, although, as we noted earlier, the psalmist understands clearly that God will only act at a time acceptable to God (Ps 69:13).

The style of prayer in Psalm 13 incorporates an open questioning of one conversation partner by the other and a demand for a response. It knows no privileged position for either of the participants, even God. There is no sense either of offence being given by this questioning, or of offence being taken. The psalmist presumes a right to question God. The prayer could be characterized as honest or even brazen. There is room in it for expressions of anger, and a sense of betrayal.

In the concluding section of the psalm the psalmist states his/her trust in God in the past and anticipates a response of salvation to that trust. The psalmist then promises to praise God.

> ⁵ But I trusted in your steadfast love;
>   my heart shall rejoice in your salvation.
> ⁶ I will sing to the LORD,
>   because he has dealt bountifully with me.[1]

The movement from complaint, to plea, and finally to praise is clear although the way this movement takes place is not clear. J.L. Mays has said about Psalm 13: 'The psalm leads those who read and pray it from protest and petition to praise; it holds all three together as if to teach that they cohere in the unity of prayer.'[2] In an earlier study he said that the psalm was not to be seen as indicating a temporal sequence in its structure. 'We do not begin at one end and come out at the other. The agony and the ecstasy belong together as the secret of our identity.'[3]

This insight is helpful. It suggests that an expression of protest is not to be equated with a lack of hope, or for that matter, a lack of faith itself. In fact, since it is a protest *to God* it embodies a level of trust and expectation. It also recognizes that the movement toward hope does not simply negate or dispense with all sense of protest. Nor is this hope simply a denial of the real pain behind the complaint. The reality of the hope expressed is only fully understood when the reality of the silence of God and the desperation of the circumstances are confronted. On the other hand, it can also suggest that we do not have to be at the point of despair before we can pray this psalm or those like it. A desire to praise God may still have room to recognize the need for protest and petition. This is the prayer of a mature faith.

Mays' insight, however, does need some qualification. While, in one sense we 'do not begin at one end and come out at the other', we do, in fact, still read the psalm that way and live our lives within the dimensions of time and space. Moving through the psalm from beginning to end does have significance for the pray-er. If we understand Mays' remark to mean that we can dispense with the idea of a temporal sequence entirely, then we run the danger of dissipating our hope in God, who has engaged the world in Jesus Christ, to answer prayer. The opening of the psalm indicates that we can cry to God out of the deepest despair. It locates the

---

[1] The translation of the Hebrew word *kî*, 'because', in v. 6 raises some issues. The last half of v. 6 could be translated 'as soon as he has dealt bountifully with me' (so Craigie, P.C. (1983), *Psalms 1-50*, Word, Waco, p. 140) or 'when he has dealt bountifully with me' (so Broyles, C.C. (1989), *The Conflict of Faith and Experience in the Psalms: A Form-Critical and Theological Study*, JSOTSup 52, Sheffield Academic Press, Sheffield, pp. 186). Thus v. 6b could be a promise of praise either after some future deliverance or following deliverance that has already happened.

[2] Mays, J.L. (1994), *Psalms*, John Knox, Louisville, p. 79.

[3] Mays, J.L. (1980), 'Psalm 13' *Interpretation*, Vol. 34, pp. 281-2. Cf. Westermann, C. (1965), *The Praise of God in the Psalms*, John Knox, Richmond, pp. 70ff.

pain.[4] The rest of the psalm locates the possibility of moving toward praise. It assumes that God can answer the psalmist's plea. In the end the psalm keeps us in both contexts. It reminds us that despair and hope do cohere. It also reminds us that movement from despair to praise is possible. The psalmist formulates his/her prayer in the midst of this tension.

Psalm 90

Lament psalms were not only written for individuals but also for the community as a whole. Psalm 90, while in some ways not typical of the community laments (see e.g. Pss 12, 44, 74 etc.), is instructive in its understanding of prayer. It begins with a meditation on the relation of God to the community (vv. 1-2):

> [1] Lord, you have been our dwelling place
> in all generations.
> [2] Before the mountains were brought forth,
> or ever you had formed the earth and the world,
> from everlasting to everlasting you are God.

The confident statement in v. 1 has its basis in the knowledge that the reign and status of Israel's God preceded even God's act of creating earth. This is in contrast to some other ancient Near Eastern myths where the god who creates earth wins power over the cosmos in that very act. The parallel in Psalm 90 between the community having trust in and relating to God 'in all generations' (v. 1), and God ruling 'from everlasting to everlasting' (v. 2) not only expresses the foundation of the community's trust, but also the unassailability of the relationship with God. It is a statement not only of past trust, but also of future hope.

Having proclaimed this firm foundation of relationship, the psalmist recalls the transitoriness of the human situation. He/she meditates on the frailty of the human condition (vv. 3-6). The eternal nature of God's reign, in which the community trusts, is contrasted with the temporal nature of humankind. While in God's sight a thousand years are like a fleeting thought, humanity barely sees out the passing of a 'day.'

> [3] You turn us back to dust,
> and say, 'Turn back, you mortals.'
> [4] For a thousand years in your sight
> are like yesterday when it is past,
> or like a watch in the night.
> [5] You sweep them away; they are like a dream,
> like grass that is renewed in the morning;
> [6] in the morning it flourishes and is renewed;
> in the evening it fades and withers.

---

[4] McCann, J.C. (1993), *A Theological Introduction to the Book of Psalms: The Psalms as Torah*, Abingdon, Nashville, pp. 92-93.

The focus now moves to the frailty of humanity, but not simply in contrast to the eternal nature of God. The word translated 'sweep' (v. 5) recalls the action of a flood sweeping all before it. It implies a destructive intention on God's part. The idea of God's anger is then developed in vv. 7-12. This seems to be in stark contrast to vv. 1-2, but it reminds us that both security in God's presence and vulnerability before God's judgment are part of the community's experience of the one God. The vulnerability leads the psalmist to recognize that this is an opportunity for the community to become wise (v. 12). However, this does not mean that the community simply acquiesces before the judgment of God, and sees change within itself as the only hope in the present circumstance. There needs to be a balance in prayer between a sense of security in God's presence, and one of vulnerability before God's judgment. Both realisations depend on the recognition of God's rule over all, and both are necessary for the generation of hope.

The psalmist's argument changes dramatically in vv. 13-17. From a desire for God to assist the community to change, the psalmist petitions God to change. This is where the sense of security in God's presence comes to the fore. The psalmist seeks the Lord's compassion and favour. There is a sense of urgency or even impatience in the plea in v. 13:

> Turn, O LORD! How long?
> Have compassion on your servants!

There are three important things to note. First, v. 13 begins with an imperative addressed to the Lord: 'Turn, O LORD!' The same word is used here as in v. 3 where God is said to turn humans back to dust. Verses 5-12 make it clear that humans cannot return or repent. Dust is their destiny. Their only hope for satisfaction or gladness is for God to turn from anger. Secondly, while the psalmist contemplates the consuming power of God's anger in v. 11, he/she pleads in v. 16 that God's 'glorious power' will be made manifest to God's people. The psalmist recognizes another side to God's power; one that is for blessing and not for judgment. Thirdly, the psalm ends (v. 17) with a plea for the favour of God to be on the people. This verse encapsulates the general sentiment of the psalm. Humans cannot commend themselves to God. Both their transient nature (vv. 4-6) and their sinfulness (vv. 7-8) prohibit that. However, the end of the psalm also seeks to return to a position of favour similar to that presumed in v. 1. The psalmist asks that the work of human hands be taken up into the work of God. If such a desire is to be authentic, the psalmist must have a clear understanding of the depth of God's compassion and the utter constancy of his steadfast love (vv. 13-14). He/she must also have a sense of security in God's presence, which allows them to challenge God to change, as well as to change the community.

There is freedom in this prayer for the psalmist to acknowledge the ambiguities of life. Having described at length God's anger at the sinfulness of the people, the psalmist has the audacity to ask how long the community needs to bear its current affliction. The boldness of this prayer lies in the acknowledgement that it is only God who can in any way repent or return. Prayer is the place where God is acknowledged as the necessity and only hope for community life and security.

This acknowledgment is based on the reign of God over all creation. True humility before God not only knows human vulnerability but also demands that God reassess the community's situation. This is neither arrogance nor hubris, but rather a belief that God is compassionate (v. 13), and will satisfy the people again with their needs (v. 14). This is the only genuine hope the community can have. It assumes that God can repent and turn, so prayer is not a useless activity. It assumes that the community can gain a wise heart (v. 12), which one writer has defined as 'the capacity to submit, relinquish, and acknowledge the decisive impingement of (the Lord) on one's life.'[5] This impingement is not only in terms of judgment but also in terms of compassion on the people. While the evidence of the people's life reveals both their transitoriness and God's judgment, that evidence is not determinative for the people's future. The psalmist audaciously asks for deliverance knowing that there is another reality beyond that of their sinfulness, namely God's compassion. It is the latter for which the psalmist strives in prayer. It is a great expression of hope, faith and trust in the God of eternity.

Psalms 113 and 65 – Praising God

Psalm 113

Psalm 113 is the first in a group of psalms that has played an important role in Jewish liturgy. Psalms 113-118 is collectively known as the 'Egyptian' Hallel-psalms. 'Hallel' means 'praise'. In ancient Judaism, these psalms were used in the liturgy at the three great pilgrimage festivals, Passover, Weeks and Tabernacles, as well as at the festivals of the New Moon and the Dedication of the Temple. Psalms 113 and 114 have also been sung at the beginning of the family Passover meal, and Psalms 115-118 at its conclusion.

Psalm 113 begins and ends with the invocation *hallelujah*, 'Praise the Lord!' This gives a clear context of praise to this psalm and sums up its theme. The body of the psalm develops what it means to 'praise the Lord'. It begins by expounding on this call to praise.

> [1] Praise the LORD!
>> Praise, O servants of the LORD;
>> praise the name of the LORD.
> [2] Blessed be the name of the LORD
>> from this time on and forevermore.
> [3] From the rising of the sun to its setting
>> the name of the LORD is to be praised.

Verses 1-3 are also framed by words declaring praise. The first three lines and the last line of this section begin with forms of the verb *hallel* 'to praise'. Equally prominent is the phrase 'the name of the Lord', which occurs three times. Thus,

---

[5] Brueggemann, W. (1984), *The Message of the Psalms*, Augsburg, Minneapolis, p. 111.

what the servants, or worshippers, of the Lord are to do, and to whom they are to direct their activity, is made very clear.

The psalmist has created a chiasm in vv. 2-3 to impress upon the reader that praise is an act which takes place everywhere and in every time. The lines 'Blessed be the name of the LORD' and 'the name of the LORD is to be praised' enclose lines describing the appropriate times and places for praise, namely 'from this time on and forevermore' and 'from the rising of the sun to its setting'. That is, praise should be continually offered in every place. The praise of the individual or community, which is focused at a particular time and place, participates in this wider circle of praise. At the same time it calls other servants of the Lord into that circle. It both participates in an act of praise that stretches beyond the limitations of the pray-er(s), and seeks to enhance that greater act. It seeks to further the human relationship with the Lord and proclaim the way of the Lord in the world.

The psalm fits the general structure of psalms of praise. It calls for praise and then gives the reasons for praise. Although a clause beginning 'because' does not mark the latter, the psalm does outline a number of attributes of the Lord and actions by the Lord that call for praise. Verses 4-6 give the first reason, namely the incomparability of the Lord.

> [4] The LORD is high above all nations,
>   and his glory above the heavens.
> [5] Who is like the LORD our God,
>   who is seated on high,
> [6] who looks far down on the heavens and the earth?

There are other statements on God's incomparability in the Old Testament, for example Deut 3:24; 1 Kgs 8:23 etc. In this psalm the Lord is said to be not only high above the nations, but also his glory is above the heavens (v. 4). Implicit in this is that the Lord is not only above all earthly powers, but is also sovereign over all other gods. In this psalm there is the sense that God is wholly other, and the psalmist refrains from any effort to comprehend God. The great distance between God and the world is evident.[6] However, in spite of this incomprehensible distance the people can still call God 'their God' (v. 5), a statement that assumes God's care for them.

Thus, in this context the prayer of praise incorporates both a statement of faith about the wholly otherness of a God who can yet be in close relationship with the people, and a political statement. This prayer is self-consciously both a political statement as well as a faith utterance. It declares allegiance to the one who stands beyond all other powers, heavenly or earthly. A prayer of praise is not simply adoration of the creator and redeemer of all. It involves a declaration of alignment with the Lord over against all other powers that would seek to supplant God. And this is the case whether we are aware of it or not.

Verses 7-9 provide a second reason for the praise of the Lord, namely his compassion for the poor and barren.

---

[6] Weiser, A. (1962), *The Psalms*, Westminster, Philadelphia, p. 707.

[7] He raises the poor from the dust,
      and lifts the needy from the ash heap,
[8] to make them sit with princes,
      with the princes of his people.
[9] He gives the barren woman a home,
      making her the joyous mother of children.
  Praise the LORD!

The Lord raises the poor and needy from the place of utter desolation (cf. Job's situation in Job 2:8) and establishes them alongside those of privilege and status in the world. The Hebrew verbs used in the psalm help tie the various parts together and contribute to discerning meaning. The verb used for 'raising' the needy (*rûm*, v. 7) is the same one used to describe the 'exalted' or 'high' status of the Lord above the nations (v. 4). In v. 8, the verb *yašab* 'to sit' is used to describe the sitting of the poor and needy with princes. That same verb is used to describe the Lord being seated on high (v. 5) and the establishment of the barren woman in a home (v. 9). In comparison to the latter image, it is used in relation to marriage in Ezra 10:2, 14; and Neh 13:23, in the sense of giving a home to someone.[7] The use of these verbs indicates that what the Lord does with the needy or barren etc. is consistent with his own nature. It also suggests that the compassionate acts of the Lord in relation to the poorest of humankind, has its basis in the cosmic realm.

The prayer of praise in Psalm 113 goes beyond political and religious statements. It involves matters of social justice and privilege as well as personal security and acceptance. The one who prays this prayer of praise is committed to addressing issues of privilege and need. He/she is also faced with questions of social and personal acceptance. This is the scandal of this prayer. Praise is again not just a matter of adoration in isolation. It incorporates matters of society, care and relationship as well as politics and faith. It is not only a matter of the remembrance of glory above the heavens, although some psalms focus on that, but it incorporates a celebration of God honoring those at the lowest point of life. It is not just about God's glory but also about his raising others to share in that glory. This particularity in praise is to become the praise of all times and places. It is the ground for all other expressions of praise.

While this psalm focuses on praise grounded in God's acts of compassion, one could also ask whether the reverse is not the case also. Can we deem genuine acts of social justice, personal acceptance etc. as acts of praise? If so, praise is not just caught up in words, be they of prayer or song. Nor is it confined to specific occasions of adoration. It is, in fact, embodied in the life of discipleship.

The issues raised in this prayer of praise were part of Israel's story. The raising of the needy is reflected in the exodus tradition and in many other stories (e.g. Isa 52:13-53:12). Moreover, the image of the barren woman becoming a mother is a constant theme (e.g. the matriarchs from Gen. 11:30; 25:21; 29:31; Samson's mother in Judges 13; Hannah in 1 Sam 2:1-10; and Isaiah 54). In fact,

---

[7] Allen, L.C. (1983), *Psalms 101-150*, Word, Waco, p. 99.

Psalm 113 is often associated with the Hannah story, especially 1 Sam 2:2, 4-8, and with the story of Mary the mother of Jesus in the Magnificat in Luke 1:46-55.

Psalm 65

Some scholars have argued, based on the portrayal of a rich rural scene in the last four verses of this psalm, that the psalm was written for a time of harvest. The psalm divides naturally into three sections. The first begins with the acknowledgment that praise is due to God.

> [1] Praise is due to you, O God, in Zion;
>> and to you shall vows be performed,
> [2] O you who answer prayer!
>> To you all flesh shall come.
> [3] When deeds of iniquity overwhelm us,
>> you forgive our transgressions.
> [4] Happy are those whom you choose
>> and bring near to live in your courts.
>> We shall be satisfied with the goodness of your house,
>>> your holy temple.

Each line in vv. 1-2a begins in Hebrew with the words 'to you'. God is clearly the one to whom praise is rightfully offered. The basis for the statement is hidden in the way God is addressed. The one called 'God, in Zion' is also the one 'who answers prayer'. The pray-er turns to God with praise because God has already responded to him/her in answering prayer. While this can be true about a specific situation, as one might imagine the case for the psalmist, it also holds truth for prayer in general. The pray-er turns to God, because God has already responded to him/her. In the Christian context this involves God's work in Jesus Christ. In v. 2b the psalmist anticipates that all flesh will come to God.

Verses 3-4 develop the initial statement in two ways. First, the sinfulness of the people is acknowledged (v. 3). Praise is offered from a position of self-awareness and vulnerability.[8] Secondly, the magnitude of God's forgiveness is stressed. Sins may overwhelm the pray-er but God's forgiveness is greater. The one whom God has chosen and brought near to his house is blessed (NRSV 'happy'). The goodness of that place is sufficient for the pray-er. The prayer of praise is a response to the abundance of God's forgiveness and blessing (v. 4, cf. Ps 23:6).

The second and third sections of the psalm (vv. 5-8 and 9-13 respectively) develop the idea of God's answer to prayer. Verses 5-8 emphasize God's answer to prayer in the mythic realm.

> [5] By awesome deeds you answer us with deliverance,
>> O God of our salvation;

---

[8] Cf. Brueggemann, *The Message of the Psalms*, p. 135.

you are the hope of all the ends of the earth
    and of the farthest seas.
[6] By your strength you established the mountains;
    you are girded with might.
[7] You silence the roaring of the seas,
    the roaring of their waves,
    the tumult of the peoples.
[8] Those who live at earth's farthest bounds are awed by your signs;
    you make the gateways of the morning and the evening shout for joy.

The psalmist's language in this section recalls God's power over the forces of chaos in the cosmos. Combined with this are allusions to the deliverance of the people. This is evident in the phrase 'God of our salvation' (v. 5) but also in the words 'awesome deeds' and 'signs' in vv. 5 and 8 respectively. The former is connected with the exodus out of Egypt (cf. Exod 34:10; Pss 66:5; 106:22) while the latter is associated with the plagues in Egypt (cf. Pss 78:43; 105:27; 135:9).

In the tradition concerned with God's power over the raging seas (with v. 7 cf. Isa 51:9-11; Ps 89:5-10) God defeats evil or chaos. In the exodus tradition the people are delivered from slavery. In both traditions evil is overcome at the foundational or mythic level. Evil, or the destructive power of chaos, is not confined to the arena of human affairs. The latter is continually in danger of being overwhelmed by chaos in any of a number of forms. The psalm acknowledges the work of God in the mythic realm and recognizes the dependence of the worldly realm on that work.[9] Prayer is thus seen as a conversation incorporating consideration of the mythic realm. It is not simply about the things we experience here and now. In short, prayer provides an opportunity for the interplay of the worldly and the mythic to take place. It not only reminds us of but also lets us participate in a reality beyond the mundane and familiar.

In vv. 9-13 the psalm returns to the worldly sphere with a recall of God's blessing of abundant fertility on the earth. The psalmist responds with praise of God, but, as vv. 12-13 make clear, this praise echoes that already offered joyfully by the pastures, hills and valleys with their crops and flocks.

[9] You visit the earth and water it,
        you greatly enrich it;
    the river of God is full of water;
        you provide the people with grain,
        for so you have prepared it.
[10] You water its furrows abundantly,
        settling its ridges,
        softening it with showers,
        and blessing its growth.
[11] You crown the year with your bounty;
        your wagon tracks overflow with richness.

---

[9] Quoted in Kraus, H.-J. (1989), *Psalms 60-150*, Augsburg, Minneapolis, p. 30.

¹² The pastures of the wilderness overflow,
      the hills gird themselves with joy,
¹³ the meadows clothe themselves with flocks,
      the valleys deck themselves with grain,
      they shout and sing together for joy.

The psalmist's response is continuous with the process of the earth living up to its potential. Praise is thus broadened beyond a rational, wordy, conscious, human endeavour. It is embodied in the very life of the creation and the human prayer of praise is but a part of the chorus. We are called on to recognize that, and in our prayers of praise to be lost in the wonder of the life of the world around us. It would seem that our ingrained consumerist attitudes, our objectification of creation, and our self-centred attitude to life foster a loss of wonder at the world around us. Praise is reduced to something we offer to God, usually at the beginning of a service of worship. We lose our sense of God as creator and of the life of the creation, including our own, as praise.[10]

Psalm 107 – Giving Thanks

Psalm 107

The main part of this community song of thanksgiving is marked by a clear and repetitive structure. It begins, however, in vv. 1-3 with a call for the 'redeemed' to give thanks for God's everlasting faithfulness. The redeemed have been gathered from the four corners of the world.

¹ O give thanks to the LORD, for he is good;
      for his steadfast love endures forever.
² Let the redeemed of the LORD say so,
      those he redeemed from trouble
³ and gathered in from the lands,
      from the east and from the west,
      from the north and from the south.

It then speaks about four different groups who give thanks to God: refugees who are hungry and thirsty (vv. 4-9); prisoners (vv. 10-16); the sick (in Hebrew 'fools', vv. 17-22); and sailors (vv. 23-32). A parallel structure runs across these four sections. It consists of a description of the distress, a refrain 'Then they cried to the LORD in their trouble, and he delivered them from their distress', a notice of deliverance appropriate to each group, and either a further statement of deliverance (vv. 9 and 16) or a final exhortation to thank God (vv. 22 and 32). The first section below illustrates the structure (the lines repeated elsewhere in the psalm are in italics):

---

[10] Brueggemann, *The Message of the Psalms*, p. 136.

⁴ Some wandered in desert wastes,
    finding no way to an inhabited town;
⁵ hungry and thirsty,
    their soul fainted within them.
⁶ *Then they cried to the LORD in their trouble,*
    and he delivered them from their distress;
⁷ he led them by a straight way,
    until they reached an inhabited town.
⁸ Let them thank the LORD for his steadfast love,
    for his wonderful works to humankind.
⁹ *For he satisfies the thirsty,*
    and the hungry he fills with good things.

The choice of the four groups of people who cry to God has been debated. The difficulty lies with the fourth group. Israel was not a great seafaring nation, and the ways of ships and sailors would have been unknown to most. The other three groups are familiar but could also remind an audience of the exodus tradition. With the reference to the redeemed coming from all corners of the earth in vv. 1-3, we could see the psalm set in the post-exilic period when a number of people returned from exile to their homeland.

The psalm concludes with a statement that God is the one who controls creation (vv. 33-38). God can turn prosperity (rivers, pools, and fruitfulness) into places of sterility because of sin (vv. 33-34), but God can also reverse that (vv. 35-38) turning the desert place into a spring or place of harvest, a home for the hungry who were mentioned in vv. 4-9. The psalm concludes with an assertion that God can deliver his people when they are low (vv. 39-41), and a closing injunction for the upright to rejoice in this and for those who are wise to consider 'these things' and God's faithful acts. Verses 33-38 constitute a statement of God's absolute power over nature and history. However, by speaking about God's power to turn deserts into places of fertility after telling of his power to turn places of fertility into deserts, the point is made that even God's acts of redemption can overcome his judgment.

In this psalm thanksgiving is the response of those who recognize the goodness and 'steadfast love' of God (v. 1). That is, God's nature is what gives rise to praise in thanksgiving. It is not that God is good to those who praise him. The psalm reminds the pray-er that thanksgiving arises after deliverance from many types of situations. Both the innocent sufferer and those who suffer as a result of sinfulness (see vv. 11 and 17) receive deliverance. The psalm is an exercise in the common response of thanksgiving to the Lord's common act of deliverance. It is also an exercise in the constant call for thanks to God in light of the constancy of his acts of deliverance. Verse 43 invites us to consider prayer itself as an occasion to ponder this *hesed* ('steadfast love' in the NRSV or 'covenant loyalty' or 'faithfulness') of God. It is an incentive to those who are faithful to maintain their prayer. The past and its acts of deliverance constitute a cause for hope for the future. Thus prayers of thanksgiving and praise are an important element in the relation of prayer and experience, but not just as one point on a never-ending cycle.

The repetition in this psalm does not signal a hopeless movement back and forth between petition and thanksgiving. Rather it points to the constant overcoming of distress by deliverance and thanksgiving. The pray-er is always moving toward praise and thanksgiving, even if there are many experiences of distress along the way.[11]

Psalms 121 and 27 – Trusting God

Psalm 121

This psalm is the second in the group Psalms 120-134. These psalms are designated by their Hebrew titles as 'Songs of ascents' or possibly 'Pilgrimage Songs', although there is nothing overtly connecting the group with pilgrimage. While that is true of the group, there are indications that Psalm 121 could be a pilgrimage psalm. It begins:

> [1] I lift up my eyes to the hills –
>> from where will my help come?
> [2] My help comes from the LORD,
>> who made heaven and earth.

These verses have often been read as the words of a pilgrim who, about to commence a journey maybe either to or from Jerusalem, expresses some uncertainty as to his/her safety. The hills, or more properly 'mountains' in the Hebrew, are seen as a place of potential danger. We might imagine the threats of bandits or wild animals. The psalmist reassures him or herself in v. 2 that help comes from the Lord.

However, the beginning of the psalm can be understood in other ways. Some scholars have read v. 1b not as a question but as a statement: 'I lift up my eyes to the hills from where my help comes'. The mountains are the place where the Lord resides and hence they are a promise of protection. We could compare Pss 48:1-3 and 87:1-3, which make similar statements about mountains, and Ps 123:1 where lifting up the eyes is also a statement of trust. The problem with this interpretation is that the word translated 'from where' in Ps 121:1b when used elsewhere is always involved in a question. One scholar at least sees a third possibility in which the question is retained but the mountains are seen positively as a source of protection. He translates: 'I look up to the mountains to see where my help comes from'.[12] Whichever way we read v. 1, it is clear that the question is answered by the declaration in vv 3-8, that the psalmist can put his/her trust in the Lord as protector. The Hebrew verb *šamar* 'to keep, guard, or protect' is used six times in these verses and forms the central theme of the psalm. The reason that the psalmist can have confidence is that the Lord is the creator of heaven and earth (v.

---

[11] Cf. Miller, P.D. (1986), *Interpreting the Psalms*, Fortress, Philadelphia, p. 66.

[12] Allen, *Psalms 101-150*, p. 151.

2b). The personal trust of the psalmist is founded on the cosmic sovereignty of the Lord.

An important aspect of this psalm is that while vv. 1-2 are in the first person, 'I', vv. 3-8 are in the second person. Someone else addresses the psalmist in these verses, possibly another pilgrim or, as many have suggested, a priest. It seems unlikely that the psalmist simply reflects and reassures him or herself. There are none of the normal indications in the Hebrew that the psalmist is reflecting personally. Thus a dialogue is set up in the psalm. One might imagine the psalmist being assured by a Jerusalem priest, as he/she is about to return home from pilgrimage to the holy city. The change in pronouns from vv. 1-2 to vv. 3-8 accompanies a change in form from a statement of trust (v. 2) to one of promise, which is both the foundation of trust and that which sustains it along the way. There is also a movement from statements on the cosmic scale ('my help comes from the LORD, who made heaven and earth') to ones more concerned with the well being of the individual ('he will keep your life'). The trust of the individual, and the promise under girding that trust, are grounded in the one who is creator and sovereign of all.

Verses 3-8 then divide into two sections, vv. 3-5 and 6-8.

> ³ He will not let your foot be moved;
>> he who keeps you will not slumber.
> ⁴ He who keeps Israel will neither slumber nor sleep.
> ⁵ The LORD is your keeper;
>> the LORD is your shade at your right hand.

In these verses the word *šomer* 'he who keeps, keeper' occurs three times and the psalmist, addressed as 'you', is five times mentioned as the object of that keeping. There is a sense of total protection. It is there when the psalmist feels helpless, which is the sense of the reference to the foot being moved in v. 3a (cf. Pss 38:16; 94:18) as well on every other occasion. The Lord who protects does not sleep. The psalmist's assurance lies in the fact that the one who is creator beyond time is yet concerned for the least time of danger to the psalmist. The image of preventing the foot from slipping also brings to mind the rough mountain journey.

The poetic structure of these verses reinforces the assurance of the psalmist. While at first the psalmist's protector is described anonymously as 'he', in v. 5 the Lord's name is twice used. The promised protector of the psalmist is one who can be named and potentially held accountable. This is no off hand commitment. In addition, in v. 3b 'he who keeps *you*' is parallel to '*your* keeper' in v. 5a. Between these two lines the protector is described as 'he who keeps Israel'. The psalmist has the extra assurance that the one who has kept the people from time immemorial is the one who is now promised as their personal protector. The Lord as creator, who is beyond not only time but also any source of danger that may come, is the one who has kept the psalmist's community throughout its history. The psalmist thus stands in a greater context than he/she at first possibly perceived. His/her future is assured.

In vv. 6-8 the psalm moves from the possibility of danger on a particular journey to the situation of life itself. The trust that the psalmist can have in the Lord is connected to both the particulars of life as well as to life itself.

> ⁶ The sun shall not strike you by day,
>   nor the moon by night.
> ⁷ The LORD will keep you from all evil;
>   he will keep your life.
> ⁸ The LORD will keep your going out and your coming in
>   from this time on and forevermore.

These verses open with a reference to the difficulties of the journey, particularly the heat of the day and the dangers of night. In the psalmist's world the night represented a time of danger and particular vulnerability. The reference also recalls the mention of the protector who neither sleeps nor slumbers. However, it broadens its scope giving a sense of the Lord's protection in all the endeavours of life. The verb *šamar* again appears three times, but this time in the form '(he) will keep' and the psalmist, addressed as 'you', is the object of those verbs on four occasions. In everything the psalmist does, the Lord keeps him/her. The psalmist knows that in the particular journeys in life trust can be placed in God He/she also knows that trust can be placed in God in the greater journey of life itself.

In this psalm the words 'the Lord will keep you' function almost as a mantra. The repetition of them under girds the assurance. The words spoken to the psalmist promise the Lord's protection at every turn, at every moment. But the psalmist also knows and proclaims in other places that even one who is faithful does not attain a life preserved from all harm in every situation (e.g. Psalm 17). Many lament psalms arise out of innocent suffering. Nevertheless, the assurance in Psalm 121 has the power to strengthen the believer to face many difficulties and hardships. The prayer of the psalmist is thus not limited by personal experience and circumstance. He/she asserts the possibility of trusting against the grain of experience. While the promise of the Lord's protection and presence can be understood neither simplistically nor literally, trust in that promise is grounded in a reality that goes beyond personal experience. It is grounded in the Lord as creator and in the fact that the larger community of faith has discovered the Lord as one in whom trust can be placed. A prayer of trust is not simply an isolated word about the pray-er's immediate well-being. Of course, in its particulars it is that, but it is more. It evokes and participates in a relationship that stretches beyond both the experienced world and the present. To pray a prayer of trust is to commit oneself to a relationship, or a web of relationships, that incorporates creation and history. And the promise of security, which incorporates our individual needs, spreads to the end of the world and time. One writer quotes words from a hymn by Paul Gerhardt which expresses this same kind of faith:

> Who points the clouds their course,
> Whom winds and sea obey,
> He shall direct thy wandering feet,

He shall prepare thy way.[13]

It is little wonder then that the psalm is set up as a dialogue and the promise (vv. 3-8) is spoken by someone other than the psalmist who is called to trust. Of course, this dialogue might make the psalm seem strange if we pray it today but that need not be a difficulty. If we pray the psalm on our own behalf, it is more than fitting if we hear the words of promise come from another voice, even that of an ancient priest. It helps ground us in the call to trust and promise of security that span the centuries. On the other hand, if we pray the psalm in relation to another who seeks assurance, we can evoke the promise for the other as part of the larger community of faith called to trust and proclaim the promise. This psalm gives the pray-er permission to express every anxiety and seek assurance. It also draws us all into the larger community of trust.

Psalm 27

Psalm 27 has often been regarded by scholars as a mixed psalm, or even as two distinct psalms joined. Verses 1-6 contain a clear statement of trust while vv. 7-12 contain a lament or complaint. However, while there are two distinct parts to the psalm, there are unifying elements. Key words occur in both sections: 'salvation', vv. 1, 9; 'adversaries', vv. 2, 12; 'heart', vv. 3, 8, 14; 'seek', vv. 4, 8; 'hide', vv. 5, 9; 'rise', vv. 3, 12; and 'life', vv. 4, 13. Vv. 1 and 14 also form a frame or inclusio around the psalm. The psalm begins and ends in Hebrew with the word 'Lord' and the word occurs twice in each of these verses. Moreover, v. 14 is marked off from vv. 7-13 by being in the second person, addressed to the psalmist rather than continuing the psalmist's own words to the Lord. Vv. 1 and 14 complement each other in that, while they both urge trust in the Lord, v. 1 expresses it in a 'negative' fashion,

> [1] The LORD is my light and my salvation;
>> whom shall I fear?
> The LORD is the stronghold of my life;
>> of whom shall I be afraid?

and v. 14 through a strong 'positive' statement:

> [14] Wait for the LORD;
>> be strong, and let your heart take courage;
>> wait for the LORD!

Thus, I will treat the psalm in its unity, and see what the distinctive sections contribute to an understanding of prayer.

Verse 1 is a general statement of trust. The psalmist proclaims that there are no potential sources of fear because of his/her relationship to the Lord. The implicit

---

[13] Quoted in Weiser, *The Psalms*, p. 748.

assumption is that there is no challenge to the Lord, no adversary who is stronger than the Lord. That is the basis of the psalmist's trust. Verses 2-3 spell this out further in terms of the assaults of enemies, using metaphors of ravenous beasts in v. 2a and siege and warfare in v. 3. In spite of the threats, the psalmist repeats the confidence of v. 1, dismissing any fear as in v. 1, and concluding that the enemies are the ones who will stumble and fall. He/she concludes with the clear statement in Hebrew at the end of v. 3: 'yet I will trust'.

Verses 4-6 form the central statement about the psalmist's attitude toward the Lord.

> [4] One thing I asked of the LORD,
>   that will I seek after:
> to live in the house of the LORD
>   all the days of my life,
> to behold the beauty of the LORD,
>   and to inquire in his temple.
> [5] For he will hide me in his shelter
>   in the day of trouble;
> he will conceal me under the cover of his tent;
>   he will set me high on a rock.
> [6] Now my head is lifted up
>   above my enemies all around me,
> and I will offer in his tent
>   sacrifices with shouts of joy;
> I will sing and make melody to the LORD.

The psalmist wishes only to dwell in the house of Lord all their days, to gaze on the Lord's beauty, and to inquire of the Lord, that is, to seek out the Lord's will. Technical priestly language is used here. The basis of this desire is introduced in v. 5 with 'because'. There is refuge in the Lord's house, which in turn leads to rescue (v. 6). The elevation of the psalmist over his/her enemies recalls the earlier image of the enemies falling (v. 2b). These words of confidence are not a form of boasting.[14] While they are confident, they are also words of humility undermining any sense of self-confidence on the part of the psalmist. This will lead to the psalmist offering sacrifice and rejoicing in the place of the Lord. The psalmist's trust in founded in his/her desire to worship and be in the presence of the Lord where there is protection. Worship is both the foundation of trust as well as an expression of it. This is the heart of the psalm and concludes the general statement of trust before the lament, which relates that trust to a specific occasion for fear. It is a statement that echoes both the words and sentiment of the end of Psalm 23.

In terms of prayer, we note that the psalmist recalls the basis of his/her trust – communion with and worship of God – at the point where he/she needs to rekindle that trust again. Prayer gives the opportunity to enter this place of

---

[14] See Craigie, *Psalms 1-50*, p. 225.

communion, and to reorient oneself in the world. It allows the possibility of recognizing what gives life and peace, and gives opportunity to voice that desire.

Verses 7-12 then form an extended plea to the Lord to be faithful to this relationship.

> [7] Hear, O LORD, when I cry aloud,
>   be gracious to me and answer me!
> [8] 'Come,' my heart says, 'seek his face!'
>   Your face, LORD, do I seek.
> [9]   Do not hide your face from me.
>
>   Do not turn your servant away in anger,
>   you who have been my help.
>   Do not cast me off, do not forsake me,
>   O God of my salvation!
> [10] If my father and mother forsake me,
>   the LORD will take me up.
>
> [11] Teach me your way, O LORD,
>   and lead me on a level path
>   because of my enemies.
> [12] Do not give me up to the will of my adversaries,
>   for false witnesses have risen against me,
>   and they are breathing out violence.

The psalmist's trust in the previous verses does not dispel the difficulties in life that now face the psalmist. He/she seeks, even demands, an answer to their plea (v. 7). Eight imperatives addressed to the Lord come from the mouth of the psalmist in these verses. The basis for his/her demands includes the general statement of trust in vv. 1-6, as well as the psalmist's reliance upon the lord, the Lord's past action, and the present danger. The psalmist proclaims faithfulness on his/her part. The statement of general trust becomes the bargaining point with God over the issue of faithfulness. For the psalmist, arguing with God with cogent and strong arguments is not beyond the bounds of prayer. In fact, prayer in this psalm seems to be an argument that God act according to the past experience of God's way of doing things. This is made quite explicit in v. 11 where the psalmist seeks to follow in the 'way' of the Lord.

The psalmist asks that the Lord not hide his face. The use of the word 'hide' in v. 9 picks up on what the Lord would do for the psalmist in the Lord's house (v. 5). Now, however, it is the Lord's face that seems to be hidden in anger. The psalmist wishes to turn this 'hiding' around so that it is no longer the Lord who hides but the psalmist who is hidden in the lord. The words 'O God of my salvation!' in v. 9 recall the phrases of v. 1 and remind the Lord again of the past relationship. The reference in v. 10 to the potential for a father or mother to abandon the psalmist, does not speak literally of the psalmist's present plight.

Rather, it reveals what the psalmist believes is the depth of the Lord's concern. It is greater than the natural concern of a parent for a child.

Finally the psalm ends with a strong statement of trust and hope (vv. 13-14).

> [13] I believe that I shall see the goodness of the LORD
> in the land of the living.
> [14] Wait for the LORD;
> be strong, and let your heart take courage;
> wait for the LORD!

The psalmist makes a firm statement of trust in v. 13. However, the speaker in v. 14 is not clear. One might presume the psalmist now reflects and speaks words of encouragement to him or herself. But this seems unlikely since there is nothing in the Hebrew to indicate that someone is reflecting and there is the presence of four imperative and the words 'your heart'. The suggestion (also noted above in Psalm 121) that another person, possibly a priest, now addresses the psalmist and urges hope in the Lord seems most reasonable. The word translated 'wait' in the NRSV literally means 'hope'. This is not just an urging of patience. It focuses the hope of the psalmist in the Lord, even as he/she trusts in the Lord entirely. It urges the very thing that the psalmist states confidently in v. 13.

We can make a number of general points from this psalm about trust that are relevant for our consideration of prayer relating to the psalms of trust.[15] First, the point of the unity of the psalm is that it brings trust and anxiety into relationship. The psalm might very well consist of a general statement of trust and a lament psalm, but brings these two together *as one prayer*. In that context, the statement of trust becomes more than pious words, and the lament psalm more than anxiety. Verse 13 could function in the lament as the statement of trust, but by enveloping the lament within the statements of trust and hope, the psalm more fully underlines the nature of trust. Secondly, worship is the foundation of trust. In that context, we learn of and renew the relationship that lies at the heart of our trust, and our trust itself is informed, challenged, and grows. Finally, in the psalm the opposite of trust in God is fear of humans. This is particularly so in relation to the language used by human opponents, which is false in its statements. The sanctuary, or place of worship, is the place where truth is spoken, and prayer is the occasion when it is declared over against the falsehood of the 'enemies' of truth. Prayer enables one to contemplate this and assert it in one's life.

Psalm 51 – Confessing Sin

Psalm 51

Psalm 51 is probably one of the best-known psalms. It is used in the various lectionaries for Ash Wednesday each year as the Church marks the beginning of

---

[15] See Mays, J.L. (1994), *Psalms*, John Knox, Louisville, pp. 132-3 for a further discussion.

Lent. Verses 10-12 and 15, have been used widely in prayers of general confession or in the liturgy of the Daily Office or Daily Prayer. At the time of the Reformation, this psalm was among the texts to which Luther appealed for his doctrine of justification.[16] It is one of seven psalms, the so-called 'penitential' psalms, concerned with confession and forgiveness.

Verses 1-2 set the theme for the psalm.

> [1] Have mercy on me, O God,
>> according to your steadfast love;
> according to your abundant mercy
>> blot out my transgressions.
> [2] Wash me thoroughly from my iniquity,
>> and cleanse me from my sin.

Without any introduction, the psalmist seeks God's mercy, not for relief from any oppression but because he/she has sinned. No qualification is added to this confession. The four imperatives in these two verses anticipate the long list of imperatives to come later. The psalmist seeks God's action in the matter and uses language ('blot out', 'wash', and 'cleanse') drawn from atonement rituals in temple worship. The piling up of words for sin ('transgression', 'iniquity', and 'sin') points to the seriousness of the issue. While vv. 1d-2 contain three requests for forgiveness, they are preceded by the request that God grant mercy on the basis of God's steadfast love and compassion (*hesed*, NRSV 'mercy'). The psalmist is aware that he/she is totally dependent on God. One writer states: 'The *sola gratia* shines forth from every verse.'[17] God's grace is the only hope this psalmist can have.

The psalmist then provides the reasons for the request (vv. 3-6). He/she is constantly aware of his/her own sin (v. 3). It is not just a matter of acknowledging something that he/she has to live with, or of recognizing some minor imperfection in his/her being. The psalmist's whole life is marked by sin (v. 5). No excuse or mitigating circumstance can be offered in vv. 3-6 to support the request in vv. 1-2. The psalmist can only plead that God lift this terrible affliction. Verses 3 and 5, which state the psalmist's awareness of his/her own sin, surround the statements that he/she has sinned against God alone and that God is justified in judgment (v. 4).

Three points deserve comment in these verses. First, the psalmist says he/she has sinned against God *alone*. This could sound as though it dismisses the wrong that can be done to other humans, or creatures, or to the creation in sin. It is unlikely this is meant. The context within which the editors of the psalms have interpreted this text according to the heading attached to the psalm, namely that of the story of David, Uriah, and Bathsheba (2 Sam 11:1-12:23), is one which shows the grave consequences of sin within the human domain. Nevertheless, even within that story it is stressed that David has sinned against the Lord (2 Sam 12:9, 13-14).

---

[16] Kraus, H.-J. (1993), *Psalms 1-59*, trans. H.C. Oswald, Fortress, Minneapolis, p. 506.
[17] *Ibid.*, p. 507.

In other texts, sin against other humans is regarded as sin against God (cf. Gen 39:9; Prov 14:31; 17:5). Far from dismissing the earthly consequences of sin, the psalmist goes to the very heart of the problem. All sin affects the relationship between the psalmist and God. While an offence against other humans or creatures may be grave in its consequences, the depth of the offence against God cannot be underestimated and no forgiveness can be attained or restitution made without attention to that relationship as primary. As some writers have put it, the psalm affirms that sin is essentially a theological problem.[18] Dealing with sin involves a reckoning with God.

A second issue concerns v. 5: 'Indeed, I was born guilty, a sinner when my mother conceived me'. This has sometimes been understood to refer to the Christian doctrine of original sin. However, the point is not that sin is transmitted in the act of conception or that there is something inherently sinful about sex. Rather, the psalmist makes a similar point in v. 5 to that made in v. 3. Sin has had an inescapable hold on the psalmist his/her whole life long. He/she has never been out of its grip. Verse 5 points to the 'depth of the sinner's conviction of sin.'[19] Verse 6 relates to v. 5 in this context, although the meaning of v. 6 is not completely clear. Both verses begin in Hebrew with *hen*, 'indeed, behold'. The translation of two words in v. 6 as 'inward being' and 'secret heart' is tentative and the two words could possibly be rendered as 'dark, hidden spaces' and 'closed space'. They could be a reference back to the womb and God's own desire to find truth and impart wisdom even from the beginning, in the hidden places where the body forms.

Finally, in Psalm 51 there is no complaint that God acts unjustly, or that the psalmist is innocent of wrongdoing. The sentiments are, in fact, quite the opposite. This psalm, therefore, stands in sharp contrast to many of the lament psalms that declare the innocence of the psalmist (e.g. Pss 7:3-5; 17:3; 26). It is clear that the psalmist anticipates occasions when it is proper to complain that God acts unjustly, or doesn't act at all when God should, or that the pray-er is not guilty of sin in a particular context. He/she recognizes also that on other occasions we must acknowledge that we are caught in a complex web of sin. There is a fine line between these two situations. At what point does a complaint against a perceived wrong by God become arrogance or self-delusion? Or when does an awareness of our being utterly lost in sin become either self-denial or cause for self-pity? No clear answer is given to this but there are some points to be noted in the psalms. In Psalm 51 it is said that the psalmist is acutely aware of his/her own sin. One can presume that God knows of the psalmist's awareness. This is clearly stated elsewhere and is the very hope of the psalmist when he/she proclaims their innocence, as in Pss 69:5. Psalm 139, discussed in detail elsewhere in this book, describes the total knowledge God has of the psalmist.

Thus, God is totally aware of the psalmist's situation. God knows the psalmist's innocence in certain circumstances, their culpability in others, and

---

[18] Mays, *Psalms*, p. 200, and Brueggemann, *The Message of the Psalms*, p. 99.

[19] Miller, P.D. (1998), 'Preaching Repentance in a Narcissistic Age: Psalm 51', *Journal for Preachers*, Vol. 21/2, pp. 3-8, esp. p. 5.

his/her general inability to escape from sinfulness. While that could be a threatening situation, it is, in fact, hope for the psalmist who knows also that the one who knows him/her is not only just but also compassionate. Psalm 103 declares:

> ⁶ The LORD works vindication
> and justice for all who are oppressed.
> ⁷ He made known his ways to Moses,
> his acts to the people of Israel.
> ⁸ The LORD is merciful and gracious,
> slow to anger and abounding in steadfast love.
> ⁹ He will not always accuse,
> nor will he keep his anger forever.
> ¹⁰ He does not deal with us according to our sins,
> nor repay us according to our iniquities.
> ¹¹ For as the heavens are high above the earth,
> so great is his steadfast love toward those who fear him;
> ¹² as far as the east is from the west,
> so far he removes our transgressions from us.
> ¹³ As a father has compassion for his children,
> so the LORD has compassion for those who fear him.
> ¹⁴ For he knows how we were made;
> he remembers that we are dust.

This ultimate reliance upon the compassion of God, coupled with total honesty on the part of the psalmist, is the way in which the conversation in prayer regarding confession and forgiveness must proceed.

Ps 51:7-15 contain an extended plea to God for forgiveness and renewal. There are some patterns in the construction of these verses that hold the psalm together. The language of 'washing' etc. (vv. 7, 9, and 10) recalls v. 1, as do the various words for 'sin' and 'sinners' (vv. 9 and 13). In vv. 10-12 each second line begins in Hebrew with the word *ruach*, 'spirit'. Finally, vv. 12-15 present a series of three requests, each followed by a statement of the result that will follow when God carries out the request.

The section contains a series of fourteen imperatives or similar constructions requesting action from God. There is nothing in these verses to justify the psalmist or to counter the just sentence that God passes in v. 4. He/she is aware that he/she depends solely on the freedom of God to grant forgiveness and compassion in spite of the justice of God's sentence. This is not self-pity on the part of the psalmist. He/she does not dwell on their sin, which was expressed briefly in vv. 3-6, but focus on God's capacity to forgive. That is at the heart of this psalmist's confession. It is important to note also that the psalmist is talking about a state of sin in these verses. He/she is not just speaking about isolated sinful acts.[20]

---

[20] Cf. Mays, *Psalms*, p. 203.

But the psalm also makes it clear that confession and forgiveness involve renewal. It is fitting that the first imperative in these verses is from the verb *bara'*, 'to create', a word used only with God as subject and which recalls the creation story in Genesis 1. Moreover, the final sequence of imperatives and results in vv. 12-15 urges renewal. The psalmist seeks a 'clean heart' and a 'right spirit', which in other words are a mind and a will oriented toward God and open to God's renewing activity.[21] Not only does the psalmist seek to remain close to God but desires to experience joy and praise once more. He/she desires to be involved again in the service of God teaching others the meaning and nature of confession and forgiveness. He/she wishes to pass on to others what he/she has learned and what is expressed in the psalm itself. Verse 15, 'O Lord, open my lips, and my mouth will declare your praise', is often used at the beginning of Daily Prayer services, and it could be seen as the start of the next section of the psalm which describes the 'sacrifice' that God does desire. However, it is also fitting that it be the last desire of the psalmist in this sequence. The end of confession can only be praise.

In vv. 16-17 the psalmist describes what is most desirable to God.

> [16] For you have no delight in sacrifice;
>   if I were to give a burnt offering, you would not be pleased.
> [17] The sacrifice acceptable to God is a broken spirit;
>   a broken and contrite heart, O God, you will not despise.

These verses could be read as an 'anti-sacrificial' statement by the psalmist; one in which he/she expresses the belief that the ritual sacrifice of the temple, especially that associated with atonement, is ineffectual. But that seems to disregard the rest of the psalm. There are other ways of reading the psalm as a unity. Rather than being a polemical statement, vv. 16-17 get at the heart of what has been said already. There is in the contemplation of forgiveness a need for a deep understanding of the severity of sin and its effects. This is the broken and contrite heart that God desires. This is what is needed in confession, for it is only this kind of heart that understands the depths of God's grace in forgiveness. It is not a matter of 'works' here, as if the psalmist can generate his/her own 'broken spirit'. That would be simply to replace a thoroughly negative view of sacrifice in v. 16 with a 'broken spirit' as a means to appease God. The psalmist is talking about a deep realization of the nature of sin and its inescapable hold on us, and of the utter dependence of the sinner on God for forgiveness. Unless the heart is broken and contrite in this way, then the pray-er will not understand the nature of forgiveness. The word translated 'contrite' in v. 17 may help in our understanding. It is the same word in Hebrew as that describing the bones of the psalmist back in v. 8b, namely *dakah* 'to crush'. While in v. 8b the bones of the psalmist were crushed by God in punishment for sin, in v. 17 the heart will be 'crushed' in forgiveness. According to the psalmist, in punishment for sin the outer being is broken, whereas in forgiveness, the inner being is broken.

Finally we come to vv. 18-19.

---

[21] *Ibid.*

[18] Do good to Zion in your good pleasure;
  rebuild the walls of Jerusalem,
[19] then you will delight in right sacrifices,
  in burnt offerings and whole burnt offerings;
  then bulls will be offered on your altar.

As noted above, it has often been suggested that these verses are an addition to the psalm by an exilic or early post-exilic writer. They presume that Jerusalem is in ruins. They could be read as a 'corrective' to an 'anti-sacrifice' piety proclaimed in vv. 16-17. As such, they would be a justification for the place of cultic activity in the acknowledgement and forgiveness of sin. However, this suggestion is not the only possible explanation. It leaves the final form of the psalm in a state of tension. In the end are we to read the psalm as for or against sacrifice? Alternatively, one could see the development of the psalm in stages so that vv. 16-17 reflect a period when Jerusalem and the temple were not available for worship, and hence portray a temporary piety for the exile. Verses 18-19 express the hope that things will return to what they were before the exile.

  Another alternative is to read the whole psalm as exilic or early post-exilic, with the hope for rebuilding as a way to allow the cult to function again. At the same time the psalmist sees the possibility of rebuilding Jerusalem as an example of the utter graciousness of God in forgiveness of his people. In many texts the exile is seen as the result of the past sins of Israel (e.g. 2 Kgs 23:26-17; Lam 1:1-5; Zech 8:14-15; Isa 40:1-2 etc.). Thus, in the experience of exile the psalmist has realized a need for the recognition of the depth of sin and the nature of forgiveness, not only on the individual level but also in terms of the community. The activities of the cult (vv. 18-19) and a deep 'inner piety' (vv. 16-17) need not be seen at odds, with one a 'corrective' to the other. Rather they act as complementary aspects in the processes of confession and forgiveness. The one is the outer public proclamation of these processes, incorporated in space and time. The other is the inner spiritual experience of contrition. They belong together. This would make sense of the presence of the technical cultic language ('washing', 'cleansing' and 'blotting out' and the various words for 'sin') throughout the psalm. The temple worship and all its activities are not dismissed, but need to be accompanied by a right spirit in the heart of the pray-er.

Chapter 5

Invited to Pray

The world of prayer in the psalms is a world shaped by many conversations. As we have seen there are psalms of praise and thanksgiving. There are wisdom psalms for times of reflection, and psalms of confession for when the psalmist has sinned. There are also psalms of complaint to God. It is a world shaped by poetic language, and one that the pray-er will find has been inhabited by many others before them. The pray-er is invited to use these prayers and be disciplined by them. Above all he/she is invited to pray, and to see his/her own life in faith in the psalms. The psalms are not just for study alone.[1] In the Jewish tradition, the Rabbis distinguished too between *'iyyun tefilla*, the study of prayer texts, and *tefilla*, prayer itself.[2]

But how might we pray using the psalms? This question can be broken down into a number of related questions. First, how can we use the psalms as individuals or groups in our own prayers to God? A related issue is how the psalms might be organized to assist us in our prayers. Secondly, how can we use the psalms in our prayers with and for others, that is, in pastoral care? Finally, how can we speak to God using the psalms in the context of public worship?

The Way we Might Pray Using the Psalms

First, we should note that we can pray either **with** a psalm or **from** a psalm. In praying **with** a psalm we adopt the words of the psalm as our own prayer. This involves an act of imagination on the part of the pray-er. He or she uses the words of the psalm, as if they were their own, but understands the words in relation to their present situation.[3] A suggested classification of the psalms according to type or genre is included in the appendix.

On the other hand, praying **from** a psalm involves using it as a source for ideas for our own prayer. This can be done in several ways.

---

[1] Garrone, G. (1965), *How to Pray the Psalms*, Notre Dame, Fides, p. 11.

[2] Blumenthal, D. (1998), 'Psalm 145: A Liturgical Reading', in J. Magnes et al. (eds), *Hesed ve-emet. Studies in Honor of Ernest S. Frerichs*, Scholars, Atlanta, pp. 13-35, esp. p. 28.

[3] This was recognised by St. Athanasius long ago in his *Letter to Marcellinus*, sect. 12, in Gregg, R.C. (ed.) (1980) *Athanasius: The Life of Antony and The Letter to Marcellinus*, SPCK, London, p. 111.

- A word, phrase, verse, or section from a psalm can become the focus for prayer. This allows the pray-er to explore matters well outside the domain of the actual psalm. In this case the psalm acts as a foil for such thoughts, as a way of examining them, questioning them, or probing them further.
- Another way is to imagine the sort of situation and people that fit a particular psalm and pray for them using some or all of the words of the psalm. It involves imagining who the 'I' or the 'we' might be in the psalm who give praise or lament. This provides a concrete context within which the words can be prayed in intercession. I will take this matter up further below.
- Alternatively, we could interpret the 'I' of the psalm as the Church, the Body of Christ, which prays. This was frequently done in the middle ages. It was promoted both through the commentaries written by the Church Fathers, who interpreted the psalms in terms of Christ, as well as by the titles and psalm collects added to psalms in the Liturgy of the Hours.[4]
- Another suggestion is to memorise (or write down) a phrase, line or verse from the psalm and to use it throughout the day as a source for meditation or as a trigger for short extemporary prayers.
- Finally, we might like to write a brief personal reflection or response to the psalm as our prayer to God.

I mentioned above a connection between the psalms as prayer and poetry. When praying either with or from a psalm it is very important to recognise the nature of the language before us, to respect that and, in turn, immerse ourselves as much as possible in that language. At a basic level this means we could read the psalm slowly or rhythmically, giving careful attention to the words. This would give us time to become involved in the poetry and seek some understanding. It can also quieten and calm us, and help focus our own prayer. At a deeper level it could involve us in other ways. First, let us consider the case where we use the psalms for our own prayers, that is, praying **with them**.

We need to remember that the poetic language of the psalms is a language of exaggeration. And so, when praying with the psalms we must reinterpret the words of the psalms within our own context. We investigate the language of the psalm with all its devices – the imagery, the word plays, the metaphors etc. – and begin to play with it, and develop it in light of our own experience.[5] Moreover, when we pray with a psalm we do not simply follow the words of the psalm literally, or slavishly, word for word trying to fit our experience to that of the psalmist as we perceive it. We are not a ventriloquist's doll, with our mouth and our life moving to the words of a psalm. Rather, we enter into the process of reinterpretation I noted above. Indeed, the psalms invite us into that process. To use another theatrical simile, we are more like the actor on the stage, who has the

---

[4] Guiver, G. (1988), *Company of Voices: Daily Prayer and the People of God*, SPCK, London, pp. 155-6.

[5] See further Brueggemann, W. (1982), *Praying the Psalms*, St. Mary's, Winona, p. 34.

words of the script before him/her but who, through their actions, intonation, and timing give the words new life. One writer describes the act of praying with the psalms as a 'form of prayer located somewhere in the continuum between the active exercise of prayerful reading and the more intense state of being associated with moments of contemplative prayer.'[6] As we bring our concerns, joys etc. to a psalm we give it new life in our prayer. We enter into a partnership with the psalm, and it is a partnership in which both the psalm and we are free to surprise each other. Thus, the poetic language of the psalms can capture our spirits in the act of prayer, as one scholar remarks:

> We must be able to abandon ourselves to a certain rhythm, consent to a certain enchantment of combined sounds and images, an almost musical experience which is perplexing to our ordinary thinking processes. We must be ready to situate ourselves in a certain region of the unknown, out of which the prayer of the psalms rises with irrepressible fervor. Otherwise the psalms as prayers are unattainable.[7]

What he says here relates to psalms of praise but is equally applicable to laments where the pray-er may feel the depths of abandonment or despair. The poetic language of the psalms, being open and understated, makes it possible to pray with the psalms and not just be reading the words of another person's prayer.

Another writer who has given thought to what I have called here praying 'with' a psalm is D. Blumenthal. In a study of Psalm 145 he makes some further suggestions about how to pray with the psalms. What he says about Psalm 145 can be applied to any psalm. He outlines several ways people can pray the psalm.[8]

- The pray-er could 'perform' the words of the psalm by imagining and feeling what the words of the psalm say. This should be done at a measured pace.
- The pray-er could recite the words of the psalm slowly, even breaking between words, and noting the repetition of words and various other word patterns. He suggests that for a group reading this could be done ahead of time and the psalm printed in such a way as to highlight these patterns with bold or italic fonts etc.
- The pray-er could 'weave' the verses of the psalm together. Blumenthal bases this suggestion on a quote from C.S. Lewis on Psalm 119:

> It is a pattern, a thing done like embroidery, stitch by stitch, through long, quiet hours, for love of the subject and for delight in leisurely, disciplined craftsmanship.[9]

---

[6] Casey, M. (1983), 'The Prayer of Psalmody', *Cistercian Studies*, Vol. XVIII/2, pp. 106-120, esp. p. 106.

[7] Garrone, *How to Pray the Psalms*, pp. 14-15.

[8] Blumenthal, 'Psalm 145', pp. 13-35.

[9] Lewis, C.S. (1977), *Reflections on the Psalms*, Fount, London, p. 52.

Blumenthal suggests that the pray-er imagine the verses of the psalm weaving across each other, the first verse going across, the second verse up and down, the third across etc. as if weaving a tapestry with them. The psalm could also be written out in this way. Alternatively, the verses could be woven in a sphere around the pray-er; the first verse horizontally in a circle, the second vertically and so forth until the pray-er can imagine standing inside a sphere made up of the verses of the psalm.

Blumenthal is trying to break the mould of thinking of prayer in strictly intellectual terms. The psalms are more than just intellectual works. In the act of prayer, as well as in our prayers themselves, intellectual, aesthetic, spiritual, emotional, and psychological elements are involved.

If we use the psalms to help generate new prayers, that is, we pray **from** the psalms, then the poetic language of the psalms can inform us in other ways. The use of metaphor and imagery in the psalms reminds us of the need for new images in our own prayers, especially those we compose for public worship. It also reminds us that we must give attention to the rhythms and cadences of the language we use. We might consider taking a lead from the psalms by using parallelism by either repeating ideas with new words, and thus exploring the idea further, or by using a repetitive structure within our own prayers. Such repetition is not a sign of a lack of imagination. For the psalmist, and in our own prayers, it can be a way of taking thoughts further and exploring issues more deeply.

Finally, if we are responsible for prayers that are to be used in public or community worship, then we need to pay careful attention to the language of the prayer since we aim to allow the hopes or anxieties of others to be touched and gathered up in the prayer. It is here, especially, that some attention should be given to the poetic language of the psalms. Prayers that pay more attention to concise, concrete language, to imagery, and to structure are more likely to be effective for those who would pray through them.[10] While it is important for a prayer to be clear and to the point in its content, the language used needs to have the qualities of the poetry of the psalms, including a level of openness, which allows others to reinterpret the prayer within their own context. The imagery and other poetic devices we use need to be concrete, simple, and unadorned. There needs to be room for other pray-ers to work with the imagery etc. in their own way.

The Order of the Psalms in Prayer

We do not have any incontrovertible evidence that the collection of psalms was intentionally constructed for reading or use in its present order.[11] Over the millennia, numerous Jewish groups and Christian groups or denominations have organized the collection into set patterns for reading or praying, either in part or

---

[10] Hughes, G. (1992), *Leading in Prayer*, JBCE, Melbourne, p. 19.

[11] See Whybray, R. N. (1996), *Reading the Psalms as a Book*, JSOTSup 222, SAP, Sheffield, for a full discussion.

whole. In Christian circles this has been a regular practice in relation to the lectionary for Sunday services, as well as in orders of service for daily worship in religious houses and churches. In Judaism, certain psalms have been used in the set prayers for daily worship and Sabbath services.[12]

Dietrich Bonhoeffer suggested people should pray several psalms a day in order to go more deeply into them. Moreover, he suggested that the psalms be prayed as they come in the Book of Psalms, namely from 1 to 150.[13] Praying the psalms in their canonical order, even if only one per day, has the advantage of not letting our own preferences determine our praying. It would also allow us to experience the move in our prayer cycle from predominantly lament to praise. It would allow a good part of our praying to be intercessory if we prayed many of the laments on behalf of those who suffer.

Besides praying the psalms in their numerical order, other lists of psalms for prayer have been developed. Some of these are listed below and others could undoubtedly be added. They give either selected psalms for prayer at different times of the day or year or suggest an order in which a pray-er might work his/her way through the whole collection of psalms. Individuals or groups would ideally select an arrangement that best suits their needs.

a) G. Garrone suggests a listing of psalms associated with various seasons of the Christian year.[14] His list would not presume that all psalms will be used, nor that one might use a psalm in prayer each day. It simply suggests psalms appropriate for the season. His list is as follows.[15]

Advent:	Pss 80(79), 85(84)
Christmas:	Pss 2, 98(97), 110(109)
Epiphany:	Pss 66(65), 72(71)
Lent:	Pss 32(31), 51(50), 130(129)
Passiontide:	Pss 69(68), 88(87)
Holy Week:	
Holy Thursday:	Ps 142(141)
Good Friday:	Ps 22(21)
Holy Saturday:	Ps 27(26)
Easter:	Pss 16(15), 30(29), 118(117)
Ascension:	Pss 24(23), 47(46)
Pentecost:	Pss 48(47), 67(66)

---

[12] The weekly cycle of psalms is as follows: Sunday, Psalm 24; Monday, Psalm 48; Tuesday, Psalm 82; Wednesday, Psalm 94; Thursday, Psalm 81; Friday, Psalm 93; Sabbath, Psalm 92.

[13] Bonhoeffer, D. (1970), *The Psalms: The Prayer Book of the Bible*, trans. J.H. Burtness, Augsburg, Minneapolis, pp. 25-6.

[14] Garrone, *How to Pray the Psalms*, pp. 43-88.

[15] The psalm numbers shown are according to the numbering in the Hebrew Bible and NRSV, while those in brackets are those actually noted by Garrone, who follows the numbering in the Septuagint and the Vulgate.

b) The Roman Catholic Breviary is a book which contains the 'liturgy of the hours', also known as the Divine Office, or the Office of the Hours. In its modern guise it is structured in terms of three periods of prayer each day, morning, noon, and evening. The purpose of the office is to sanctify the day and hence all human activity through regular prayer and to contribute toward fulfilling our Christian obligation to pray continually. While saying the office is mandated for clergy and members of religious orders, it is also urged for the laity. I noted above that from earliest times psalms have been a major element of the office. In medieval times, when there were many more times of prayer, or 'Hours', in the day, and when many members of religious orders devoted their lives to prayer, the complete collection of psalms was covered every week. In the present form of the Divine Office, approximately 80 per cent of the psalms in the Book of Psalms are used over a four week cycle. The selection of psalms does not follow the canonical order. Each service has one, two or three psalms or psalm portions assigned to it. A number of psalms are repeated during the cycle, either because of their importance or because the mood of the psalm fits the time of day or week. For example, penitential psalms occur on Fridays. Psalm 51 occurs in each of the four Friday morning services. Longer psalms are divided and spread over some days, usually to be said at the same time of day. Psalm 119 is divided up according to its 22 Hebrew stanzas but with two of these sections repeated within the four week cycle. Other psalms are included on a numerical basis. These facts would make it difficult to spread the cycle out over a longer period for those for whom prayer three times a day, as suggested by the office, is difficult to maintain. Such an action would sever the specific connections between certain psalms and the time set in the four week cycle. One way in which the cycle could be extended, without totally ignoring the intentions of the compilers, would be to note which psalms are repeated specifically in relation to certain days of the cycle, e.g. Psalms 51 and 119. These could be retained in their designated positions while the remainder of the psalms could be spread over a longer period. Those psalms omitted from the cycle could also be incorporated on this basis.[16]

c) In the Anglican Church in Australia the daily office consists of two prayer services, morning and evening prayer. These are usually observed in churches, but a wider use of the services by individuals, families, households and small groups is also encouraged. Recitation of psalms is incorporated into each service. Psalms are set for each day, two for each of the morning and evening services.[17] Some of the longer psalms are divided into portions within this and wherever possible these portions are read on the one day. Psalm 119 is the main exception. It is read over seven evenings. As far as possible the psalms are read in their numerical order. Variations on this are mainly due to the length of a psalm or the desire to use a particular psalm for a saint's day or a special festival. The system allows for the coverage of the whole collection of biblical psalms in about

---

[16] See *The New Companion to the Breviary*, (1988), Carmelite Monastery, Indianapolis.

[17] The Liturgical Commission of the Anglican Church of Australia, (1995), *Tables of Psalms and Readings for the Lectionary: Morning and Evening Prayer on Weekdays*, Broughton Books, Alexandria, NSW.

two months. The earlier *Book of Common Prayer* arranged the cycle of psalm reading so that the whole of the Psalter was covered in a month. If it were desirable to cover the whole Psalter in a period shorter or longer than the two months, then the number of psalms used in daily prayer services could be correspondingly increased or reduced. This system is based on the monastic tradition of psalmody in daily prayer. There are some who wish to follow the cathedral tradition, reciting the psalms on a thematic or seasonal basis rather than a numerical one.[18]

d) Elsewhere I have published another psalms lectionary for use on a daily basis.[19] The psalms chosen follow a pattern that takes into account both the season in the Christian year and the different types of psalms available. In this way all the psalms are covered over a period of less than a year, although some appear more often than others, either because of their importance in the Christian tradition, or because there are fewer psalms of that type in the collection. The pattern followed is as follows:

Monday:	a psalm of praise to God.
Mid-week (Tues.-Thurs.):	psalms appropriate to the season of the Christian year.
Friday:	a lament psalm
Saturday:	a psalm of trust or similar expression
Sunday:	a hymn of praise to God.

In mid-week psalms are chosen which are suitable for the season. For example, in Lent lament psalms or psalms of confession are used, while in the Easter season, psalms of thanksgiving etc. are employed. In Holy week, and on special days the psalms set in the Revised Common Lectionary are followed. Occasionally passages recognized as hymns or prayers from other books of the Old Testament are included and the ancient Christian tradition of including the Odes or Canticles[20] with the psalms has been followed.

These are some of the ways people can use the psalms in their daily worship. It requires discipline and commitment to take up any one of these methods seriously. Even to modify them and cover the whole collection of psalms over a longer period of time requires resolve. However, the return is considerable. In each of the above systems a way is given of seeing our daily life sanctified before God. Each offers us a new way of perceiving our daily endeavours and our life in its various parts within the purpose of God in our world.

---

[18] See for example Barton, A. (1999), *The Daily Office: Exploring Patterns for Daily Prayer*, Grove Worship Series 150, Grove Books, Cambridge, p. 18.

[19] Published in the Bible study book *With Love to the World*, Strathfield, NSW: The With Love the World Committee.

[20] These include: Exod 15:1-19; Deut 32:1-43; 1 Kgs 2:1-10; Hab 3:2-19; Isa 26:9-20; Jon 2:3-10; Dan 3:26-45; Dan 3:52-88; Luke 1:46-55, 68-79; Isa 5:1-9; Isa 38:10-20; Luke 2:29-32; etc. For a brief discussion of the development and early use of these texts in relation to psalms see Guiver, *Company of Voices*, pp. 156-158.

Finally, it is important to add that we should not ask the psalms to do more for us than they can do when we use them in prayer. Even if we pray with a particular psalm we should remember that we are the ones doing the praying. The psalm might provide words for us and even guide us in our thinking about prayer and in praying, but ultimately we are the ones who pray. The psalm is an aid to our prayer. It is the vehicle for the expression of our hearts and minds. Of course, there will be times when our hearts and minds feel dried up and seem to have nothing to say to God. The psalms can be invaluable in sustaining us through such times. But even in those circumstances, while we may lean heavily on the words of the psalms, there still must be some longing within us to speak with God, however small, which forms the basis of our prayer life. No written prayers, however good, can supply that.

The Psalms in Prayer With and For Others

The Psalms and Pastoral Care

As prayers the psalms also have a place in pastoral care. They are not the solution to every pastoral problem or situation within the faith community, but we neglect a valuable resource for pastoral ministry if we do not use them. They can be used in a number of ways. If it is deemed appropriate to do so, they can simply be used when praying with others who are in need. They can also be used in intercessory prayer to pray for others. Finally, they can be used as a resource for reflection with someone in need. The carer might help another reflect on or argue with the words of the psalmist in light of the person's situation as they read the psalm together. This could involve the whole psalm or part of it, even just one line, although in the last case the carer should take care that the citation is not a thorough distortion of the overall tenor of the psalm. In any of these situations judicious use should be made of the psalms, and attention given to matters of interpretation. The use of the psalms in prayer with or for others, or in reflection, requires a lifelong discipline of study and reading for those who offer care in this way.

It is appropriate, at this point, to recall some aspects of the psalms that are particularly pertinent in pastoral care. Some of these I have already considered. The first is that Scripture can be used in pastoral care in many ways. Pastoral care theorists have reflected on these in detail.[21] Above all the pastoral carer should not use Scripture, the psalms or any other text, as something to hide behind in pastoral conversation. The relationships between the carer and the one cared in the first place, and between the one cared for and God in the second place, are of primary concern. If the carer uses Scripture, then it is to foster these relationships. It is

---

[21] There is a useful analysis of different ways the Bible has been used by several pastoral care theorists in Pattison, S. (1988), *A Critique of Pastoral Care*, SCM, London. Specifically in chap. 6, he speaks of: 1) the fundamentalist or biblicist approach; 2) the tokenist approach; 3) the imagist or suggestive approach; 4) the informative approach; and 5) the thematic approach.

therefore important, that the integrity of Scripture be maintained, part of which is recognizing that it comes to us from some distance, both historically and culturally. There is an 'otherness' or 'strangeness' to Scripture which cannot be ignored. If it is duly acknowledged, then it helps maintain a sense of conversation with the 'other', especially the God who stands behind the text. Having said that, however, I would want to add that while the text comes from a distance we are also aware that contemporary readers play a very important part in the process of perceiving meaning in a text. The pastoral carer needs to be aware that different people will have different perceptions of the text and those perceptions need to be honoured as part of the conversation, even if they might need to be challenged from time to time for pastoral purposes. Scripture should not be thought of as having one fixed meaning, be it that of the carer or the one cared for. It is there to encourage the relationship with God.

Following on from this, we need to note *the openness of the language of the psalms* with their often unspecified subject, 'I' or 'we', and the equally open designation of the 'poor' and the 'enemies.' When we use the psalms to pray or reflect with someone for whom we are caring, we offer him/her words that can be claimed as their own prayers or with which they might readily associate. He/she may even be more ready than we to take some of the imprecatory psalms, for example, as their own prayers to God, or as words that express their feelings. We also noted that *the psalms reflect a wide variety of human experiences*. They include words for all occasions in the life of faith and give to those words a form that relates to each situation. The psalms shape the expression of despair before God, or complaint to God, just as they offer a way of giving praise. They teach us how to pray or reflect in the circumstances we encounter. And even if we do not follow their words, they offer models for our own prayers and reflections. Thus, the psalms can help the one cared for express their feelings and thoughts to God.[22] The person for whom pastoral care is offered might not have been able to express these things in his/her own words, or they might not have thought such words and feelings appropriate expressions to voice in God's presence. The psalms give aid, and sometimes even permission, to pray the prayer that needs to be prayed or say the words that must be said. The words of the psalms grant freedom to speak.

I also stressed earlier that *when praying the psalms we are not alone*. We use the same words that have been used by countless others in the community of faith over the millennia, including the great figures of faith and prayer. With the psalms, the person to whom care is given, prays or reflects as part of a community over time and space, offering the same words of despair, thanks or trust to God as others have done. He/she may be able to identify with others who have had a similar experience, and may even find hope in the experience of the other. Moreover, as we submit to the spiritual and theological discipline of the community, our prayers are not limited by our own imagination or experience, but are shaped by the experience of that larger community. Both we, and those for whom we care, can find ourselves challenged by new understandings of God, and

---

[22] So also Molzahn, D. (1994), 'Psalms: Lament and Grief as a Paradigm for Pastoral Care', *Affirming Diversity*. The Society of Pentecostal Studies, Wheaton, IL, pp. 5-6.

of ourselves before God. Such challenges, however, come to us in the psalms in a form that has been shaped under the guidance of the Spirit in the tradition of our faith. We are also prevented from being caught in a realm isolated from all else. The pastoral conversation in prayer or reflection is naturally extended to include others beyond the pastoral carer and the one cared for. We use prayers that have come from other contexts, other political, historical, or personal circumstances. As both carer and cared for we are drawn into a wider circle of prayer and care.

Finally, I noted earlier that *the psalms are poetry* and that the language of poetry has important connections to prayer. The pastoral theologian, Donald Capps, has argued that while there has been much support for a 'narrative' approach to pastoral care in recent times, and by that he means relating the personal story of the one cared for to the larger Christian story, contemporary poetry also has value for pastoral care. Poetry is episodic, so that we see the person in the poem only in relation to the one event or scene described in the poem. The poem is also open-ended, and often challenges our present ways of looking at life's experiences. Capps argues that there is an affinity between poets and pastors. Both are explorative, questioning and tentative in their work, but neither is without conviction. Both are concerned with life's experiences, and use language based in experience with great care, working with both heart and head. He thus sees poetry as a great resource for pastoral care.[23] The same points that apply for contemporary poetry apply also to the psalms, in terms of their poetic character, their openness and often questioning nature, and the often passionate language of the psalmist focussed on experience. If, as Capps argues, contemporary poetry is a valuable resource for pastoral care, then so are the psalms.

It could be helpful at this stage to draw attention to a recent discussion relating to the therapeutic value of lament psalms with those who are grieving, ill, lonely, dying, or facing loss in some other way. Not only do the psalms offer language in such situations to help the one who is suffering express his/her difficulties and feelings, but they also offer symbolic language whereby the person's experience and life can be restructured to lead to a new manner of living.[24]

Donald Capps has also been involved in this discussion. Another participant has been Walter Brueggemann. The latter has written on the form of the lament in Israel as a way of enhancing and articulating the experience of suffering, but also as a way of limiting the experience so that the sufferer could cope with it within the perspectives and resources of the community.[25] Nuances in the form allowed the community to define grief in such a way that the experience of the sufferer might be changed. These nuances included: the fact that there was no attempt to flatter

---

[23] Capps, D. (1993), *The Poet's Gift: Toward the Renewal of Pastoral Care*, Westminster/John Knox, Louisville.

[24] See further Meyer, S.G. (1974), 'The Psalms and Pastoral Counselling', *Journal of Psychology and Theology*, Vol. 2, pp. 26-30. Other studies in the area also attest to this, for example, Roseberry, Q.G. (1988), *Terminal Anxiety and Psalms of Lament*, Unpublished DMin Thesis Project, Princeton, Princeton Theological Seminary.

[25] Brueggemann, W. (1977), 'The Formfulness of Grief', *Interpretation*, Vol. 31/3, pp. 263-275.

the Lord in the lament; there was characteristically an affirmative ending, a vow of praise; and that Israel's God could enter the pathos of the psalm. The God of the psalms was one who could be confronted and yet could also enter the pathos of the situation. The affirmative ending meant that the focus of the lament was primarily on the presence and fidelity of God, who could transform the psalmist's situation, and not on the anger itself.

Brueggemann then compared the form of the laments with the stages of the grief process in the modern world as outlined by Elizabeth Kübler-Ross. According to her the grief process includes five elements: denial and isolation; anger; bargaining; depression; and acceptance. Brueggemann noted that the similarities include elements of the expression of anger, and some bargaining, while the differences include: Israel's covenantal address of God in the lament psalms instead of statements of denial as in the grief process; expectant petitions to God rather than words of depression; a focusing of the lament form on intervention which is treated ambiguously if not denied in modernity and in the grief process; and the rhetoric of the lament form being set in the larger context of covenant relationship. Also the lament form is essentially a dialogical form rather than a monologic one. That is, the one suffering in the lament is not simply voicing his or her own feelings, but enters into dialogue or conversation with another, principally God. I discussed this above in terms of prayer in the psalms being conversational.

The primary function of the form of lament psalms, according to Brueggemann, is in the rehabilitation of a member of the community from a chaotic experience to a structured one within a particular worldview. The form of the lament helps give meaning to life in the face of chaos. The psalmist trusts in a God who can deal with the dangers of loss, grief, and death.[26] At the end of his essay, Brueggemann suggests that the lament psalms, and their form in particular, offer an important resource for Christian ministry, and the life and faith of the Church.[27]

Donald Capps has developed this approach further, especially in relation to the use of the lament psalms in grief counselling.[28] These psalms have been especially useful in allowing the counselee to vent his/her inner feelings, but the psalms have also assisted in bringing new spiritual energy to replace negative feelings. Capps explores the issue in depth and asks what can the pastoral counsellor learn from the psalms. He is not interested in the context of the psalmist behind the text, but probes the form and content of the psalms themselves, seeking to understand their strengths and weaknesses. This is an important distinction for a number of reasons. First, the pastoral counsellor, as an interpreter of the psalm text,

---

[26] *Ibid.*, pp. 273-275.

[27] Tanner, B.L. (2001), 'How long, O Lord! Will your people suffer in silence forever?' in S.B. Reid, *Psalms and Practice: Worship, Virtue, and Authority*, Liturgical Press, Collegeville, pp. 143-152, notes (p. 145) the paucity of studies on the use of lament psalms in worship following the work of Brueggemann.

[28] Capps, D. (1981), *Biblical Approaches to Pastoral Counselling*, Westminster, Philadelphia, pp. 47-97. A similar approach has been suggested by a number of writers on pastoral counselling.

is not trying to guess what it is about an unknown psalmist that can offer help today. Rather, the counsellor focuses on what we do have access to, namely the words of the psalm. The voice of the tradition of the faith speaks out of the words of the psalm itself. Secondly, as the counsellor focuses on the words of the psalm, the counselee finds company in the larger community of faith in their time of suffering. I have discussed this above in relation to the psalms and prayer. Capps offers an example of how this understanding makes a difference. Whenever the psalmist acknowledges his or her own sin in the lament psalms there is a clear lack of specificity (e.g. Pss 25:18; 32:5; 38:3, 18; 40:12; 51:2). This could be seen as a weakness, indeed an avoidance, if it is seen as the isolated act of individuals. However, this lack of specificity is characteristic wherever sin is mentioned in the lament psalms. What could be read as a weakness in some individuals, is in fact something that the community of faith has endorsed over time. The lack of specificity does not give license to avoid naming sin, but rather allows others to share in these words of confession to God, bringing a diverse community with its various sins together in the act of confession. Other aspects of the lament psalms, such as questioning God, the cry for vindication, the call for 'justice', the protestation of innocence, and the move to praise, are also part of the form and endorsed by the community of faith for our spiritual well-being. They should not be seen as the idiosyncrasies of particular psalmists.

Capps then asks how the form of the biblical lament can shape the grief counselling process in terms of methods, objectives, and counsellor-counselee relationship. To answer this, he looks critically at the analysis of Brueggemann discussed above, and takes it further. He seeks the implications of Brueggemann's comparison of laments with Kübler-Ross's stages for pastoral counselling. In Capps' view the traditional form of the lament psalm exhibits 'formfulness' compared to the relative 'formlessness' of Kübler-Ross's stages. He suggests that pastors have not given adequate attention to helping those who are grieving give 'form' to their experience: 'If grief counselling is to be shaped by the psalm of lament, it needs to deepen its understanding of the *complaint* stage and take seriously the three later stages in the lament: *petition, words of assurance,* and *vow of praise.*'[29] The complaint stage is the crucial point of entry in this process. In it the counsellor helps the one being counselled name his/her negative and self-justifying feelings. In the three later stages of petition, assurance, and vow of praise, the counsellor respectively helps the counselee clarify his/her specific needs and desires, supports his/her petitions and assures them that God hears the prayers of those who lament, and helps the counselee clarify the grounds for praise and affirms that God is also one who mourns when the counselee cannot praise.[30]

---

[29] *Ibid.*, p. 77. For detail of Capps' discussion of how these four elements of the lament form can inform grief counselling, see *ibid.*, pp. 77-92.

[30] This should not be understood as pressure applied to the counselee to move to the stage of praising God regardless. On this last statement Capps adds: 'The counselee who remains bitter toward God may be helped to see that God has deep feelings too, and could hardly have remained unmoved by the counselee's sufferings.' *Ibid.*, p. 89. For more detail and a chart comparing lament elements with stages in grief see *ibid.*, p. 91.

Capps shows how the lament form can guide the process of working through the grief experience. He draws three further points from this. First, the lament form can help define the objectives of the counselling process. Secondly, the lament form helps clarify the relationship between the counsellor and counselee in grief counselling as one in which the counsellor acts as mediator between the sufferer and God, not drawing attention to their own capacities to provide comfort and hope, but 'to open channels for the "transforming intervention" of God.'[31] Thirdly, the lament psalms reflect a nondirective method in grief counselling. The form of the lament psalms itself is open and adaptable with shifts in the experience of intervention and complaint. Thus, Capps states that grief counselling is also nondirective in both its pace and timing. The length of the process is not the important matter, nor does all the process have to take place within the counselling process itself. What is important is that the process 'follows the pattern of the lament, issuing eventually in an attitude not of frustration, disillusionment, or bitterness, but of genuine praise.'[32] The counsellor's role, while nondirective, may occasionally involve helping to keep the process moving. It is essentially to allow the 'spiritual energies' involved to work their will, and to remove any barriers to the process.

While there may be points of detail at which we might disagree with Capps, his general thesis stands. The psalms of lament can play a rehabilitative role in pastoral care. They offer a form for grief or anger that is spoken in the presence of God and the context of faith. They do not deny the legitimacy of the experience and subsequent feelings, even feelings of vengeance. Rather, they assert that the expression of those feelings does not negate faith as many, especially in a Protestant context, are apt to think. Moreover, they do not prohibit the speaking of such feelings and anger in the presence of God. In fact, as I noted earlier, they suggest that this is the proper place for these feelings to be given voice.[33]

But the use of the psalms in pastoral care should not be restricted to the lament psalms. Psalms of praise and thanksgiving can help people give voice to their praise of God in times of joy and celebration. Just as the form of lament psalms can help give the one who suffers expression to his/her feelings, so too the form of praise and thanksgiving provides a model for our praise and thanks. The fact that, as I noted earlier, the psalms of praise consist of both a summons to praise followed by a reason for praise, should limit the possibility that praise is reduced to a self-assured, disembodied, and comfortable statement which forgets the hurt or situation wherein there has been healing and the discovery of new life. It could even be that the task of pastoral care is to help the individual or congregation acknowledge the path from pain to praise and hence deepen their understanding of faith and their relationship with God.

In all this the psalms are not just prayers or poems penned by some insightful person of the community; they have been regarded not only as words to

---

[31] *Ibid.*, p. 90.

[32] *Ibid.*, p. 92.

[33] Cf. Miller, P. (1990), 'The Psalms and Pastoral Care', *Reformed Liturgy & Music*, Vol. 24, pp. 131-135.

God, but also as words from God. As we pray or reflect on the psalms with others, we use the very words God has given for our prayer or reflection. In these things, there is both comfort and assurance for those seeking to speak with God.

The Psalms and Intercession

The psalms are not only available for face-to-face individual or congregational pastoral care, they can also be used in intercessory prayer. This type of prayer is itself an important part of pastoral care. To pray for another person or community is to enter into conversation with God on behalf of another or regarding another. It involves going outside oneself in two directions: toward God with whom we converse; and toward the other, for whom we express concern. However, while it involves movement in two possibly quite different directions, it is at the same time a way of bringing God and the one(s) for whom we pray together. Our concern for the other is the focus of the conversation with God. The need of the other is related to our faith and hope in the kingdom of God. Pastoral care in this context is more than sympathy, friendship, or solidarity with another. It is a way of participating in the deep conversation between God and the one who suffers or celebrates.

When we think specifically of the use of the psalms in prayer for others a number of points come to mind. First, in praying a psalm as intercessory prayer we must realise that few psalms are intercessions in the normal sense in which we use that word. The clearest example of intercessory prayer in the psalms is Psalm 72 in which the psalmist prays for the well-being and proper and effective rule of the king. It begins:

> [1] Give the king your justice, O God,
>   and your righteousness to a king's son.
> [2] May he judge your people with righteousness,
>   and your poor with justice.
>
> [3] May the mountains yield prosperity for the people,
>   and the hills, in righteousness.
> [4] May he defend the cause of the poor of the people,
>   give deliverance to the needy,
>   and crush the oppressor.

But this is an exception. More often, the psalmist speaks out of his/her own experience or in the context of his or her own community. Consequently, as I have noted, a great number of psalms speak in the first person singular or plural, and are addressed directly to another party, be it God or the community. Thus, as we pray using the psalms, we pray with words more easily adapted to our own prayers than to a prayer on behalf of others. But the task of using the psalms in intercessory prayer is not impossible, although it clearly calls for an exercise in imagination and interpretation. In such cases sensitivity, empathy and openness to another's experience is needed. The carer needs to read the psalms over and over, and study them carefully, so that he/she becomes familiar with them and the issues they address. It will also involve the carer imagining possible situations in which the feelings and expressions in the psalm might be invoked, and then waiting, attentive to the needs of those for whom he/she has pastoral responsibility, or of those with whom he/she comes in contact, to see if they and the psalmist have experiences on common.[34] This exercise in familiarity is just as necessary in the case of face-to-face pastoral care.

Secondly, to take a psalm as part or whole of our prayer of intercession is, of course, to take words that are not our own to form our prayer. But this has a great advantage if done with imagination and sensitivity. One of the difficulties with intercessory prayer is that we can easily impose upon the one for whom we pray our own understanding of who he/she is and what they need. We cannot avoid this even in the most open of prayers. However, in using the psalms we use the words of a third party. We can begin to avoid imposing our own wills on those for whom we pray. We still face the problems of selecting a psalm, and of relating it to a specific person or situation. These are also tasks subject to our understandings of the person or situation, but at least we have set up a situation in the prayer where other voices enter the conversation.

A third point is closely related to this. If the psalm with which we pray is appropriate for a situation, then the fact that we pray in the words of one 'who has been there' can give a freshness and honesty to the words we pray, which we might not have achieved in the course of composing our own prayer. Our modern world with its communications technology is well equipped to bring us quickly news of the conflicts and difficulties faced by many people around the globe, but the effect of all this information is to numb us to the suffering of individuals in those situations. Using the words of the psalms for intercession has the advantage of letting the words come from one who knows the suffering and the feelings involved. We are not limited by the words and perceptions of our own experience, feelings, mood, or theology. It can lead to new levels of understanding of the situation or person for whom we pray and a deeper sense of prayer.[35]

Fourthly, to use the psalms as prayers of intercession means that we use words that the community attests are also words from God. This means that we not only bring someone or some situation into our conversation with God, but we recognise that the person or situation is already the topic of a conversation begun by God and continued by him. Our prayers essentially join in a conversation. Use of the psalms makes that tangible in a way that newly composed prayers cannot. The dual nature of the psalms discussed earlier underlines the point.

---

[34] See the report on an exercise in this type of intercessory prayer by Dawson, G.S. (1991), 'Praying the Difficult Psalms', *Weavings*, Vol. VI/5, pp. 28-35.

[35] Cf. Caldwell, C.F. (1990), 'A Pastoral Perspective on the Psalms', in J. Knight and L.A. Sinclair (eds), *The Psalms and Other Studies on the Old Testament*, Nashotah House Seminary, Nashotah, pp. 86-95, esp. p. 88 where he suggests that if we sometimes do not understand the words of a psalm, and I would think that might apply equally to a lack of understanding due to lack of experience as well as lack of intellectual understanding, that this helps 'purify prayer from being an exercise in human projection'.

Finally, we should remember that when we pray for others we do not pray alone, but the Holy Spirit also prays through and with us. As we take the words of the psalms for our intercessions, we should remember too, with Bonhoeffer, that these are the prayers that Christ prays for his people. We do not pray for others alone, nor do we pray simply in our own power.

There are, however, some potential problems for the pray-er in this type of intercession. The pray-er needs to be careful not to confuse his/her own feelings with those of the psalm, especially if the latter are particularly strong. The pray-er can end up praying for him/herself and not interceding for another. Also, in those psalms where we hear of God inflicting the psalmist or others with suffering, or in the imprecatory psalms where the psalmist curses his/her enemies, it might be best for the pray-er to resist any temptation to begin to debate how these psalms fit overall within Christian theology. Such theological reflection is necessary, as I have discussed earlier, but it is not the aim of intercessory prayer. This is much more concerned with acknowledging how others experience life and bringing them into our conversation with God.

Some Examples of the Use of Psalms in Pastoral Care

The psalms could be used within numerous pastoral situations. Some examples will suffice. They are in no way meant to indicate that particular psalms were written for specific contexts, nor that those same psalms cannot be used in a number of situations. When it comes to the use of specific psalms, we need to keep in mind the points made above and that we work within our own world with its problems and people. Further examples can be found in a number of recent publications.[36]

Psalm 3 A psalm for those beset by many worries and struggling with issues of faith. The enemies of the psalmist could be understood metaphorically, as the many expectations or responsibilities etc. that cause tension, or oppress in modern work and family life. In other circumstances they may be interpreted more literally. Many things are saying to the pray-er 'There is no help for you in God' denying him/her even of the hope of faith. The psalm offers an opportunity for the pray-er to reassert his/her faith that God still stands by them.

Psalm 10 A psalm to pray with or for those who have suffered exploitation in business, family, or society. They may have been the victims of greed, persecution, pride, deceit, or the abuse of power etc. The psalm allows for an expression of vengeance to God but recognizes the rule of God over all: 'the Lord is king for ever and ever'. It concludes with a statement of assurance of being heard for the victim:

---

[36] McCutchan, S.P. (2000), *Experiencing the Psalms: Weaving the Psalms into your Ministry and Faith*, Smyth & Helwys, Macon, GA. See also McCutchan, S.P. (1993), 'Illuminating the Dark: Using the Psalms of Lament', *Christian ministry*, Vol. March-April, pp. 14-17; Miller, P. (1990), 'The Psalms and Pastoral Care', *Reformed Liturgy & Music*, Vol. 24, pp. 131-135; and Caldwell, 'A Pastoral Perspective on the Psalms'.

¹⁷ O LORD, you will hear the desire of the meek;
>   you will strengthen their heart, you will incline your ear
¹⁸ to do justice for the orphan and the oppressed,
>   so that those from earth may strike terror no more.

Psalm 30 A psalm of thanksgiving that can be prayed with or for someone who has faced death through illness and has been restored to life. The pray-er infectiously calls others to join in their praise: 'Sing praises to the LORD, O you his faithful ones, and give thanks to his holy name' (v. 4). The psalm also expresses the experience of near death in terms of God's 'anger' or 'hiding his face' (vv. 5, 7). Such may not be the experience of all pray-ers but there are many who when faced with death do seek to affix blame or feel the absence of God acutely. This prayer of thanksgiving does acknowledge the past experience of hurt and grief.

Psalm 32 A psalm of confession for a person who has experienced a sense of deep forgiveness after acknowledging some wrong on his/her part. The prayer also acknowledges the sense of personal guilt, or even the physical effects that can result from it: 'While I kept silence, my body wasted away through my groaning all day long' (v. 3). It ends with the desire for the one forgiven to share his/her joy with others:

> ¹⁰ ... steadfast love surrounds those who trust in the LORD.
> ¹¹ Be glad in the LORD and rejoice, O righteous,
>   and shout for joy, all you upright in heart.

Psalm 41 A psalm which can be prayed with or for one who has a life-threatening illness, who feels abandoned in the face of it and who has been made to feel that it arises from some 'sin', misdeed, or shortcoming. It ends with a statement of confidence in God's presence:

> ¹² But you have upheld me because of my integrity,
>   and set me in your presence forever.

Psalm 55 A psalm to pray with or for someone who feels thoroughly betrayed or abused by a close companion or friend – in business, marriage, or family – and who dreads the loneliness of his/her plight. The psalm allows the person feeling betrayed to express feelings of vengeance upon the perpetrator of the offence (vv. 15, 23), although these are couched in the context of trust in God. There is an opportunity for a minister, priest or friend to provide words of assurance (v. 22).

Psalm 74 While this psalm, which speaks directly of the destruction of the Jerusalem temple by the Babylonians in 587 BCE, may seem too specific to be of use today, there are congregations that have lost their sanctuary, meeting place, or other property through fire, other disaster, or vandalism. This psalm could be used as a prayer of lament for a congregation in such circumstances. It not only expresses the anguish of such an experience, but also has a concern for the continued witness of God in the community (v. 20: 'Have regard for your covenant'), the fact that such events can be seen as 'God denying' in the larger community (v. 22: 'Rise up, O God, plead your cause; remember how the impious scoff at you all day long'), and the need to carry on the Church's work of care in the community (v. 21: 'Do not let the downtrodden be put to shame; let the poor and needy praise your name'). It also acknowledges the pain of rebuilding in the question 'How long?' (v. 10). Alternatively as a prayer of intercession it could be prayed for those of other faiths, especially Muslims or Jews, whose mosques and synagogues and other meeting places have suffered damage or attack because of anti-Islamic or anti-Jewish feelings that are wickedly voiced in times of insecurity.

Psalm 88 A psalm to pray with or for those who feel absolutely abandoned by God and by companions (vv. 8, 18) for reason of social stigma, disability, physical or mental disease. This lament, which has no vow of praise, allows the pray-er to vent his/her feelings fully and lay their desperation at God's feet without a sense of a total loss of faith:

> [13] But I, O LORD, cry out to you;
>   in the morning my prayer comes before you.
> [14] O LORD, why do you cast me off?
>   Why do you hide your face from me?

Psalm 94 A psalm to pray on behalf of those who suffer injustice in legal and social contexts and for whom there seems to be no support in government, legal or business circles.

Psalm 107 A psalm of thanks for deliverance from a time of trouble. The psalm itself cites examples of deliverance from hunger and thirst, from prison, from illness, and from threat of disaster at sea. These can be expanded to include any disaster that is faced, whether it is brought on by the sufferer's own carelessness or actions, or by forces beyond his/her control. It especially speaks of thanks on occasions when deliverance has been dramatic and through a reversal of 'expectations'.

Psalm 116 A general prayer of thanks for deliverance from difficult and trying times. It might be especially helpful to pray with or for someone for whom faith in God has been a significant part of his/her deliverance (v.10) or who has been falsely accused of something (v. 11).

The examples above assume we are praying **with** a psalm. I also said above that we can pray **from** a psalm. In prayers of intercession, as in pastoral care, the psalms do not have to be used in their entirety. Words or lines from the psalm can be used in conjunction with contemporary prayers. For example, the following prayer was developed for worship on Trinity Sunday when Psalm 8 was set in the *RCL* (Years A and C).

Lord, our God,
>Father, Son, and Holy Spirit,
>how majestic is your name in all the earth!

How majestic is your name in all the earth?

How can we worship your glory above the heavens
>when the mouths of babes and infants are silenced?
Your enemies ignore the cry of the abandoned baby,
>they dismiss the sighs of the dying aboriginal child,
>they are deaf to the screams of battered infants.

The mouths of babes and infants are choked with tears.
>They cry out in anger for justice.

Hear their cries, O Father,
>Let them sing again your glory above the heavens.

How can we worship your glory above the heavens
>when men and women deny each other's beauty?
Your enemies do not remember women as you remember them,
>they do not care for men as you care for them;
>they deny women dignity, recognition and justice,
>they respect only strength, hardness and resolve in men.
>They would rather be like gods, than a little less than God.

Your people suffer through the misuse of power.
>They cry out in anger for justice.

Hear their cries, O Lord Jesus Christ,
>Let them glory in the cross that bears your name in all the earth.

How can we worship your glory above the heavens
>when humans ruthlessly rule the work of your hands?

Your enemies consume your creation,
>they drive the beasts from their habitats,
>they wantonly hunt wild birds.

Your creation is choked with decay and the remains of your creatures.
>It cries out in anger for justice.

Hear its cry, O Holy Spirit,
>Let life be renewed in all the earth.

Lord, how can we worship your glory above the heavens?

Hold fast before us your love for all the earth.
Remind us again
    that from the mouths of babes and infants
    we hear your glory proclaimed;
    that in men and women we see your image.
    that in the intricate world around we see your care;

Lord, our God,
    Father, Son and Holy Spirit,
    how majestic is your name in all the earth!

                                          Amen.

The usual categories for intercessory prayer have been included, namely prayers for the whole creation, for the peoples of the world, for the Church, for the local community, and for those in need. Psalm 8 contains a bold affirmation of the majesty of God's name in the whole earth and a declaration of God's sovereignty over all life. In the prayer this is made to stand in tension with the many situations for which we might offer intercession. Intercession is offered in the form of a lament for those situations in which the praise of God seems a remote thing. This allows the positive statements of the psalm to be turned into questions, which is consistent with the psalmist's own practice of questioning God. It also allows the prayer to explore the way in which God's majesty can be seen in the world. The mention of babes and infants, human beings and the creatures of the world in the psalm suggested the sections for the intercessions. Phrases from the psalm are used in the prayer and create a regular pattern between the stanzas. At the same time the psalm invites some reflection on how we do perceive God's majesty in the world. The prayer assumes that the psalm has been read (or sung) beforehand.

This prayer is not intended as an ideal but rather as an encouragement for others to let the psalms begin to discipline their own prayers. Prayers such as this would serve equally well in less formal or private periods of worship as in public worship.

One final word in relation to the psalms and pastoral care. Several times above we have referred to the need for the pastoral carer to be familiar with the psalms in the Bible. That will require reading and study. The congregation also needs to be familiar with the psalms. Once it could be assumed that this would happen 'naturally' as the psalms were repeated over and over in worship. That is no longer the case in a number of congregations. To be sure, the psalms are still included in the worship of some denominations, or congregations, and there has been a recovery of singing the psalms in others. However, in a good number of places, the place of the psalms in prayer, preaching, and pastoral care will have to be reclaimed. Even in denominations or congregations in which psalms still have a place in worship, it could not be said that the people are as familiar with them as once could be assumed. If the psalms are to be reclaimed in order to do their work in these other areas, their place in worship needs to be strengthened. The use of the psalms in one area of Christian life flows into others but at the heart of the community's life lies it corporate worship. It is to this matter that we will now turn.

Speaking to God through the Psalms in the Liturgy

Some may already be familiar with singing of psalms in the liturgy of the Church, either under the leadership of a cantor, or as hymns sung by the whole congregation. In the Catholic Church an increased use of the psalms has been part of general liturgical reforms since Vatican II. Recent editions of hymn books associated within Protestant denominations have included an increased number of psalms set to music, and a greater diversity of styles of music and tunes to which they can be sung.[37]

Our focus here, however, is not on the singing of psalms, but on the place and use of the psalms in the liturgy as said texts. Music is especially important in the use of the psalms and I will touch on it from time to time. But the singing of psalms is a field of study in its own right with its own complex history and debates. To do it justice would require lengthy and technical discussions on matters including music in worship in general, musical appreciation, and the relation of music to meaning. I will leave these discussions for those with the technical knowledge and experience in the field.[38] Nevertheless, many things related to the speaking the psalms in the liturgy apply equally in a situation where a psalm is sung.

Following from the discussion above, I should start by saying that the psalms can be used to speak to God in the various prayers and responses within the Sunday liturgy. If the psalm set for the Sunday is an appropriate type, it could be suitable, either in part or in its entirety, as a prayer of adoration or confession. Some modification to the psalm may be necessary.

Some of the benefits of using psalms for prayers in the liturgy are similar to those already mentioned in prayer and pastoral care contexts. However, the fact

---

[37] For example in the Methodist Church in Great Britain (1983), *Hymns and Psalms: A Methodist and Ecumenical Hymn Book*, Methodist Publishing House, London; in the United Reformed Church in Britain (1991), *Rejoice and Sing*, OUP, Oxford; among the Methodists in the USA (1989), *The United Methodist Hymnal*, Nashville, United Methodist Publishing House; in the Presbyterian Church in the USA (1993), *Psalms and Canticles for Singing*, Westminster/John Knox, Louisville; in the United Church of Christ in the USA (1995), *The New Century Hymnal*, Pilgrim Press, Cleveland; in the United Church of Canada (1996), *Voices United*, United Church Publishing House, Etobicoke; and finally the ecumenical Australian hymnal (1999), *Together in Song: The Australian Hymn Book II*, Harper Collins, Sydney. See also Williams, K.E. (1984), 'Ways to Sing the Psalms', *Reformed Liturgy & Music*, Vol. 18/4, pp. 12-16.

[38] See in this regard Apel, W. (1990), *Gregorian Chant*, Indiana University, Bloomington; Hiley, D. (1993), *Western Plainchant: A Handbook*, Clarendon, Oxford; Leaver, R.A. (1990), 'English Metrical Psalmody', in R.F. Glover (ed.), *The Hymnal 1982 Companion*, Church Hymnal Corporation, New York, Vol. 1, pp. 321-348; Leaver, R.A. (1990), 'Plainchant Adaptation in England', in R.F. Glover (ed.), *The Hymnal 1982 Companion*, Church Hymnal Corporation, New York, Vol. 1, pp. 177-193; Leaver, R.A. (1991), *'Goostly Psalmes and Spirituall Songes': English and Dutch Metrical Psalms from Coverdale to Utenhove 1535-1566*, Clarendon, Oxford; Wilson-Dixon, A. (1997), *A Brief History of Christian Music*, Lion Publishing, Oxford. My kind thanks to Peter Blackwood for his advice in this area.

that we are now thinking about worship of the whole community, other factors arise. First, as noted, the use of the psalms allows the congregation to offer the kind of prayers, or to pray about things, that it might normally not. There will likely be some in the congregation who do not feel the set psalm is relevant to them on that occasion. Others may even feel uncomfortable in praying the words of a particular psalm, especially one of the psalms containing curses. On the other hand, there could well be some who need to pray such prayers, but without having it known. Or there may be those known outside the congregation for whom the psalm would be an appropriate prayer at that time. As the congregation prays a psalm in praise, thanksgiving, confession, or petition, at the very least it prays alongside others who need to offer such prayers but who may not be able to find their own words or strength to pray them. The congregation is drawn into a world of prayer that extends beyond its own words or concerns. They offer support, even if unknowingly, to others as they pray.

Secondly, the set psalms can offer an alternative form in the prayer of confession. I have noted that there are not many psalms of confession in the Book of Psalms. On the other hand, there are many psalms of lament and the lectionaries include some of these in the readings set for various Sundays. It could be important in the life of a congregation for the liturgist occasionally to use a communal lament, or even an individual lament, for the confession. In such a prayer, the congregation could lament the presence of sin in the world without necessarily feeling it has to recite its own individual errors. While we might not seek to contribute directly toward such things as ecological disasters, mass hunger and homelessness, systemic injustice, and loss of meaning in society, we nevertheless live within a world where many human activities contribute directly or indirectly to such evils, or are affected by such things. Our best intentions and actions can sometimes seem in vain in the face of major disasters. That needs to be acknowledged and the use of lament psalms may be a way of addressing the matter.

Thirdly, lament psalms might also be used as the congregation prays in their intercessions for others who are suffering. They could also be used in times of national or community mourning, or in annual commemorations of such events, when the community is grappling with changes in ordinary life, or itself reacting to natural disasters, catastrophic accidents, or gross acts of terror or injustice. The lament psalms help keep us in touch with God when difficult times arise and God seems distant.

On occasion an entire lament or confessional psalm will be set in the lectionary for a particular Sunday or high festival. It may be that some sections of the psalm would be suitable for prayers of adoration, confession, intercession etc. in the service. Such use has a way of tying the service together.[39] Entire psalms of

---

[39] For example, in the *Revised Common Lectionary* some lament psalms have been set which can be used in several ways and places in the service. These include on ordinary Sundays in Year A, Psalm 13, in Year B, Psalm 14, and in Year C, Psalms 42-43. In the last case, the two psalms are joined together by a common refrain ('Why are you cast down, O my soul, ...' Pss 42:5, 11; 43:5). The refrain could be said by the congregation in response

praise can also be used for prayers of adoration. Either the psalm could be used straight through or appropriate sections could be interspersed with contemporary prayers or hymns of praise. In general, many more psalms of praise are set in the major lectionaries than psalms of lament. There are thus many more opportunities to employ this type of psalm in our prayers.[40]

Just as in prayer, so in worship it might be appropriate for reason of length or sentiment to use only a section of a psalm instead of the whole psalm. The people can use a verse or part verse of a psalm as a response during the prayers. A psalm verse could also be used as a response in the Great Prayer of Thanksgiving in the Service of Holy Communion. Care needs to be exercised here that the general structure of the prayer is not altered. During the prayers, the response could be either said or sung.

The example below is based on Psalm 22, which is set for Good Friday services. We have already noted that Psalm 22 is an individual lament in which the psalmist protests God's absence in the face of a distressing situation. The lament dominates the first part of the psalm. Statements of how the psalmist's forebears trusted in God (vv. 3-5), and how the psalmist has had an intimate relation with God all his/her life (vv. 9-10), punctuate the lament. The end of the psalm, vv. 21b-31, turns to praise in response to God's deliverance. The mixture of lament and

---

to the liturgist reading or singing the rest of the psalm. In the case of high festivals, whole psalms which are set or which are particularly appropriate for a season include Psalm 27 (Year C, Lent 2), Psalm 32 (Year A, Lent 1 and Year C, Lent 4) and Psalm 51 (Ash Wednesday, Years A, B, and C). Similar examples could be taken from the Anglican and Roman Catholic lectionaries.

[40] For example in the RCL for the Sunday service, psalms of praise set include: Year A, Pss 46, 99, and 149; Year B, Pss 24, 84, 111, and 138; Year C, Pss 65, 85, 96, and 146. Pss 96, 99, 111, 138, and 149 are also set for certain high festivals or in other seasons. Psalms of praise which are set in their entirety for high festivals or which are particularly appropriate for a season include the following:

Psalm	Festival, Season (and Year)
8	Naming of Jesus (A,B,C); Trinity (A,C)
29	Epiphany 1 (A,B,C); Trinity (B)
24	All Saints (B)
47	Ascension Day (A,B,C)
96	Christmas Day (A,B,C)
97	Easter 7 (C)
98	Easter 6 (B)
99	Transfiguration (A,C)
100	Christ the King (A)
111	Epiphany 4 (B)
126	Advent 3 (B)
138	Epiphany 5 (B,C)
148	Christmas 1 (A,B,C); Easter 5 (C)
149	All Saints (C)

praise in the psalm lends itself to a combined prayer of adoration and confession, and the prayer below has been shaped in this way. Words from the end of the psalm and the statements of trust in the midst of the lament have been rewritten slightly to form a prayer of adoration. The words of the psalm have been turned into direct address to God. Some of the themes of the lament section of the psalm have formed the basis for a simple three-fold confession interspersed with the *kyrie*. Finally, words from the latter part of the psalm have been used in the declaration of forgiveness following the confession. In more informal or private circumstances the last part of the psalm could be read as a reminder of God's forgiveness. While the following prayer does not depend on the psalm having been read beforehand, it would best fit in circumstances where the psalm is read at some stage. The prayer is cast in the first person plural, assuming that it is prayed in public worship, but it could equally be changed to become the prayer of an individual. The prayer is as follows:

> Let us come to God with our prayers of adoration and confession.
> Let us pray.

> Lord God,
>> you are holy, enthroned on the praises of your people.

> In you the saints of old trusted;
>> they trusted, and you delivered them.
> To you they cried, and were saved;
>> in you they trusted, and were not put to shame.

> It was you who took us from the womb;
>> you kept us safe on our mothers' breasts.
> On you we were cast from our birth,
>> and since our mothers bore us you have been our God.
> You have never been far from us
>> when trouble was near
>> and there was no one to help.

> For this we praise you.

> In penitence and faith we confess our sins.

> When we take your silence for indifference,
>> **Lord have mercy on us.**
> When we openly mock and despise others,
>> **Christ have mercy on us.**
> When we secretly despise ourselves,
>> **Lord have mercy on us.**

If this prayer were used in a service of public worship or even in a small group, a declaration of forgiveness such as that which follows would be suitable. After the confession above, the leader could say:

God does not despise or abhor the affliction of the afflicted;
> he does not hide his face from them,
> but hears when they cry to him.

In the name of the Father, Son, and Holy Spirit,
> I declare to you, your sins are forgiven.

The overall mood of this prayer is more positive than that found in the first half of the psalm. If circumstances called for a lament over the seeming absence of God in the life of the people, then the prayer developed might take a different shape. The more positive prayer presented here is, however, not unfaithful to the text from which it was developed remembering that the psalm itself ends in praise. This prayer is but one of many that could be composed based on the psalm set for the week. It is not intended as a model for all such prayers but as an incentive for seeing the ways in which these words from God that are also to God can become part of weekly worship.

The set psalm for the week may not prove suitable to be used in the prayers. It may not be suitable either in a substantive way or even in terms of offering a single line. In such cases a set of standard responses taken from psalms of various types could be developed within a congregation for use from time to time. Many such verses can be found, although in some cases some slight adaptation might be necessary. Some suitable ones include the following.

In prayers of adoration:
Psalm 51
> [15] O Lord, open my lips,
> > and my mouth will declare your praise.

Psalm 95
> [1] O come, let us sing to the LORD;
> > let us make a joyful noise to the rock of our salvation!
> [2] Let us come into his presence with thanksgiving;
> > let us make a joyful noise to him with songs of praise!

Psalm 104
> [33] I will sing to the LORD as long as I live;
> > I will sing praise to my God while I have being.

Psalm 118
> [24] This is the day that the LORD has made;
> > let us rejoice and be glad in it.

In prayers of confession:
> Psalm 51
>> [1] Have mercy on me, O God, according to your steadfast love;
>>> according to your abundant mercy blot out my transgressions.
>>
>> [10] Create in me a clean heart, O God,
>>> and put a new and right spirit within me.
>
> Psalm 103
>> [8] The LORD is merciful and gracious,
>>> slow to anger and abounding in steadfast love.

The last quotation from Psalm 103 could be used in a dialogue within the worshipping community. The leader of worship could say or sing it as a refrain between prayers of confession said by the whole congregation.

In prayers of petition or intercession:
> Psalm 27
>> [14] Wait for the LORD;
>>> be strong, and let your heart take courage;
>>> wait for the LORD!
>
> Psalm 65
>> [5] By awesome deeds you answer us with deliverance,
>>> O God of our salvation;
>>> you are the hope of all the ends of the earth and of the farthest seas.
>
> Psalm 69
>> [16] Answer me, O LORD, for your steadfast love is good;
>>> according to your abundant mercy, turn to me.
>
> Psalm 130
>> [6] My soul waits for the Lord
>>> more than those who watch for the morning,
>>> more than those who watch for the morning.
>
> Psalm 143
>> [1] Hear my prayer, O LORD;
>>> give ear to my supplications in your faithfulness;
>>> answer me in your righteousness.

In prayers of thanksgiving:
> Psalm 118
>> [1] O give thanks to the LORD, for he is good;
>>> his steadfast love endures forever!

Psalm 69
[30] I will praise the name of God with a song;
      I will magnify him with thanksgiving.

Other psalm verses could be used for ascriptions of glory or as prayers for illumination before the readings from scripture, if such are part of the service. In terms of an *ascription of glory* a number of psalms provide appropriate verses, for example:

Psalm 8
[1] O LORD, our Sovereign,
      how majestic is your name in all the earth!
   You have set your glory above the heavens.

Psalm 96
[7] Ascribe to the LORD, O families of the peoples,
      ascribe to the LORD glory and strength.
[8] Ascribe to the LORD the glory due his name;
      bring an offering, and come into his courts.
[9] Worship the LORD in holy splendor;
      tremble before him, all the earth.

Psalm 57
[11] Be exalted, O God, above the heavens.
   Let your glory be over all the earth.

And in terms of *prayers for illumination* before the reading of Scripture, Psalm 86 provides an example:

Psalm 86
[8] There is none like you among the gods, O Lord,
      nor are there any works like yours.

   . . .
[11] Teach me your way, O LORD,
      that I may walk in your truth;
      give me an undivided heart to revere your name.

It has been the tradition in many congregations to use the psalm as a response to the Word of God read in Scripture. I will consider this more fully in the next chapter, and although I will argue for a wider use of the psalms in worship in general, and the possibility of using the set psalm as a Scripture reading for the day, the use of the psalm as part of the congregation's response to the Word from God is still appropriate as long as the usage on a particular occasion is clear to the congregation. The use of the psalms in one part of the liturgy affects other parts of the liturgy. The liturgist needs to be well aware of how he/she is using the psalm in each part. Is its role as Word from God the focus at a particular point or its role as word to God? Whichever the case, the liturgist needs to make sure the psalm functions in a constructive way within the liturgy. In general, the psalms do have an ambiguous function but that ought not to lead to confusion of the congregation at a particular point in the liturgy. As a rule, it would be helpful if the number of changes in the role the psalms play in a particular service of worship could be restricted.

The place of the psalm selection in the major lectionaries for Sunday services is an important matter. I will take it up in detail below but it is necessary to anticipate part of that discussion here. In all major lectionaries the psalm is seen as a response to the first reading, which is usually an Old Testament reading. In those lectionaries where the Old Testament reading is chosen in relation to the Gospel reading, then the psalm functions as a dual response: following the Old Testament reading and in anticipation of the Gospel. If the psalm is used in the liturgy as a response, regardless of how it relates to the other readings, it becomes a set response for the congregation. The matter of the congregation then using words which either do not fit their present mood or context, or about which they might have serious questions arises again, as it did in our consideration of prayer and pastoral care. The same comments can be made here as I made earlier. The discipline of a set response over time will allow the congregation to offer responses that reflect not just their own experience, but that of the whole community of faith, over time and space. Just as Bonhoeffer noted that we need to learn how to pray, and not simply offer words to God that reflect our feelings, so the use of the psalms as responses to the readings from Scripture, can help discipline us in our overall response to God's word. They can help us learn how to respond as well as how to pray. A response of lament can be as important as one of praise and thanks. On other occasions, a response of trust or one of wise reflection may be appropriate. Moreover, remembering our discussion of the psalms as the prayers which Jesus Christ and many others of the faithful have prayed, we thus see the congregation responding to the reading of the word with words the Church has seen especially as those of Jesus. The congregation learns how to respond to the reading of the God's word as the body of Christ as it uses the words the tradition has ascribed to Christ. While this is clear for the use of the psalm as a response to the readings from Scripture, it is no less the case when the psalms or psalm verses are used as responses in the prayers of the liturgy. The Church responds to God's word as well as offering its own prayers with the words Christ has first prayed.

The liturgist needs to be aware of this situation, and indeed can use it to further the congregation's understanding of its faith, its attitude, and way of living its faith. It can also be an aspect of the pastoral care of the congregation. The psalms can thus function in worship, as in prayer in general, not only as words to give expression to all present human experiences, but also as words that disturb present experience and open up the possibility of other experiences. It may be important for a congregation that is settled and at ease in its context to be disturbed by words of lament as a proper response to Scripture. This can be for the congregation's own benefit, when in time it may need to voice its own lament, or for its understanding of those outside or even within the congregation whose individual life is not so settled or comfortable. Alternatively, if the congregation is experiencing difficulty the psalm can bring words of hope to speak in the midst of disorientation. Of course, this greater understanding of the faith and expression of experience within the faith would depend on the regular use of the psalms week by week within the liturgy.

Finally, in relation to the psalms in liturgy, we might ask how does singing the psalms, as opposed to saying them, affect their use as words to God? Where, for example, some psalms of praise or trust have been made into hymns, these could be used on occasion in place of a prayer of adoration, although I do not think the *regular* replacement of a prayer of adoration by a hymn of praise, as happens in some congregations, is a desirable practice. It can lead to a loss of appreciation of praise in forms other than hymns, or can lead to a diminishment of praise if the singing of the hymns is poor. In any event, the number of psalms available for use in this way is not large and many psalms and psalm types would not be available. In order to sing a wider range of psalms in their entirety, liturgists or church music leaders have had to rely until relatively recently on plainsong or Anglican Chant. The composer and scholar, Erik Routley, states that both these forms are demanding on singers, and can be beyond the abilities and resources of congregations. Moreover, he argues that it is foreign to almost all the psalms to have the congregation sing them through. Most psalms, he says, are suited to solo voices.[41] This argument fits with what I noted earlier, when I discussed the voices within the psalms and who is speaking to whom. Many psalms have only one or two voices in conversation with God. If psalms are to be sung to God then it makes sense to use a cantor or small singing group with a relatively simple musical form and a congregational response. In this way the congregation can make the prayer in the psalm their own.

---

[41] Routley, E. (1980), 'The Psalms in Today's Church', *Reformed Liturgy & Music*, Vol. 14, pp. 20-26.

PART III
THE PSALMS AS WORD FROM GOD

Chapter 6

The Psalms in Preaching and Liturgy

Whenever the Psalter is abandoned, an incomparable treasure vanishes from the Christian Church. With its recovery will come unsuspected power.

Dietrich Bonhoeffer[1]

Listening to the Psalms in the Church

The Church has consistently found ways to say the psalms in prayer, song, and liturgy. While there are yet new things to be explored and learned in this area, we cannot overstate the importance of the psalms in the prayers and worship of the Christian community throughout its history. But, as I argued in chapter 1, alongside the tradition of speaking the psalms to God, there has been another tradition of hearing God in the words of the psalms. It is fair to say, however, that support for this latter tradition has been neither unanimous nor unambiguous. In the Church today there are some who would want to discourage or even contest hearing the psalms in certain ways. This is particularly true in the matter of the proclamation of the word within formal worship.

The reluctance of some to preach on the psalms or to see them as texts for preaching is often based on the special nature of the psalms. Their poetic quality is stressed, or their role as prayers is noted, or it is argued that they were intended to be sung. The oft-quoted dictum that the psalms are 'the hymn book of the Second Temple' illustrates the persistence of this last view. Such views have been expressed by Hebrew Bible scholars, by professors of preaching,[2] and by other notable commentators, such as C.S. Lewis.[3] Such views favour the notion of 'authorial intention'. That is, they believe that contemporary use of the psalms is determined by the form and function of the psalm in its ancient context, i.e. as the 'author' intended it. Others have argued against the use of the psalms in preaching, not on the grounds of authorial intention but on that of liturgical intention. I will

---

[1] Bonhoeffer, D. (1970), *The Psalms: The Prayer Book of the Bible*, trans. J.H. Burtness, Augsburg, Minneapolis, p. 26.

[2] McCann, J.C. (2001), 'Thus Says the Lord: "Thou Shalt Preach from the Psalms!"' in S.B. Reid (ed.) *Psalms and Practice: Worship, Virtue, and Authority*, Liturgical Press, Collegeville, pp. 111-122, quotes some opinions, p. 112.

[3] Lewis, C.S. (1977), *Reflections on the Psalms*, Fount, London, p. 10.

return to this below when I consider the place of the psalms in the lectionaries of the Church.

However, a number of writers have put forward strong counter arguments, promoting the use of the psalms as texts for teaching and preaching. In his book *Introduction to Psalms*, Christoph Barth says that we need to expand our use of the psalms in the Church. He notes that the Psalter is often said in various ways, but that it 'is intended just as much, if not more, to be listened to'. He argues that we need more serious study of the Psalter alongside recitation of it. Thus its place is not just in the liturgy but should be equally as much 'in the pulpit, in instruction and in study groups'.[4]

The way the psalms have been treated in scholarly study over the last two centuries also belies the notion of the psalms as having a special nature. They have been subjected to the same historical and literary critique as other biblical books, and have been shown to be part of a larger body of ancient Near Eastern poetic, liturgical and pious literature. In fact the Book of Psalms has been of particular interest to scholars, ranking among the books that have received most attention in introductions, commentaries, and other studies, and figuring prominently in the development of form criticism and the study of Israelite worship. The scholarly treatment of the psalms has not distinguished them from other biblical texts in any significant way, and raises a question about a distinction on liturgical grounds.

One experience of 'rediscovering' the psalms as texts to be heard is recounted by Ted Dotts, a United Methodist minister in the US. His story relates to preaching from the psalms. He says that for a long time the psalms did not interest him as preaching texts. In his preaching, which regularly addressed issues of politics, racism, education, etc., he thought he needed to wrestle with biblical texts involving law, prophecy, parable, story and ethics. The 'comforting-lamenting-thanking Psalms' did not have a place in that. However, his experience of preaching at funerals was different. It was only in the psalms that he found echoes of the cries of grieving families. This, and a renewed attention to the many sermons on psalm texts preached by Karl Barth, eventually led him to make preaching from the psalms part of his ministerial discipline.[5] Dotts's mention of Karl Barth reminds us of other well-known theologians who have published sermons on psalms. Paul Tillich and Dietrich Bonhoeffer are two who come to mind. I will consider these and a number of others who would encourage the task of listening to the psalms as word from God in the course of the discussion below.

In what follows I will consider the place given to the psalms now in the proclamation of the Church. I will also look at the particular issues that arise in relation to preaching from the psalms. While I will concentrate on the matter of preaching from the psalms, I will also touch on other ways in which we hear the psalms in worship. As the Church reassesses its place in the world at the beginning of the twenty first century, and wrestles with how it might continue to witness to its

---

[4] Barth, C.F. (1966), *Introduction to the Psalms*, trans. R.A. Wilson, Blackwell, Oxford, pp. 74-75.

[5] Dotts, T.J. (1988), 'Recognizing the Tone: Preaching from the Psalms during Pentecost', *Quarterly Review*, Vol. 8, pp. 71-88.

Lord, it needs to hear the voice of God speaking to it in all guises. Hearing the psalms as proclaimed word could offer an important perspective in this context.

The Psalms in the Lectionaries

If, as I have argued, there is a strong tradition in the Church of listening to the psalms, then we might expect to see evidence of it in the preaching of the Church. The fact that a psalm is set for each week in the major lectionaries for Sunday worship, would seem to support this. However, it is not so straight forward. It is precisely at this point, the relation of the lectionaries to preaching, that suggestions like that of Christoph Barth above – that the psalms need to be heard more within the Church – prove justified. Within the lectionaries for Sunday worship the psalm has not always been seen in the same way as the other readings set for the week: Old Testament, Epistle and Gospel readings. This is true for both those who construct lectionaries and for many who use them.

The constructors of the lectionaries have frequently expressed the view that the psalm fulfils a different role to the other readings. It has been seen particularly as a response to the Old Testament reading. This has often been clearly stated in the instructions or notes that accompany the various lectionaries.

This is the case for the Roman Catholic Mass. The psalm set for the Sunday is to be used for the chant after the first reading, usually an Old Testament passage.[6] Since the latter is mostly chosen in relation to the Gospel passage, which sets the theme for the day, the psalm as response is also governed by the Gospel reading. The readings from Scripture and the chants between the readings constitute the main section of the liturgy of the word. The responsorial psalm is, therefore, understood to be 'an integral part of the liturgy of the word'.[7] However, it is stated that '[i]n the readings, explained by the homily, God is speaking to his people …'.[8] The chants, including the psalm, are the avenue whereby 'the people make God's word their own...'.[9] So the psalm as part of the liturgy of the word is part of a complex 'conversation' over the word. Even the refrain during the singing of the psalm can be used to focus on the theme of the readings for the week. The psalm can thus play a significant role in hearing the word of God. Nevertheless, the fact that it is not designated as one of the readings in which 'God is speaking to his people' suggests that the compilers of the lectionary do treat the psalm differently. In the introduction to the document *Lectionary for the Mass*, no mention is made of

---

[6] See *Lectionary for the Mass* (1969), Introduction, 25 May, Vatican Polyglot Press, Rome, par. 9 and *General Instruction of the Roman Missal* (1975), 4th ed. 27 March 1975, Vatican Polyglot Press, Rome, par. 36, both reprinted in International Commission on English in the Liturgy (1982), *Documents on the Liturgy 1963-1979: Conciliar, Papal, and Curial Texts*, The Liturgical Press, Collegeville, as documents 232 and 208 respectively.

[7] *General Instruction of the Roman Missal*, pars 33 and 36.

[8] *Ibid.*, par. 33.

[9] *Ibid.*

the psalm in the section dealing with the Sunday readings.[10] The psalms are mentioned only in relation to the chants between the readings, where it is admittedly noted as the 'more important' of these.[11] The effect of this could be to give the psalm a different status in the eyes of preachers and congregation alike.

The *Revised Common Lectionary* (RCL), is an ecumenical lectionary published in North America by the Consultation on Common Texts (CCT). Historically, its origins lie in the Roman Catholic Lectionary (*Ordo Lectionum Missae* or ORL) devised for the mass following the Second Vatican Council. However, the RCL does not in itself carry the canonical status in the denominations where it is used that its predecessor did in the Roman Catholic Church.

The RCL is for Sunday services and has a psalm set for each week. The psalm is explicitly regarded as 'a congregational response and meditation on the first reading and is not intended as another reading'.[12] On ordinary Sundays, that is the Sundays after Pentecost, the Old Testament readings are selected on a continuous basis, and hence are not determined solely by the Gospel reading.[13] This means that the psalm does not necessarily relate to the Gospel. This goes beyond the earlier Roman, and even earlier Anglican statements as we will see below, by explicitly declaring that the psalm is not of the same status as the other readings. In the Consultation's response to criticism on the use of the Psalter in the earlier, and experimental *Common Lectionary* (published in 1983), attention was given to trying to maintain the integrity of the psalms set, especially where it was too long for complete inclusion, while reiterating the general place of the psalm in relation to the other readings. In revising the *Common Lectionary* '… the task force affirmed that the psalm (or scriptural canticle) should be chosen as the liturgical response to the first reading, and that it should fit harmoniously within the general tenor of the celebration'.[14]

For Anglican services of Holy Communion on Sundays, a psalm or psalm portion is provided with the weekly readings. In recent years the Anglican Churches have adopted the RCL as the basic lectionary for these services. Thus, the principle of selection as well as assumed use of the psalm portion is the same as outlined above.[15] This principle is similar to that which had been operating in the Anglican lectionaries before adoption of the RCL. For example, in the earlier *An Australian Prayer Book* the psalm portion was designated 'as a devotional response following the first reading'. It was suggested that the psalm be either sung

---

[10] *Lectionary for the Mass*, par. 16.

[11] *Ibid.*, par. 9.

[12] The Consultation on Common Texts (1992), *The Revised Common Lectionary*, Abingdon, Nashville, p. 11.

[13] The readings in Year A are from the Pentateuch (principally Genesis and Exodus) and are read in their canonical order. In Year B they are from Samuel-Kings and some Wisdom literature, and in Year C they are from the prophetic books.

[14] Consultation on Common Texts, *The Revised Common Lectionary*, p. 77.

[15] Occasionally there is a change in verse selection, usually to avoid gaps.

or said as appropriate to the congregation.[16] There can also be a set of 'supplementary readings' for Anglican Churches for worship on Sunday other than the service of Holy Communion. These readings usually supplement or fill in the gaps in the lectionary for Holy Communion, assuming that the latter has been read. This is the case for the psalms as much as for the other readings. In some seasons of the Christian year the psalms in this set of supplementary readings will run numerically, for example in Lent. There is no particular principle operating in the choice of psalms, other than using resources that have not been utilized elsewhere.[17]

Of course, the lectionaries set for Sunday Eucharist or Mass in the Anglican and Roman Catholic Churches respectively, are not the only lectionaries used in those denominations. There are lectionaries for daily prayer in the Anglican tradition and for the Liturgy of the Hours in the Catholic tradition. As I noted in chapter 1, the reading of psalms has been a major part of these liturgies for many centuries, although not for all. In daily prayer services the psalms set are read in their own right and not as responses to other readings. Canticles fulfil the latter role. However, there is still some ambivalence over the reading of the psalms in daily prayer. In the Catholic tradition they are mainly used for praise, although they are open to be heard as well. In the instructions on the Liturgy of the Hours, the psalms are understood as poems of praise, and headings, psalm-prayers and antiphons are given to assist the worshipper to pray the psalms.[18] This all helps the worshipper hear the psalms at the same time as praying them. It accords with the statement of the Second Vatican Council that there needs to be 'more intensive biblical instruction, especially with regard to the psalms'.[19] This is not the case in the Sunday Eucharist or Mass, at least as the devisers of the lectionaries have intended. The ambivalence over the use of psalms is more marked in some Anglican communions. In some orders of morning and evening prayer, or in the Daily Office, there is little explanation on the purpose of the psalms. In some others, or in some resources for daily prayer produced within the Anglican tradition, the practice of having a psalm-prayer at the end of psalm has been reintroduced.[20] This presumes that the psalms are to be heard as well as prayed. The psalm-prayer picks up a theme of the psalm and puts it within a Christian context. In Anglican contexts where there is provision for a daily Eucharist, the Roman Catholic Ordo is used without change.

---

[16] The Standing Committee of the General Synod of the Anglican Church of Australia (1978), *An Australian Prayer Book*, Anglican Information Office, Sydney, p. 177.
[17] My thanks to the Rev'd Dr. Charles Sherlock of the Melbourne College of Divinity, for his assistance with Anglican lectionaries.
[18] Sacred Congregation of Divine Worship (1971), *The Liturgy of the Hours: The General Instruction on the Liturgy of the Hours with a Commentary by A.M. Roguet, O.P.*, trans. P. Coughlan and P. Purdue, Geoffrey Chapman, London, pars 103, 110-120 on pp. 40, 43-44.
[19] *Constitution On Sacred Liturgy, Sacrosanctum Concilium*, n. 90 quoted in *The Liturgy of the Hours: The General Instruction*, ch. 3, n. 1, p. 73.
[20] See for example the Society of St. Francis (1992), *The Daily Office SSF*, Mowbray, London.

We can draw the conclusion from the above that the constructors of the Sunday lectionaries have a fairly uniform view that the psalms are not to be seen as readings of Scripture in the same way as the Old Testament, Epistle and Gospel readings. Presumably this means that it is not intended to use the psalms as texts for the preaching of the word. Even if, as in the instructions for the Roman Catholic Mass, the psalm is seen as 'an integral part of the liturgy of the word', the separate treatment of it would not facilitate seeing it as one of the texts for consideration in the preparation of the sermon. This situation may even be behind the fact that in a detailed, relatively recent discussion of the history of the Church's lectionaries, the matter of the place of the psalms within the lectionaries is not addressed.[21]

Two historical factors could be involved in the treatment of psalms in the Sunday lectionaries. First, the general approach to the Old Testament in the Church's lectionaries over the centuries could be an important influence. For the bulk of the 1500 years prior to Vatican II, the Church, in both the east and the west, did not have a set pattern of Old Testament readings in its lectionaries. During this same time an annual series of readings of Gospels and Epistles had developed.[22] With little attention given to the Old Testament in general in lectionaries, it could not be expected that the psalms would receive any special regard in relation to preaching. Secondly, the continued development of the cathedral tradition of singing the psalms may have overshadowed the development of the tradition of listening to the psalms in the development of lectionaries for Sunday services.

Whether the lectionaries acknowledge the psalm readings as texts available for preaching is one thing. What psalm texts are set within the lectionaries is another matter altogether. Of course, we might expect some selectivity when setting psalms for the weekly lectionary, especially if the psalm will be chosen in relation to the other readings. On the other hand, we can ask whether the lectionary restricts the types of psalms available through its selection so that the breadth of the psalms in the canon is not represented? The answer to this is a qualified yes. In the RCL it is true that most of the types of psalms are represented. On the other hand, there is no sense of proportional representation. In the Book of Psalms, lament and penitential psalms make up just over 40 per cent of the collection. Hymns, psalms of praise in various forms, and psalms of thanksgiving or trust constitute about another 35 per cent. However, in the lectionary, hymns and psalms of praise etc. outnumber lament and penitential psalms about two to one in each of the three years. In a study of the setting of lament psalms in the Roman Catholic Lectionary of 1969 and its derivatives, Ivan Kaufman argues that lament psalms are being 'undercut by joy', that is, they are underrepresented in the lectionary compared to hymns of praise etc.[23]

---

[21] Reumann, J. (1977), 'A History of Lectionaries: From the Synagogue at Nazareth to Post-Vatican II', *Interpretation*, Vol. 31, pp. 116-130.

[22] *Ibid.*, p. 128.

[23] Kaufman, I.T. (1990), 'Undercut by Joy: The Sunday Lectionaries and the Psalms of Lament', in J.C. Knight and L.A. Sinclair (eds), *The Psalms and Other Studies on the Old Testament Presented to Joseph I. Hunt*, Nashotah House Seminary, Nashotah, pp. 66-78. The title is drawn from an essay on a similar theme by Ramshaw, G. (1987), 'The Place of Lament within Praise: Theses for Discussion', *Worship*, Vol. 61, pp. 317-322.

The integrity of individual psalms is also affected in many cases when only a portion of a psalm is set for the lectionary.[24]

The lectionaries, therefore, do not give much encouragement for preachers to see the psalms as texts for preaching. There is a general tendency to think of the lectionary as offering three readings each week and to associate the psalm with liturgical activities. However, in spite of the stated aims of the lectionaries, in practice some preachers on occasion do find themselves drawn to the psalms. While the lectionaries reflect a practice over the centuries of categorizing the psalms in terms of liturgical response to God, encounters with these poetic texts suggest that within their words, people actually do hear a word from God. The same qualities that make the psalms an important resource for devotional purposes, namely their poetic beauty and spiritual depth, make them 'a rich goldmine for the preaching task'.[25] The 'non-canonical' status of the RCL in many denominations may also reduce the influence of the lectionary on preachers.

One argument that has been made about the role of the psalms in the lectionary focuses on the matter of 'intention' in relation to the psalm selection. This argument points out that because the psalm set for a Sunday is chosen as a response to another reading, then it cannot be compared with the other readings because authorial intention, which is still privileged in the other readings, is replaced in the case of the psalm by a liturgical intention.[26] An implication that might be drawn from such an argument is that, whatever we might think of the general principle of psalm selection in the lectionary, the psalm is no longer available for preaching. I would, however, dispute that. The selection of various texts by lectionary makers, as well as the act of reading, and other aspects of the context of worship, gives a liturgical intention to each of the readings: Old Testament, Epistle and Gospel. There is also the matter of the reception of the readings by the congregation. Because only a small number of verses is selected for each reading, because readings from the same book week by week are not necessarily sequential, and because no attention is necessarily given to the context of a reading, then the author's intention in the readings is restricted or supplanted as much as it is in the case of the psalm. While the lectionary makers openly seek to impose a liturgical intention on the psalm, they nevertheless also impose one on the other readings. Thus, the difference between the psalm reading and the others is not so great. If the other readings are meant to be heard, and available as texts for preaching, then there is as good a case for also seeing the psalm in that perspective.

A movement toward acknowledging the psalms as texts for preaching is evident in some published preaching aids, especially recent Protestant ones.[27] In the

---

[24] See Kaufman, 'Undercut by Joy', for further on this. This is also true for the RCL.

[25] Lowry, E.L. (1992), *Living with the Lectionary: Preaching through the Revised Common Lectionary*. Abingdon, Nashville, pp. 57-8.

[26] See, for example, Nasuti, H.P. (2001), 'The Sacramental Function of the Psalms in Contemporary Scholarship and Liturgical Practice', in S.B. Reid (ed.), *Psalms and Practice: Worship, Virtue, and Authority*, Liturgical Press, Collegeville, pp. 78-89.

[27] The examples given here might be compared to the Catholic volume, Fuller, R. (1984), *Preaching the Lectionary: The Word of God for the Church Today*, rev. ed., The Liturgical

series *Preaching the Revised Common Lectionary*,[28] it is stated in the introduction to the first volume, published in 1992, that although the psalm set for each week is intended as a response by the people, that in no way suggests that it cannot be used as a text for the sermon.[29] In the body of the volumes, the structure of the comments on the psalms is no different to that used for the other readings with the exception that the heading to the psalm is always 'The Response'. There would thus seem to be some tension within the series between an acknowledgment of the stated intention of the constructors of the Lectionary, that is that the psalm is for congregational response, and the writers of the preaching notes who see the psalm as available for preaching. The situation, however, is not ambiguous in the more recent series *Texts for Preaching*.[30] The question of whether the psalms are intended as texts for preaching is not discussed. Moreover, the treatment of the psalms is much the same as for the other readings each week. One is left to conclude that the psalm is understood as a fourth reading available for preaching.

In spite of the intended practice of the Church, as reflected in the approved lectionaries, it seems that at least some preachers and professors of preaching are hearing for themselves and responding to the type of call Christoph Barth has voiced. They are 'listening' to the psalms, at least in the context of preaching, as well as praying and singing them. It might well be an irony in the situation that the very development and wide spread use of lectionaries in many denominations in the post-Vatican II period, with the inclusion of a psalm each week for the congregation's response to the word of God, is leading to people hearing the word of God in the very words given to them as their response. If this is the case it simply demonstrates the dual nature that the psalms already have in scripture and tradition.

Issues in Preaching the Psalms

Preaching from Prayers

One reason some have expressed reservations about preaching from the psalms is that they question whether it is proper to preach from texts that are prayers. The lectionaries for Sunday readings include very few prayers.[31] Many would hold that

---

Press, Collegeville. In that work the psalm is treated more briefly than the other readings. The comments are more directed to an appropriate inclusion of the psalm in the liturgy in general than to provide notes for preaching.

[28] Soards, M. et al., (1992-), *Preaching the Revised Common Lectionary*, Abingdon, Nashville.

[29] *Preaching the Revised Common Lectionary*, 1992, p. 11.

[30] Brueggemann, W. et al., (1995-), *Texts for Preaching: A Lectionary Commentary Based on the NRSV*. John Knox, Louisville.

[31] An important exception here is the Lord's prayer, which in the *Revised Common Lectionary* is included in the reading Luke 11:1-13 (Year C: Sunday between 24 and 30 July). It is worth noting, however, that the Matthew passage on the Lord's Prayer (Matt 6:9-

it is impossible to preach from prayers.[32] A major reason for this view is the fact that the psalms consist mostly of words addressed to God, and they believe a sermon is not meant to be an expression of our longings and praises to God. But while it is valid to say that a sermon is not the same as a prayer, this does not mean that sermons cannot be preached on prayer texts.[33] There has not always been a hesitancy to preach on prayers in the Church. The Anglican tradition of preaching occasionally on the collect for the day and the Methodist custom of preaching on a hymn both illustrate this.

There are some important things to be gained by preaching on prayers and the psalms in particular. First, there is the matter of the importance of the psalms for growth in the Christian life and faith. The psalms are the prayers of Israel, and, as I have argued, through Jesus Christ and the Church as the body of Christ, they are the Church's prayers as well. It is arguable that as the Church's use of and familiarity with the psalms decline, it loses an important source for maintaining a sense of discipline and theology in its prayers. It is imperative that the Church preaches from the psalms so that they can become the Church's prayers. The dual roles of the psalms that I considered in chapter 1 have a significance of their own. The one role is interdependent with the other.[34]

Secondly, I argued in chapter 2 that the psalms do not only offer us words with which to pray, but shape a world of prayer for us. That world presumes a certain theology, or theologies. As we pray with or from them, they set before us theological assumptions and in turn challenge our present assumptions, especially about prayer itself. As we listen to the psalms we begin to understand the nature of our conversation with God. To pray the lament psalms requires a theology that not only expects God to answer prayer, but assumes God understands suffering. To move toward praise requires a theology that demands a sense of God's sovereignty in the world. All prayer is built on a set of theological assumptions. Understanding those assumptions can only deepen prayer. If we set aside certain types of psalms so that we do not or cannot hear them, we risk forming a prayer life that hides from difficult questions, cannot cope with suffering, or neglects praise. Of course, there are other ways in which questions raised by the psalms could be addressed. For example, sermons on the Book of Job cannot help but raise the issue of suffering. However, in that context the issue is objectified. We think theologically about the suffering *of another*. In the psalms of lament, and especially in those in which the psalmist speaks as 'we' or 'I', we face theologically the issue of our own suffering. As we pray them we engage in a conversation with God on the issue. Thus, the

---

13) is omitted from the lectionary altogether. On Ash Wednesday in each year the Gospel reading (Matt 6:1-6, 16-21) skirts around the prayer.

[32] See Achtemeier, E. (1984), *Preaching as Theology and Art*, Abingdon, Nashville, p. 60 and her comments at the beginning of (1984) 'Preaching from the Psalms', *Review and Expositor*, Vol. 81/3, pp. 437-450.

[33] Contrary to the comments by Jenson, R.W. (1979), 'Psalm 32', *Interpretation*, Vol. 33/2, pp. 172-6, esp. p. 172.

[34] This argument is put forward in other words by Achtemeier, 'Preaching from the Psalms', p. 442.

matter of listening to the psalms is important for both our understanding of prayer, and our engagement in prayer.

Thirdly, I spoke above about the conversational mode of prayer in the psalms. Each partner in this conversation, God and the pray-er, has a full part to play. The psalms model this conversation for us, and invite us into that world. Preaching from the psalms is one way of calling people (back) into that conversation. It can give them permission to begin a conversation with God where none seems to exist. Alternatively, it can help them either to hear the voice of God, their conversation partner, when God seems to have fallen silent or the pray-er has become too accustomed to hearing his/her own voice. It could also help the pray-er gain a voice in the conversation when he/she has been submissive or unsure what to say. The prayers of the Bible, and particularly the psalms, model the speech that is required for and within communion. They model words of supplication: 'Hear my cry, O God; listen to my prayer' (Ps 61:1); words of irritation at God's silence: 'O God, do not keep silence; do not hold your peace or be still, O God! (Ps 83:1); words of anger at others: 'Let them curse, but you will bless. Let my assailants be put to shame; may your servant be glad' (Ps 109:28); or even words of thanks and praise that do not always come easily: 'Happy are those whose transgression is forgiven, whose sin is covered' (Ps 32:1). In this context, preaching on biblical prayers, and especially the psalms, would seem to be an imperative for the Church.[35]

Fourthly, there is good news to be proclaimed in preaching from the psalms as prayers. While a sermon ought not be just instruction on prayer, those on the psalms can proclaim whom this God is who engages us in conversation and what language, feelings, ideas, hopes and joys can be part of this conversation. The psalms cover the whole range of human experiences. Their words, addressed to God, are often emotionally charged and sometimes speak about things not often discussed.[36] In proclaiming the word of the psalms, the preacher calls the congregation to speak to God about all things in their life. The preacher directs the people to words with which to praise, complain, contemplate, give thanks, doubt, challenge, grieve, or trust in their communion with God. In terms of the content of the psalms, there is good news about God who cares for creation, is our refuge, cares for and persists with the people through their times of struggle and sin, and answers their prayers. This same God is open to both the cries and the questions of the people. The fact that these words with which we can pray to God on any occasion, are given to us by God, is itself good news.

Fifthly, if we take the idea of Jesus as the 'singer of the psalms' seriously, especially in the way Bonhoeffer understood it, then the psalms, and particularly those of lament, can become a way of proclaiming the incarnation of God in Jesus, the depth of God's love for his people, and the fullness of the world's redemption

---

[35] Cf. Brueggemann, W. (1989), *Finally Comes the Poet*, Fortress Press, Minneapolis, pp. 49-50, on the need for preaching to stimulate conversation with God. The examples Brueggemann uses in his book are all from biblical prayers, many from the psalms.

[36] See Sedgwick, C. (1992), 'Preaching from the Psalms', *Expository Times*, Vol. 103/12, pp. 361-364 for further discussion.

in Christ. In the psalms, Bonhoeffer saw the prayer of human nature assumed by Christ. Preaching on the psalms, and in this case especially those used by the Gospels to interpret the life and work of Jesus, allows the preacher to proclaim Christ who both stands in our place and brings the pain and suffering of humans to God.

Finally, while it must be acknowledged that the psalms can teach us a great deal about prayer, that is not their only contribution. To focus only on the role of the psalms in relation to prayer is to let the original form and function of these texts determine their present role. Their usefulness is not limited by any original intent we might determine for them. Even to contemplate defining their original use and setting goes beyond what is possible. The language of the psalms is open to the point of obscuring their origins. They are shaped so that they are available for new situations and contexts. The complex formation of the Book of Psalms has further obscured their origins. And now some scholars would even argue that the whole collection has a specific theological or instructional role beyond any original intention of the writers of individual psalms. All this suggests that, alongside their use as prayers and songs to offer to God, the psalms are texts from which we can learn about the faith, and which can be proclaimed.[37]

The Congregation and the Anonymity of the Psalms

While there are things to be gained in preaching from the psalms as prayers, there are matters which either need attention or must be noted. These relate to both the content of the psalms and the context of preaching. The anonymity of the psalms is one matter. I noted in the discussion on the psalms and prayer that most of the psalms are not time or space bound in terms of content. The speaker and others in the psalms remain anonymous, often referred to only as 'I' or 'we', or as unspecified 'enemies'. Many of the psalms cannot be associated with a particular historical or social context. There is thus the temptation to read the psalms in terms of timeless truths or in relation to 'the general human condition'.[38] Because they speak about or to no one in particular, we can assume they speak to everyone in general. But this can also be an advantage if the preacher is aware of the ability of the psalms to be appropriated by individuals or communities in their own particularity. In their anonymity, an individual hears or reads words in a psalm that touch upon the very particular pain he/she is bearing, or a community finds words with which to shout their joy and praise. If the preacher lets the congregation identify with the words of the psalms, then they can become fruitful texts for preaching.[39] Israel's words to God can become the words and responses of the congregation. The important point here is that preacher *lets the congregation identify* with the words of the psalm, or to put it in another way, let Israel's words become the congregation's words. The psalms invite the pray-er into their world by their very language. To preach from them is not to force an interpretation on the

---

[37] Cf. also McCann, 'Thus Says the Lord', pp. 113-116.

[38] Achtemeier, 'Preaching from the Psalms', p. 440.

[39] Achtemeier, *Preaching as Theology and Art*, p. 60.

psalm. At most, it might be to suggest some situations that fit the psalm. In any event, it is to let the congregation engage with the words of the psalm themselves, so that it can become their prayer, or a prayer that they could offer for others. Dietrich Bonhoeffer moves in this direction with his sermon on Psalm 42 discussed below. If the psalms, which become texts for sermons, represent over time the broad range of psalms, then the congregation will be encouraged to express their faith in the many different experiences which the psalm reflect.

Prayer and Praise within Preaching

Another important matter in relation to preaching on the psalms is the context of preaching, namely the service of worship. We are particularly interested in the Sunday service, or the Mass or Sunday Eucharist according to denominational terminology. Although these services will have varying foci depending on the season of the Christian year or the local calendar, the ultimate aim of the service is the praise of God in its various forms. In services that include the Eucharist, or Holy Communion, the eucharistic prayer functions as the climax of praise toward which other liturgical elements lead.[40]

The sermon also leads toward this praise. Chrysostom, Augustine, and Calvin, to mention just a few preachers, all used an ascription of praise at the end of the sermon. It was not simply a formality, but indicated the intention of the sermon to bring others to praise.[41] It is the task of the modern preacher to model praise for the congregation, giving them permission to praise, and summoning them to praise.[42] The psalms can contribute substantially to this aim in that nearly all of them, including the laments, contain an element of praise, and, moreover, the shape of the whole Book of Psalms leads the pray-er toward unhindered praise of God. The end of the conversation between God and the person of faith, indeed the end of the life of the faithful one, is praise.[43] The fact that the psalms touch upon the entire range of human experiences means that the praise modelled on these texts will not be some glib offering without any roots in both the joys and pains of life. It will be, like the praise of the psalmists themselves, praise which knows the hardships of life, and the reasons why it sings of the glory of God. The reluctance on the part of the lectionary makers to consider psalms as texts for preaching deprives the preacher of a valuable resource for both engendering praise within the congregation.

Attention to Form

More needs to be said about the form of the psalms. The fact that most of the psalms are poems, and in many cases might have been intended for singing, should

---

[40] Wainwright, G. (1985), 'The Praise of God in the Theological Reflection of the Church', *Interpretation*, Vol. 39, pp. 34-45, esp. p. 39.

[41] *Ibid.*, p. 37.

[42] Brueggemann, *Finally Comes the Poet*, p. 74.

[43] *Ibid.*, p. 67.

not deter the preacher when preaching from them. To state the obvious, many of the Old Testament readings in the Sunday lectionaries and a few of the New Testament ones are also poetic texts. Preaching from them requires sensitivity to the genre of the text, but it does not rule the task out. Giving attention to the poetic language and the generalized references in the psalms is part of the challenge of preaching from them. The very form of the psalms as prayers allows these texts to speak to the people in a way that some other texts cannot. They have a power of their own to move and change the hearer/reader. They are passionate texts that draw us into their world.[44]

The fact that the psalms are poetry suggests that, just as poetry and prayer belong together both going beyond the bounds of the ordinary to speak of another reality, so then preaching that incorporates a level of poetic language and imagination is appropriate with the psalms. It can also help sermons lead toward praise. Too often preaching is seen as a rational task, explaining, critiquing, interpreting, exhorting, or involving a moral argument, or having an instructional aspect to it. At times it will be these things. We are concerned with the human response to God, with exploring the nature of discipleship, or faith, for example. But the tasks of critique, communication, and celebration, which are all part of the larger theological enterprise,[45] are also part of the task of preaching. If one of chief elements of preaching is to focus people's thoughts on God and engender praise, then the aesthetic faculties of humankind are at least as important as the rational in proclaiming the word. Preaching may at times be required to lift the spirits, to give people a glimpse of the 'Immortal, invisible, God only wise, in light inaccessible hid from our eyes'. Preaching is sometimes called on to help people praise the great name of 'the Ancient of Days'.[46] In such contexts the sermon needs to have a touch of the poetic about it, creating a new world for people and calling on them to embrace that world. As poetry, the psalms offer the hearer/reader a new view of the world, of his/her experience, and of God. They let him/her see things in a new way, challenge old perceptions, or break open existing ones, evoking new perceptions of reality.[47] A reluctance to see the psalms as texts for preaching deprives the preacher not only of prayers as texts for proclaiming the word, but also of a substantial amount of poetry that could help lift the spirits.

To preach on a psalm requires that attention be given to their poetic form. But as in the case of praying the psalms, the preacher does not have to become a good poet to preach on a psalm. Nor are we talking about rhetoric for its own sake or simply to impress. But careful attention given to the poetic form of psalms will prove a beneficial thing in the development of sermons. Preaching is an art form in its own right and the preacher has most to learn in this art from the poet. As in the

---

[44] Sedgwick, 'Preaching from the Psalms', pp. 361-364.

[45] The present Anglican Archbishop of Canterbury, Rowan Williams, made this remark in an address at Trinity College, University of Melbourne, 1996. See also Wainwright, 'The Praise of God in the Theological Reflection of the Church', pp. 34-45.

[46] Hymn No. 143, *Together in Song*. Words by W.C. Smith.

[47] Achtemeier, *Preaching as Theology and Art*, pp. 51-52. See also Long, T.G. (1988), *Preaching and the Literary Forms of the Bible*, Fortress, Philadelphia, ch. 3, pp. 43-52.

case of prayer, we could describe preaching as a kind of poetry. It is a task that must employ all the devices of poetry – vivid metaphor, imagery, various word plays, alliteration, assonance, short lines, repetition etc. – to convey its message.[48] The point is that in the psalms there are many examples to be followed or developed which can enhance the shape and content in our proclamation of the word.[49]

I have mentioned only hymns of praise so far, but there are also difficult times in life when a sermon has to grapple with questions of 'how long?' or 'why?'. In this case, the poetry of the lament psalms can be a way of expressing what cannot be explained too easily or too quickly. I quoted before the beginning of Psalm 13:

> [1] How long, O LORD? Will you forget me forever?
>   How long will you hide your face from me?
> [2] How long must I bear pain in my soul,
>   and have sorrow in my heart all day long?
>   How long shall my enemy be exalted over me?

The fourfold repetition of the question 'How long?' drags the issue out, with words of forgetfulness and pain filling lines enclosed by phrases of time, 'forever', and 'all day long'. The anguish and distress of the psalmist is manifest and extended over several lines to stress the length of the psalmist's suffering. The questions dominate the psalm and are never fully answered. Similar devices can be used when a sermon is required to address questions of pain and suffering. Of course, in preaching we are also concerned with the proclamation of good news. To pose questions of 'how long?' as if there were no answer could be less than faithful preaching, and ultimately inconsistent with the lament psalms and their vows of praise. Nevertheless, in preaching it is possible to develop the poetry of lament so that neither the lament itself nor the good news is forgotten.

The Practice of Preaching the Psalms

I turn now to examine how some preachers in relatively recent times have used the psalms. We are, of course, restricted in this discussion to published sermons, and a written sermon will always remain, at best, the text of a sermon. We cannot capture the oral/aural events that were the sermons themselves, nor always appreciate the theological, social, and historical context which shapes the sermon's preparation and affects its hearing. Nevertheless, the text of a sermon can give us some information. In our case, we can see how the preacher handles the psalm, what links he/she tries to make to the contemporary situation, and how he/she relates the

---

[48] *Ibid.*, p. 52. See also Achtemeier, E. (1980), *Creative Preaching: Finding the Words*, Abingdon, Nashville.

[49] See also the suggestions of Achtemeier, E. (1985), 'Use of Hymnic Elements in Preaching', *Interpretation*, Vol. 39, pp. 46-59.

psalm to Jesus Christ and Christian theology in general. Looking at some of these issues will be informative for our own preaching from the psalms.

I have already referred to Dietrich Bonhoeffer in relation to the psalms and prayer. His daily use and love of the psalms is well known. Some of his sermons and meditations on the psalms can be found in *Dietrich Bonhoeffer: Meditating on the Word* edited by D.McI. Gracie.[50] In particular, the book juxtaposes two sermons on psalms which show the development in Bonhoeffer's approach to the Bible and preaching. Gracie says that Bonhoeffer's earlier sermons were 'flowery in their language and loftier in their themes' than the later ones.[51] The first sermon was preached in 1928 when Bonhoeffer was only twenty-two and an assistant pastor in a German congregation in Barcelona. The text was a single verse, Ps 62:1: 'For God alone my soul in silence waits; from him comes my salvation.'[52] Bonhoeffer focused on the words 'silence', 'wait', and 'salvation'. He discussed two reasons why so few people realize this state of silent waiting, and finished the sermon by addressing the question of what people need to do to rectify this. Already in this sermon we see some of the themes that become important to Bonhoeffer in his consideration of the psalms and prayer. He speaks of the need to practise prayer and learn the right language with which to communicate with God. 'Prayer must be practiced (sic.)' he says, and goes on: 'It is a fatal error to confuse religion with sentimentality.'[53]

Bonhoeffer preached the second sermon, on Psalm 42, in 1935 at the seminary at Finkenwalde.[54] The psalm had been one of Bonhoeffer's childhood favourites. While the sermon had some similar traits to the earlier one, it had some marked differences. One reason for this was that by the time he was giving instructions on meditation to the seminarians Bonhoeffer was also giving greater focus to the Bible. He confessed this increased attention to the Bible in a letter to a friend, Dr. Rüdiger Schleicher, written in April 1936. Bonhoeffer stated:

> I want to confess quite simply that I believe the Bible alone is the answer to all our questions, and that we only need to ask persistently and with some humility in order to receive an answer from it.[55]

Bonhoeffer admitted that this sounded a rather 'primitive' approach, but we should not assume he was talking about a simplistic literalism or a mechanistic approach to faith and scripture. His reading of the Bible was always accompanied by persistent questioning of the text. The sermon on Psalm 42 is an example of this meditation.

---

[50] Gracie, D.McI. ed. and trans. (1986), *Dietrich Bonhoeffer: Meditating on the Word*, Cowley, Cambridge, MA.

[51] *Ibid.*, p. 57.

[52] *Ibid.*, pp. 57-63. The biblical translation is that supplied in Gracie's book from the Psalter of the Book of Common Prayer.

[53] *Ibid.*, p. 61.

[54] *Ibid.*, pp. 64-72.

[55] *Ibid.*, p. 43.

His attention to words and their meaning, already there in the earlier sermon, was present in the latter but was shaped in a new way. Bonhoeffer went through the whole of Psalm 42, taking a verse or two at a time, and developed the thought of the psalm. The sermon on Ps 62:1 was essentially theocentric, not stepping beyond the reference to God in the text, but the one on Psalm 42 was thoroughly Christocentric. Bonhoeffer saw every verse in the psalm as a witness to Jesus Christ. As I noted earlier, this is not a simplistic reading of Jesus Christ into the psalms. Bonhoeffer knew that the psalm was that of an ordinary human in despair. But behind those human words, he heard the words of Christ in his humanity and suffering. The trust expressed in the psalm was completely recognisable in Jesus.[56]

In the earlier sermon on Ps 62:1, Bonhoeffer developed a line of argument based on the text, which he addressed directly to the congregation. In contrast, the sermon on Psalm 42 was more akin to a meditation on the psalm in the presence of the congregation. He addressed the questions the psalmist asked and responded to the psalmist's statements. At some points, the sermon became little more than an amplified paraphrase of the psalm. Bonhoeffer took the pronouns of the psalm seriously. He often employed the changes in pronouns in the psalm, and the speech of the psalmist, to engage the congregation. When the psalmist spoke personally, to him or herself, or to God or others, so Bonhoeffer reflected personally or on behalf of the congregation. When the psalmist addressed his/her audience as 'you', Bonhoeffer turned to address the congregation as 'you'. In this way he created the possibility of a more intimate engagement between the congregation and the text. Thus, his sermon was not so much an independent argument intended to explain the meaning of the psalm to the congregation. It was rather a development of the thought of the psalm with God, the preacher, and the congregation in 'conversation'.

It might be helpful to quote a portion of the sermon. On v. 2 of the psalm Bonhoeffer said:

> *2 My soul is athirst for God, athirst for the living God;*
> *when shall I come to appear before the presence of God?*

> Thirst for God. We know the body's thirst when there is no water; we know the thirst of our passion for life and good fortune. Do we also know the soul's thirst for God? A God who is only an ideal can never still this thirst. Our soul thirsts for the living God, the God and Source of all true life. When will God quench our thirst? When will we come to appear before his presence? To be with God is the goal of all life and is itself eternal life. We are in God's presence with Jesus Christ, the crucified. If we have found God's presence here, then we thirst to enjoy it completely in eternity.

> Jesus says that whoever is thirsty should come to him and drink. (Jn 7:37)

---

[56] Miller, P.D. (1994), 'Dietrich Bonhoeffer and the Psalms', *Princeton Theological Seminary Bulletin*, Vol. 15, pp. 274-282, esp. p. 275.

— Lord, we long to come more and more into your presence. Amen.[57]

Each section of the sermon ended, as this one did, with a brief prayer. In these prayers, the 'lessons' for the congregation were gathered up, but not in a summary or moralistic fashion. These prayers actually embodied the form of the psalm text – as prayer – at the same time as they elicited response from the congregation. In this way Bonhoeffer maintained a sense of the text as prayer while not letting his sermon become a prayer. The congregation heard God speaking to it, through the preacher and the psalm text, about prayer, and that prayer was modelled in the brief prayers at the end of each section as the congregation responded.

In these sermons Bonhoeffer demonstrated two ways of preaching from the psalms. In terms of form and structure, the sermon on Ps 62:1 could be regarded as the more 'conventional' of the two. The sermon on Psalm 42 raises the possibility of the preacher employing both the use of the pronouns in some psalms, with their lack of specific reference, and the prayer form of psalms, to engage the congregation in conversation with God, with themselves and others. Bonhoeffer's sermon on Psalm 42 especially raises the issue of a Christological reading of the psalms in preaching and presents a good model. Bonhoeffer is faithful to the psalm in its theocentric thought in that he does not read the psalm as a simple foretelling of Christ, nor as only concerned with Christ. Bonhoeffer does not deny the psalm as an expression of ordinary human faith and feeling. On the other hand, Jesus Christ can be heard, seen, or witnessed in almost every word of the psalm. Other preachers might prefer to give greater place to historical-critical issues relating to a psalm, especially those where some information is available. What Bonhoeffer does here is more akin to a literary-critical approach with a strong Christological emphasis.

Other well-known theologians, biblical scholars, and preachers have published sermons on the psalms. Some of Karl Barth's sermons on psalms or psalm texts appear in several works, particularly in *Deliverance to the Captives*, a collection of sermons and prayers Barth prepared for his ministry at the prison in Basel, Switzerland.[58] For the most part Barth preaches on individual verses from psalms (Ps 34:5; 39:8; 68:20; and 111:10) in a manner similar to that of Bonhoeffer's sermon on Ps 62:1. He expounds in detail on individual words or phrases in the verse. He relates his readings to Jesus Christ as Lord but he is in no way as thoroughgoing in his Christological approach as Bonhoeffer is in his treatment of Psalm 42. Other sermons on psalms have been published in several books containing Barth's sermons.[59]

---

[57] Gracie, *Dietrich Bonhoeffer: Meditating on the Word*, pp. 65-66.

[58] Barth, K. (1961), *Deliverance to the Captives*, Harper and Row, New York.

[59] Barth, K. (1967), *Call for God*, SCM, London, pp. 29-38 and 39-48 on Pss 50:15 and 31:16 respectively. There are also sermons on psalm verses in Barth, K. and Thurneysen, E. (1935), *God's Search for Man*, Round Table Press, New York, pp. 131-142 on Ps 131; and (1933), *Come Holy Spirit*, Round Table Press, New York, pp. 1-12 on Psalm 24. The latter sermon gives a slightly more extended treatment of the psalm.

Paul Tillich also published sermons on psalms in his book *The shaking of the foundations*. In this work he has two sermons that give extended treatments to Psalms 139 and 90 and several others which touch on psalms in less extensive ways.[60] The sermon on Psalm 139 called 'The escape from God' is a good example of how a sermon can develop a detailed treatment of the content of a psalm. Psalm 139 speaks about God's knowledge of us. This knowledge, which the psalmist contemplates, leads to attempts to escape the presence of God, or to do away with God, because this knowledge lays the psalmist, and all humans, open and vulnerable in the private, most mysterious, hidden parts of their lives. Yet the psalmist also recognizes the divine wisdom as a friendly presence rather than as a destructive force. This situation is, for Tillich, like any love affair. When there is greater intimacy, there is a greater revelation of oneself – a revelation of knowledge that could in the end prove destructive. It is a question of how the relationship is approached. Either it is based in trust that the other will deal lovingly with the knowledge revealed, or in fear that it will be used in animosity.

In a sermon entitled 'Dereliction', Frederick Buechner has given good historical-critical attention to Psalm 74 and its vivid description of the destruction of the temple in 586 B.C.E.[61] He looks at the cause of that destruction according to Jeremiah and concludes that '...the Temple fell to the Babylonians like a house of cards not because God was a pushover but because a house of cards is what God's people had made it'.[62] He compares that to the situation of the Church in our own time and remarks 'The church is intact in many ways, ... But is it possible that something crucial is missing the way something crucial was missing in the Temple at Jerusalem in 586 B.C., which is why it fell like a ton of bricks?'[63] Buechner peppers his sermon with questions about the state of the Church and its future, just as the psalmist continually asks questions about the future. Buechner says he will not answer his own questions because he does not know the answers. He concludes with a prayer quoting part of v. 3 of the psalm: '"O God, direct thy steps to the perpetual ruins" that can never ruin thee. Direct thy steps to us and to thy church in its emptiness and darkness. Thine is the day, but thine also is the night. Thine also is the night.'[64] In the references to day and night and darkness he is alluding to v. 16 of the psalm which says in part 'Yours is the day, yours also the night' and to v. 20 with its mention of the dark places of the land. Thus, Buechner makes subtle use of the imagery in the psalm while respecting the spirit of the psalm in questioning God as to how long this situation of the derelict temple can go on. Buechner maintains the integrity of the psalm's form and spirit while freely developing analogies to the contemporary situation of the Church.

---

[60] Tillich, P. (1949), *The Shaking of the Foundations*, SCM, London, pp. 38-51 and 64-75 on Pss 139 and 90 respectively.

[61] Buechner, F. (1984), *A Room Called Remember: Uncollected Pieces*, Harper & Row, San Francisco, pp. 115-126.

[62] *Ibid.*, p. 118.

[63] *Ibid.*, pp. 121-122.

[64] *Ibid.*, p. 126.

Walter Brueggemann has also published some sermons on psalms. Four are included in the work *The threat of life: sermons on pain, power, and weakness.*[65] He has one sermon on Psalm 23, and three on Psalm 69. The latter were preached in an Episcopal Church at an extended Good Friday service with three homilies. Psalm 69 is part of the lectionary for that service. With the opportunity of preaching three times during the service, Brueggemann was able to treat the psalm in its entirety. This is important in this case because the psalm is one of the so-called 'imprecatory psalms' and this one has an extended list of curses that the psalmist wishes upon his/her enemies (vv. 22-29). The Good Friday setting also raises the question of the relation of the psalm to Jesus Christ, a question that is heightened by the vindictive words of the psalm. In his treatment of the theme of power, which Brueggemann addresses via the psalm, he says that Jesus becomes 'for us the lens through which we reread power, social relations, and formal policies'. But Brueggemann also sees Jesus as the lens through which to read the psalm. In his sermons, the psalm becomes the prayer of Jesus and Brueggemann proclaims: 'Jesus stands alongside all the powerless in his abrasive prayer, demanding justice on earth from God'.[66] The abrasive prayer of Jesus is precisely Psalm 69, which Brueggemann recognizes as something of an 'embarrassment to us, because we do not expect such speech, especially on the lips of Jesus'.[67] The remarks I made earlier in relation to the psalms becoming our prayers, even with words we do not like, are thus also pertinent in the context of preaching.

Hearing God through the Psalms in the Liturgy

I have focussed on hearing the psalms in preaching. However, the psalms can also be heard as a word from God in other parts of the Sunday liturgy. We can best explore this area by looking at some examples.

A verse or line from the set psalm in which God speaks, or the psalmist speaks for God, can be used in the declaration of forgiveness, or in the blessing. For example, in the case of the *declaration of forgiveness*:

Psalm 34

[15] The eyes of the LORD are on the righteous,
     and his ears are open to their cry.

...

[22] The LORD redeems the life of his servants;
     none of those who take refuge in him will be condemned.

---

[65] Brueggemann, W. (1996), *The Threat of Life: Sermons on Pain, Power, and Weakness*, Augsburg Fortress, Minneapolis, pp. 90-115.

[66] *Ibid.*, p. 108.

[67] *Ibid.*, p. 105.

Psalm 91
        [14] Those who love me, I will deliver;
                I will protect those who know my name.
        [15] When they call to me, I will answer them;
                I will be with them in trouble,
                I will rescue them and honor them.

Although it is cast in the words of the psalmist, Psalm 103 provides a lengthy but excellent introduction to a declaration of forgiveness. It can easily be understood in the context of a word from God:

Psalm 103
        [8] The LORD is merciful and gracious,
                slow to anger and abounding in steadfast love.
        [9] He will not always accuse,
                nor will he keep his anger forever.
        [10] He does not deal with us according to our sins,
                nor repay us according to our iniquities.
        [11] For as the heavens are high above the earth,
                so great is his steadfast love toward those who fear him;
        [12] as far as the east is from the west,
                so far he removes our transgressions from us.
        [13] As a father has compassion for his children,
                so the LORD has compassion for those who fear him.
        [14] For he knows how we were made;
                he remembers that we are dust.

In each of the above cases it would be appropriate to conclude the declaration with a clear statement of forgiveness in the name of Jesus Christ, or the Trinity, for example: 'and so I declare to you, in the name of Jesus Christ (or 'in the name of the Father, Son and Holy Spirit') that your sins are forgiven.'

In terms of the *blessing* at the end of the service, a number of psalm verses are appropriate. These include:

Psalm 29
        [11] May the LORD give strength to his people!
                May the LORD bless his people with peace!

Psalm 67
        [1] May God be gracious to us and bless us
                and make his face to shine upon us.

Psalm 115
        [12] The LORD has been mindful of us;
                he will bless us;
        ...

[13] he will bless those who fear the LORD,
   both small and great.

If we are taking the psalm as another reading it may still be appropriate to sing or chant the psalm. This could be desirable if there are two or three other readings as well. However, as Erik Routley warns, the psalm should be understood primarily as a Bible reading and not as another hymn, regardless of whether it is proclaimed by a reader, a soloist, or a group of singers.[68] The congregation could still respond to the reading through an antiphon or response, which in this case need not be a verse from the psalm but could be a suitable verse from one of the other readings. As Routley notes, this mixing in the sung psalm can set up a helpful theological dialogue between the readings. He states: 'The Psalms serve us best when there is genuine conversation between the choir and the singing congregation.'[69]

These are some of the ways the psalms can be heard within the liturgy other than through preaching. Other ways and examples could be added. Hearing the psalms, whether it is in reading and sermon, or at some other point in the worship of God's people, is consistent with the tradition of the Church. While the psalms are words spoken to God, they, in turn, speak to God's people with the authority of God's word. God has given them in order that they might be both said to God, and heard from God. It is in the saying and the listening that they serve their purpose among the people of faith.

---

[68] Routley, E. (1980), 'The Psalms in Today's Church', *Reformed Liturgy & Music*, Vol. 14, pp. 20-26, esp. p. 21.
[69] *Ibid.*, p. 24.

Chapter 7

Preaching from Individual Psalms

Psalms have a contribution to make to the preaching and proclamation of the Church. I have argued already that the psalms have been and ought to be considered as a possible fourth reading for weekly community worship. I will turn now to look at what a number of psalms could contribute to the proclamation of the Church.

Only a small selection of psalms can be discussed here. About two-thirds of the canonical psalms are used in the Sunday lectionaries. However, any of the psalms in the lectionaries could provide the text for the proclamation of the word. Even psalms outside the lectionaries could offer themselves on occasion as suitable texts for sermons. The psalms below are representative of the whole collection in terms of the theological issues they raise and deal with, as well as in terms of the issues they raise for preaching.

The discussions below are not put forward as either sermons or sermon outlines. Writing a sermon is the task of the preacher in the local congregation or situation. My aim here is to explore the psalms with an eye to preaching from them, to bring out the theological and preaching issues, and to touch on difficulties where they arise. I can only treat a small number of psalms in this context. It is hoped that preachers might be encouraged to explore the psalms both theologically and homiletically. They are worth listening to and proclaiming.

Psalm 8 – Creator, Creation and Humankind

Gazing at the night sky is both an exhilarating and a humbling experience. We become aware of the immensity of the universe within which we live. In recent times astronomers and other scientists have been busy discovering more detail about those stars and galaxies at which we gaze, details that challenge our imaginations in terms of distance and time. We are discovering in a new way that 'the universe is big, really big' to quote the words of Douglas Adams in *The Hitchhikers' Guide to the Galaxy*.[1] While stargazing makes us aware of the enormous size of the universe it also makes us aware of our own small place in the larger scheme of things. The story is often recounted that when the *Apollo 11* spacecraft went to the moon in July, 1969 it left there a disk with messages from the leaders of the nations on earth. The text sent by Pope Paul VI was that of Psalm

---

[1] Adams, D. (1989), *The Hitchhiker's Guide to the Galaxy*, Harmony Books, London.

8.[2] The psalm's focus on the heavens, and the dominion of humankind, in spite of their insignificance in the scheme of things, makes it an obvious choice in light of the wonder and celebration of a great achievement in space travel. However, what it has to say about humans in the larger scheme of things also makes it an apt reminder to keep things in this world, and especially the place of humans in it, in perspective.

The psalm poses many questions for the both humans in general and the Christian community in particular. Some are clearly voiced within the psalm: 'what are human beings that you are mindful of them, mortals that you care for them?' Others are implied. At various times in its life the Church has focused on what the psalm has to say about God, or how it is related to Jesus. In recent decades, the psalm's views on humankind or the heavens and earth have been our concern. While issues of theology, anthropology, ecology and Christology each claim our attention from time to time as we continue to read, this psalm, by its very nature and place within Scripture, insists that we cannot isolate any of these matters. It proclaims that the relationship between these issues is as important as the individual issues themselves. Perhaps that is the important thing to hear from Psalm 8 at the start of the twenty-first century. Perhaps that is what we ourselves should hear from this text.

The many questions posed by the psalm might suggest that the preacher's task is to attempt to answer them. This, however, would ignore the genre of the psalm, and the especially the nature of the question that lies at the centre of the psalm. As a hymn the psalm also invites praise and wonder and a sermon on the psalm should seek to foster those very things as much as, or even more than, explore its questions. Reason is not paramount in this psalm and addressing the question facing the psalmist does not result in logical deduction and a reasoned conclusion. It results in proclamation, praise and wonder. A sermon on such a psalm should 'go and do likewise'. But also a sermon on Psalm 8 should take seriously the fact that many interrelated questions are raised by the psalm. To focus on the view of humankind portrayed in the psalm without some acknowledgement of the theological, Christological, or ecological issues raised at the same time would be simply to repeat the 'sins' of some who have preached on the psalm before us.

We are first confronted by the 'shape' of Psalm 8, by its *inclusio* - the occurrence of the same verse ('O LORD, our Sovereign, how majestic is your name in all the earth!' [vv. 1a, 9]) at the beginning and end of the psalm, - and by its general 'hourglass' shape. There is also a clear sense that this is a psalm of praise, a hymn, with every single verse addressed to God. The *inclusio* gives a sense of completeness to the psalm. All things about which this psalm speaks, or which are implied by the psalm, are enclosed within the sovereignty of YHWH in all the earth. This envelops all – in heaven and on earth. God's sovereignty is the beginning and end of all things. The 'middle' of the psalm then deals with the question of how this is proclaimed or known in the earth, and the one with whom the middle of the psalm is most concerned, namely humankind, is the same one

---

[2] Quoted in Limburg, J. (2000), *Psalms*, Westminster John Knox, Louisville, p. 24.

who in the person of the psalmist declares YHWH as 'our sovereign' at the beginning and end of the psalm.

The body of the psalm begins with reference to the heavens (v. 1b). This might seem out of place having just declared the majesty of YHWH's name in all the earth (v. 1a), but not so in the scheme of the whole. There is a movement within the body of the psalm from the heavens down to the earth. This immediately introduces us to a major difficulty with the psalm. It is not clear to scholars how to translate v. 1b, whether YHWH's glory is 'set', 'chanted', 'sung', 'worshipped' etc.,[3] nor how v. 1b is related to v. 2. But, whatever solution we opt for, it is clear that what happens to YHWH's glory happens 'above the heavens', in the farthest reaches above the skies.

The first part of the movement in the psalm then takes place quickly (vv. 3-4) as the psalmist's gaze shifts easily from the heights of the heavens, and the work of YHWH's fingers there, to the realms of human life. It then passes on from the human sphere (v. 5) to the air, the sea and the uttermost paths of the sea (vv. 6-8), corresponding in this last movement to the beginnings of the psalm with its mention of the farthest reaches above the skies. The statement on the humans in vv. 4-5 is at the centre of the psalm, but we move into that from the expanse of the heavens, and out from it into the expanse of the earth, thus giving the 'hourglass' shape to this hymn. All of this interconnectedness and movement, in both the heavens and the earth, and from heavens to earth, is enveloped by the sovereignty of YHWH. In fact, it comprises both the field in which the majestic name of YHWH is made known, and the means by which this is accomplished.

Verse 2 has always presented problems for interpreters. One problem is its relation to v. 1b, as noted above. Another concerns what the words in v. 2 refer to in their present context. One way interpreters have understood them is as a statement that even the utterances of the weakest of humans praise God and somehow become a stronghold against the Lord's enemies. This interpretation is as old as the New Testament itself where we note Jesus' quotation of v. 2 in Matt 21:16, and the possible influence Ps 8:2 has had on I Corinthians 1 and 2. Alternatively, it has been suggested that v. 2 is an allusion to an ancient myth about the children of the god El.[4] In either case, the enemies, whoever and wherever they are, are conquered or overcome.

In vv. 3-4 the psalmist's attention moves from the wonders of God's handiwork in the heavenly spheres to the insignificance of the human being in the

---

[3] See the various English versions and commentaries for the options. A majority of scholars would take v. 1b as an independent statement, with no connection to v. 2. Some, however, see it as the context of or related to v. 2. For example, in the former case the NRSV reads: 'You have set your glory above the heavens. Out of the mouths of babes and infants you have founded a bulwark because of your foes, to silence the enemy and the avenger.' And in the latter case the REB reads: 'Your majesty is praised as high as the heavens, from the mouths of babes and infants at the breast. You have established a bulwark against your adversaries to restrain the enemy and the avenger.'

[4] Smith, M. (1997), 'Psalm 8:2b-3: New Proposals for Old Problems', *CBQ*, Vol. 59, pp. 637-641.

grand scale of things. But it is not so much the insignificance of humans that catches the psalmist's attention as the interest that God, who has established all the heavenly wonders, shows in humans. The psalmist makes a quick change of image, from the grandeur of the heavenly spheres to the relative smallness of the human frame, at the same time as he/she shifts from a statement to a question. As readers our thoughts subsequently slow down and we too find ourselves pondering the psalmist's question. Our own thoughts of insignificance when we have gazed at the heavens might even come to mind. The following verse (v. 5) keeps our minds working at a slower pace, but at a deeper level. The psalmist moves back to making a statement, but one which stands in stark contrast to the question in v. 4. Humans are a 'little lower' than God (or gods) and crowned with 'glory and honour'.

The words used to describe humans in vv. 5-6 are important. Even as the psalmist attributes a certain 'insignificance' to humans in the scale of things in v. 4, the language in vv. 5-6 elevates them to great heights. Within the Book of Psalms the 'glory (*kabod*) and honour (*hadar*)' with which humans are crowned in Psalm 8 are attributes usually associated with God (e.g. Pss 19:1; 29:1-2, 9; 96:3-6; 104:1, 31; 145:5,11,12 etc.). While the same language is used occasionally of humans (Pss 16:9 [where *kabod* is translated as 'my soul']; 45:13; and 49:16, 17 [trans. 'wealth']; and 84:11 [trans. 'honour']), it is also used for the king (Pss 21:5)

The reference to 'crowning' humans with glory and honour in v. 5 introduces the additional royal language of v. 6. Again this language, especially that of giving humans 'dominion', is used elsewhere in relation to both God and human monarchs (cf. Pss 22:28; 72:18; and 145:3). This echoes the royal language used of God in vv. 1 and 9 and ties in with the royal associations with the theme of creation in vv. 1-3. The work of God's hands in v. 6 calls to mind the 'work of God's fingers' in v. 3. The remainder of the body of the psalm (vv. 7-8) lists the creatures under human dominion - domestic and wild animals, birds of the air, fish and the creatures of the deep. The list recalls the Genesis 1 creation account, and takes us out from the human sphere to the uttermost parts of the sea. The two movements from the expanse of the heavens down to the humans, and then out from the humans to the expanse of the earth, correspond to each other with their fulcrum in the statement on humans in vv. 4-5. The wonder of the heavens brings to mind the insignificance of the humans. On the other hand, the fact that they have been crowned with almost the status of their creator ('a little lower than God'), and have been granted dominion, sets humans in a place above all other creatures. The symbols of God's dominion in creation may belittle humans in the span of all things, but the divine gift of dominion raises those same insignificant creatures to new heights.

There is a natural tendency to read this statement from an anthropocentric perspective. But as we have seen in relation to vv. 1 and 9, statements about humans need to be seen first and foremost in relation to God. We should note here, too, that the vision of the cosmos gives rise to an awareness of the insignificance of humans, which is not itself the focus. Rather, it is God's concern for humans. The wonder that the psalmist experiences is not in humans themselves as much as in God's grace toward them. In fact, the psalm states clearly that there is no wonder in human beings themselves. This sense is picked up by the psalmist in Ps 144:3, where he/she quotes Ps 8:4, and wonders at God's attention to such an insignificant creature with so fleeting an existence. On the other hand, the writer of Job quotes Ps 8:4 only to enter into a savage parody of the psalm. This close scrutiny by God of such a small and frail creature as a human can become oppressive, even to the point where the human feels trapped and suffers greatly (Job 7:17-21; cf. also Job 15:14). At this point the writer of Job is acutely aware of the question of human sin (Job 7:20-21), and that adds to the feeling of oppression under God's close scrutiny. On the other hand, the psalmist is also aware of human sin (e.g. Ps 51:3-5). While human sin cannot be forgotten, neither can the role granted to humankind in the created order.[5]

We could characterize the sentiment of Ps 8:4 by saying that in regard to humans and their place in creation, 'size doesn't matter'. But that is only part of the story. The psalm also wants to talk about the things that do matter in respect to humans and the world they inhabit. It is about the balance between the significance and insignificance of humankind.[6] We have already noted that while there is movement from the expanse of the heavens to the earth and then out again, there is also a good deal of cross-referencing within the movement. We are not dealing with a simple hierarchy, moving from greater significance and power to less, but rather with an intricate and interrelated whole. We noted above the use of royal language for both God and humans, and the reference to the work of God's hand/fingers in the two halves of the psalm. In addition, the 'all things' which are put under human feet in v. 6 recalls the 'all the earth' within which God's name is majestic in vv. 1 and 9. With the *inclusio* in vv. 1 and 9 also in mind we can say that the sovereignty of God, which encompasses all, is expressed in the place of humans in creation, or finds its expression in them. However, part of the irony of this is that the insignificance of humans in the grand scheme of the heavens and earth, would not suggest that God give any attention to them. In other words, the attention of God is unmerited on the part of humans. It stems from God, and seems to be at the behest of God. To underline this, the only verb the psalmist has associated with human action is 'looking' in v. 3. The ultimate focus of the psalm remains on God. In this psalm neither nature nor humans, even with their exalted state, is to be elevated to the position of God. Even the most exalted creature is still 'a little lower than God'.

Of course, if the sovereignty of God finds expression in the action of humans it implies that the power vested in them is potentially very great. Humans rule over the 'work of God's hands', that is over all God has established (v. 4). But we do not require the psalmist to tell us that. We can see it clearly for ourselves as we contemplate the height and size of our cities, the expanse of farmlands, our ability to harness tremendous power in rocket or bomb, as well as a growing ability to manipulate the biological building blocks of life. The psalmist does not need to tell us what we can easily observe. However, while the psalmist states the obvious,

---

[5] Cf. Kraus, *Psalms 1-59*, p. 185.

[6] Mays, J.L. (1994), 'What is a Human Being? Reflections on Psalm 8', *Theology Today*, Vol. 50, pp. 511-520, esp. 514.

that humans in spite of their insignificance possess great power, he/she also says that it is God who has given humans this power: 'You have given them dominion over the works of your hands; you have put all things under their feet'. God has granted this position to humans and that over which they have dominion is God's own work. Thus the question of the responsible use of power is raised.

One way this is addressed is in terms of the shape of the whole psalm. It reminds us that over and above all things in creation is the sovereignty of God. That is the foundation of everything. All the heavens and creatures on earth are 'the work of God's fingers/hands'. Human dominion over other creatures is part of the glory and honour granted to humans by God, but as such it does not stand outside of the domain of God's own sovereignty, nor is it an end in itself. All relationships within the created order as well as responsibility for various parts of it are also part of the created order. They are as much a part of the whole as are the physical entities in the heavens and earth. The position of humans within the cosmos, as well as their responsibility for all else, stems from and finds its end in the sovereignty of God over all. To use the language of the *inclusio*, human dominion serves to proclaim God's majestic name in all the earth. That is the benchmark against which all human action within the world should be measured.

Another aspect of this is found in vv. 7-8. Human dominion is extended to what is, physically speaking, beyond human control. Among the things put under their feet are 'the beasts of the field, the birds of the air, and the fish of the sea, whatever passes along the paths of the seas'. While modern technology and the sheer impact of the human presence in the world means that a lot of these things are now under human power or influence, in the mind of the ancient Israelite they were largely beyond the realm of human influence. Moreover, the reference to 'whatever passes along the paths of the seas' could be an allusion to 'the great sea monsters' of Gen 1:21 or Leviathan of Ps 104:26 etc. Thus in the psalm, human dominion is not simply defined by the limits of human action and control, nor by the possibilities of the human imagination, nor even by what is deemed tamable and safe. Human dominion relates more to how things are encountered in their natural state, than to whether and how they can be exploited by humans. It is as much a statement about human standing in the created order as about human control and responsibility. The language used about humans in vv. 5-6 is royal, as I have mentioned, and suggests that humans themselves occupy a position of sovereignty within creation, albeit in the service of the overall sovereignty of God. A similar thing could be said about humankind in Gen 1:26-28. Power and authority are not just the prerogative of the king (cf. Psalm 72) in whom power is publicly acknowledged, although the psalmist does not deny the place of positions of authority.[7] Nevertheless, in Psalm 8 there is a devolution of the power, authority and majesty of kingship over all humankind. The psalm is speaking of both the honorific position of humans in creation and their responsibility within it. That casts a slightly different light on the way humans are considered in the psalm. We are not simply talking about the relation of humans in general to nature, and about

---

[7] Note the many royal psalms within the canonical collection (e.g. Pss 21; 72; 89; 132 etc.) and the association of the psalms with David, the archetypal king.

the exercise of the human intellect and power in controlling or using the non-human world. On the one hand, human dominion is exercised in valuing the integrity of all within the created order as we encounter it, and not just as we would reshape it. On the other hand, human dominion also concerns the relationships between humans if all humans are considered 'royal'. Human dominion involves a respect for the value of all humankind within the created order. Thus, the psalmist not only rejects the notion of human exploitation of the created order, he/she also promotes the 'equality' of all humans in relation to it. And both sets of relationships have their reason for being focused in the sovereignty of God over all.

The use of Ps 8:4-6 in the New Testament is also a significant issue when preaching on the psalm. The psalm takes on a new meaning in the eyes of the writers of 1 Cor 15:27; Eph 1:22; and Heb 2:6-8. In each case the psalm is interpreted in terms of the life, death and work of Jesus. What was said to be the case for humankind in general in the psalm is made specific in the case of Jesus. Moreover, in Jesus who is seen as representative of humankind, the words of the psalm find their fulfilment, especially those relating the subjection of all things to him. This New Testament reading of the psalm depends on an ambiguity in the Hebrew of the Psalm. The Hebrew preposition used in the phrase translated 'a little lower than God' can be used of degree, as implied in this NRSV translation, or of time, i.e. 'for a little while'. The ancient Greek translators of the Old Testament understood it in this second, temporal, way. The writers of the New Testament, using that Greek translation (the Septuagint, LXX) have understood the phrase in temporal terms and applied it to Jesus in his incarnation. Hence, we have the quotation as found in Heb 2:7: 'You have made them *for a little while* lower than the angels'.[8] The fact that Jesus' incarnation involves his death, takes up the point made by the writer of Job 7:17-21 who sees Ps 8:4 involving human suffering. As Brevard Childs notes in his treatment of the psalm, the New Testament use of it means that we can no longer speak of the human relationship with God and the whole created order, a focus of the psalm, without speaking of it in Christological terms. On the other hand he also says that we cannot just see this psalm in its Christological interpretation. What is said about Jesus, on the basis of the psalm, also has anthropological, theological (in the strict sense of 'a word about God'), and creation dimensions.[9]

In terms of Psalm 8 and ecological issues, a similar intertwining of matters can be seen. James Limburg has remarked in relation to the psalm and matters of ecology: 'This psalm assumes that the God-praising community and the earth-caring community are one.'[10] In answer to the question in the title of his essay,

---

[8] Note also that the word *elohim*, 'God' can also mean 'gods' and has been taken in the LXX to refer to the heavenly beings attendant on God, often referred to in post-Old Testament times as 'angels'.

[9] Childs, B.S. (1970), *Biblical Theology in Crisis*, Westminster, Philadelphia, pp. 151-163, esp. pp. 157-163.

[10] Limburg, J. (1992), 'Who Cares for the Earth? Psalm Eight and the Environment', in A.J. Hultgren et al., (eds), Word & World 1, *All Things New: Essays in Honor of Roy A. Harrisville*, Luther Northwestern Theological Seminary, St. Paul, pp. 43-53, esp. p. 51.

'Who cares for the Earth?' he answers 'God does' and so ought God's people. While human dominion over all creation has been misunderstood and misappropriated, both in the Psalm and in Genesis 1, it is not the point of view expressed in the psalm that lies at the heart of the present ecological crises.[11] It is rather that humankind have seen the statements about human dominion over creation in the psalm in isolation from the theological and creation statements contained therein, and even from the Christological statements related to the psalm by the New Testament writers. In the task of preaching from the psalm, it is not so much the place of humankind vis-à-vis creation that is of primary concern, as the place of humankind vis-à-vis God. Humankind's ability to live in awe and praise of God is what the psalm questions. How humankind then shapes its 'dominion' over creation flows from that. It is not the psalm that stands behind our ecological crises, but our lack of understanding of the perspective put forward by the psalm.[12]

Psalm 73 – God and Injustice in the World

Psalm 73 does not appear in any of the major lectionaries for Sunday worship in the churches. Does that mean we need not think about it in relation to preaching? There are several reasons for answering 'no' to that question. First, it raises the further question of how strict our adherence to the lectionary readings needs to be and this is a question that the preacher ought to consider. We might answer it differently depending on our tradition. There are some who would adhere quite closely to the lectionary, only diverging if the occasion made it absolutely necessary. Others feel a greater sense of freedom with the lectionary readings. There is certainly much to be gained when the preaching Sunday by Sunday is governed by a lectionary. A sense of continuity is achieved at the same time as the congregation is exposed to the diversity of scripture. It provides a handy discipline for the preacher who is encouraged to consider a variety of texts and issues. On the other hand, no lectionary, regardless of our commitment to following it, should be used uncritically.

Some preachers may occasionally feel justified in adjusting the reading set, either for reasons relating to the reading itself or because of the occasion or the development of the sermon. Some may even want to change the passage entirely. If one is to preach on Psalm 73, then it clearly has to be substituted for another Psalm or Old Testament reading. In general, a case could be made for this on a few

---

[11] Although on this point cf. the views of Hunter, A.G. (1999), *Psalms*, Routledge, London, pp. 124-128; and Carley, K. (2000), 'Psalm 8: An Apology for Domination', in N.C. Habel (ed.), *Readings from the Perspective of Earth*, The Earth Bible 1, SAP, Sheffield, pp. 111-124. The latter outlines what he sees as the less sanguine features of the psalm, especially the focus on and exercise of God's power over the earth (p. 115). However, I would ask whether the issue for most people today in terms of ecojustice is not so much the proclaiming of the power of God over all creation, as the denial of it.

[12] See Nordin, J. (1993), 'Preaching Psalms', *Currents in Theology and Mission*, Vol. 20, pp. 259-264; esp. p. 260; and Mays, 'What is a Human Being?' pp. 517-520.

Sundays. While Psalm 73 does not appear in the lectionaries, a portion of Psalm 37, a psalm of similar genre and interests, is set in a few of the lectionaries on one or two occasions.[13] Psalm 73 offers a strong critique of the view put forward in the body of Psalm 37, addressing what can be seen as the naïveté of Psalm 37, and so it would not be inappropriate to use Psalm 73 to address matters of theodicy, the justice of God in the face of evil or injustice in the world. Alternatively, the issue of theodicy is raised specifically within the Book of Job. To employ Psalm 73 as the psalm on days when readings from Job are included would also be appropriate.

A second reason for including Psalm 73 at an appropriate point in the lectionary is that it provides a fine example of a type of psalm not frequently encountered in Sunday readings. Scholars have vigorously debated the specific genre of Psalm 73, but there is no denying that wisdom forms and language have at least influenced it. It is a marvellous example of a writer pondering one of the basic statements of faith and wrestling with it in light of the so-called realities of life, and this is done in the context of prayer. It is also an excellent reminder that many psalms and other biblical texts need to be read in their entirety if we are to hear what they have to say. So while the writers of the Sunday lectionaries have not found a place for Psalm 73, the preacher may feel inclined to let it be heard on occasion. In any event, those who pray with the psalms on a regular basis are bound to encounter it from time to time and would benefit from giving some closer attention to this masterpiece of theological reasoning.

A number of points about preaching from the psalms are raised when we read Psalm 73. I will deal with these after we have delved into the psalm itself. The psalmist wrestles with the seeming contradiction between the promise of God being good to the upright and the suffering of the innocent faithful. We confront this same problem daily in our newspapers or on the nightly TV news. It is the problem at the heart of the Book of Job. But the psalmist has a particular interest in the matter. He/she is not so much concerned with why a good God allows suffering in the world, or whether suffering is indicative of a sinful life, or even with the experience of the sufferer. The psalmist uses the issue of suffering and the injustice associated with it as a way of seeking greater understanding of the nature of our communion with God. The innocent suffering in the world and the seeming ease of the wicked are matters which concern the faith of the psalmist and which need investigation. Other psalms also tackle these matters but do so in less satisfying ways. Psalm 1 ends with the statement (v. 6):

> for the LORD watches over the way of the righteous,
> but the way of the wicked will perish.

---

[13] In the *Revised Common Lectionary* Ps 37:1-11 and 39-40 are set for Epiphany 7. In the lectionary for the US Episcopal Church and Lutheran Churches, Ps 37:1-18 or 3-10 is set for the Sunday Proper 22/Ordinary 27 in Year C, while in the Episcopal Church Ps 37:1-18 or 1-6 is set for Epiphany 4.

There is no development of how the Lord watches over the way of the righteous, nor how the wicked perish. Psalm 37, as I alluded to above, offers some rather naïve statements on these matters, for example:

> [25] I have been young, and now am old,
>   yet I have not seen the righteous forsaken
>   or their children begging bread.
> [26] They are ever giving liberally and lending,
>   and their children become a blessing.

Neither of these statements, if taken literally, holds up to any scrutiny. The psalm goes on to speak in vv. 27-28, as did Ps 1:6, in very general terms of the perishing of the wicked and the blessing of the righteous. It presumes a crude mechanical retribution correcting the present injustice of the prosperity of the wicked and the suffering of the righteous. These are but temporary situations. Psalm 49 likewise holds a cynical attitude to wealth and prosperity. It is as fleeting as this earthly life: 'for when (the rich) die they will carry nothing away; their wealth will not go down after them' (v. 17). The psalmist hopes in some future deliverance by the Lord (v. 15).

The psalm begins with what in ancient Israel would have been a widely held view: 'Truly God is good to the upright, to those who are pure in heart' (v. 1).[14] This verse is similar in theme to Psalm 1:6 noted above.[15] It presumes a view of the world with a well-defined order and moral structure. But, just as with Psalm 1, the statement in Ps 73:1 only raises new questions. Who are the upright and the pure in heart? We could respond that the upright are those to whom God is good but then we start to go in circles. What is God's goodness? The questions are left hanging for the moment, although Martin Buber's observation that those who are 'pure in heart' are not to be equated too easily with those to whom God is good already points toward the solution of the psalmist's dilemma. This is the case even though the parallelism in v. 1 might suggest they are equivalent.[16]

The psalmist says in v. 2 that this beginning statement had become a point of danger to him/her. The psalmist had almost stumbled. The reason for this unsteadiness is only revealed in v. 3 where the psalmist sees the prosperity of the arrogant and wicked. The Hebrew word translated 'prosperity' in the NRSV is the word *shalom*. The wicked are not only well off, but they lead peaceful lives (vv. 4-12). Verse 4 can be translated 'For they have no pains at their death; their bodies

---

[14] There is a textual problem with this verse. The Hebrew Masoretic Text reads 'Truly God is good to Israel, to those who are pure in heart'. This is translated in most standard English Bibles. The emendation of 'Israel' to 'upright', which involves relatively few changes, is argued by some to give a better parallel set of lines in the verse. The emendation does not affect the overall interpretation of the psalm.

[15] Cf. also Deut 7:12-15; or from the reverse perspective cf. Job 4:7-9; 8:20-22; and 11:13-20.

[16] Buber, M. (1983), 'The Heart Determines: Psalm 73', in J.L. Crenshaw (ed.), *Theodicy in the Old Testament*, Fortress, Philadelphia, pp. 109-119, esp. pp. 109-110.

are healthy'[17], and while v. 7 may sound unattractive to us ('Their eyes swell out with fatness; their hearts overflow with follies') in Israel's world of lean diets and low consumption it was a picture of material well-being (cf. Ps 104:15). However, the psalmist lets us know that such prosperity is the result of ill-gotten gains. The ideal picture of verse 7 is surrounded in vv. 6 and 8 by words like pride, violence, malice, and oppression. Thus, for the psalmist, there is conflict between the apparent *shalom* of the wicked and the way they conduct their lives.[18]

If the arrogant and wicked seem to share in God's goodness, i.e. if all seems well for them, then what does that say for the one who has endeavoured to be 'upright' or 'pure in heart' and yet has not experienced that 'goodness'? The assumption could be made from v. 1 that there is a simple relationship between God's goodness and prosperity and peace in life. But to assume this is to enter those same slippery places the psalmist encountered. The psalmist saw the prosperity of the wicked and was jealous. How then is God's goodness to be understood, if it is not seen in the well-being of God's faithful people?

The first section of the psalm ends with the words of the wicked: 'How can God know?' The prosperity of the wicked can lead them to a point where they not only do not give thanks to God for their situation, but they do not even see God as the source of their blessing. God is superfluous to them.[19]

The further we delve into Psalm 73 the more complex matters become. The psalmist had almost stumbled over v. 1. There is the further danger that he/she can also begin to believe what the wicked say. If God is good to the upright but the wicked seem to participate in God's goodness in terms of prosperity then does God really know or care if people are upright or not? There is a logic to the statement by the wicked, albeit perverse. The next section of the psalm (vv. 13-17) begins at v. 13 with the Hebrew word *'ak* 'surely'. That is also how v. 1 began. In this section the psalmist ponders his or her own faith. According to Psalms 1 and 37 the righteous are said to be in the Lord's care. But here the psalmist asks whether the faithfulness he/she has shown has been in vain (vv. 13-14):

> All in vain I have kept my heart clean
> and washed my hands in innocence.
> For all day long I have been plagued,
> and am punished every morning.

In vv. 15-16 the psalmist's dilemma seems two-sided. On the one hand he/she says that if they keep talking on in this way then they will betray the

---

[17] Cf. Tate, M. (1990), *Psalms 51-100*, Word Books, Waco, p. 227.

[18] Here the psalmist echoes the thoughts of Jer 12:1, 'Why does the way of the wicked prosper?'

[19] The question which the wicked ask here concerning God, as well as the situation giving rise to it, are similar to that noted in Mal 3:14-15. Cf. also Job 21:7-33. See further Crenshaw, J.L. (1984), 'Standing Near the Flame: Psalm 73', in *A Whirlpool of Torment: Israelite Traditions of God as an Oppressive Presence*, Fortress, Philadelphia, pp. 93-110, esp. pp. 97-103.

faithful. Just how this is meant is not entirely clear. Is the psalmist speaking about repeating v. 1 or is it a reference to the psalmist's questioning? On the other hand the psalmist cannot resolve the dilemma he/she perceives (v. 16). They struggle with the conflict between the circumstances in which they find themselves and the faith statement of the past represented by v. 1. However, it is important to note that it is precisely at this point, from v. 15 on, that the psalmist starts to address God directly. In the psalmist's own words the close relationship with God envisaged at the end of the psalm is modelled. The solution to the psalmist's problem, and the direction in which that solution is to be found, are embodied in the shift of the psalmist's speech.

The resolution of the conflict is seen in v. 17.[20] It is perceived when the psalmist enters the sanctuary of God. The new insight the psalmist has is described in the next section of the psalm. Just how it is gained is left unexplained. What does the psalmist see in the sanctuary? We will explore the nature of this experience later. For now, it is sufficient to note that something led the psalmist to a new understanding of his/her faith and God's ways.

Verse 18 begins the final section of the psalm. It too starts with the Hebrew word *'ak* 'surely' and, therefore, reminds us of v. 1 and the questions of who are the upright and how is God good to them? However, while to this point the psalmist has been addressing others or pondering his/her own thoughts, now he/she turns to address God. The psalmist realizes that his/her perception has been wrong in the past. He/she now has a new understanding of the old statement in v. 1. The imagery of the psalm has also been reversed. The psalmist has not really been the one in slippery places (v. 2), but rather the wicked have been (v. 18).

In vv. 21-26 the psalmist again refers to their bitter struggle and anger toward God but this time the struggle is resolved. The solution to his/her dilemma lies, according to vv. 23-26, in an awareness of the closeness of the faithful to the Lord even in difficult situations. A new realisation is evident and a new position on statement in v. 1 is found. It is not that the statement is incorrect, but rather a 'new' understanding of it has been perceived. Ps 73:1 is understood in the light of vv. 23-26. In contrast to the seeming *shalom* of the wicked, the psalmist realizes that all that one can indeed 'have' or 'desire' in heaven or on earth is the nearness of the Lord (vv. 25-26). That is really *shalom*. A clue to this within the text is found at the start of v. 23. It begins with the Hebrew word *we'ani* 'but as for me', which is the same word as at the start of v. 2. The point of realisation of the truth of the matter for the psalmist is marked in the text in the same way as the point of danger. The point of danger has been overturned and replaced by the new realisation.

Finally, in vv. 27-28 the psalmist's solution is stated clearly. The end of the psalm returns to the theme of v. 1: 'Surely God is good to the upright, the pure in heart'. The psalmist explains precisely what the nature of God's goodness to the upright is. Those far from God will indeed perish, but what is good for the psalmist

---

[20] Cf. McCann J. C. (1987), 'Psalm 73: A Microcosm of Old Testament Theology', in K. G. Hoglund et al., (eds), *The Listening Heart: Essays in Wisdom and the Psalms in Honor of Roland E. Murphy, O. Carm.*, JSOT, Sheffield, pp. 247-258, esp. p. 250, who sees the whole of the section vv. 13-17 as the 'turning point' of the psalm, especially v. 15.

is to be near the Lord. The goodness that God gives is his very nearness, and the upright are those who are near the Lord. Those who are secure, well off, yet who are proud, scoffers, arrogant etc., are in fact at some distance from God. The psalmist reinterprets v. 1 in terms of nearness to God, rather than in terms of material or physical well-being. To underline the point the psalmist begins v. 28, the final verse, with the same word which began vv. 2 and 23, namely *we'ani* 'but as for me'. The new realisation is made explicit at the end of the psalm.

In Psalm 73 the psalmist struggles with questions to do with faith in the real world. What is the *shalom* or peace which God promises those who are faithful to him? How do we assess the obvious well-being of some who are proud, violent, malicious, or oppressive? Where is the justice in that when others who are faithful to God suffer and struggle in life? These questions, which are no less our questions than the psalmist's, point to a contradiction between what the psalmist has heard is the goodness of God, and what he/she actually sees to be the case in the world around them. Those who prosper, who appear to have God's *shalom*, are not necessarily the righteous. So is prosperity a sign of God's goodness? We have heard the psalmist's solution to this contradiction, but it is just as important to note the context in which the psalmist worked out the problem. Let us go back to the psalmist's experience in the sanctuary in v. 17.

The solution to the contradiction confronting the psalmist is perceived in the sanctuary, in the place where one comes near to God. While the psalmist's experience is not entirely clear we can still say some things about it. One problem is that the Hebrew word for 'sanctuary' in v. 17 is plural and not singular as the NRSV translation and others would suggest. If we take the plural 'sanctuaries' literally, it might suggest that the psalm has been written after the destruction of the old sanctuaries of God in the northern kingdom (i.e. after 722 BCE), and the writer has toured these destroyed sites and concluded that in the end those unfaithful to God will be destroyed. But this confines the meaning of the psalm to some supposed historical situation, or particular locations. We do not have to take the psalm literally at this point. At this point Buber does not see a reference to the temple or even multiple sanctuaries at all, but understands v. 17 as speaking about the 'sphere of God's holiness, the holy mysteries of God'.[21] It is not so much the specific location of the perception that is important, as the fact that it is a 'place' where God is encountered. Some further things can be said about this 'place'.

First, the solution, which the psalmist perceives in the sanctuary, does not involve an escape from reality. That is, when the psalmist struggles with the contradiction in faith caused by the prosperity of the wicked and the suffering of the faithful, he/she does not simply retreat from the world to take refuge in the sanctuary where everything *seems* to be in order once again. Rather the psalmist gains another perspective on the truth of the situation perceived outside the sanctuary.

The psalmist is aware that there is something deceptive about the usual interpretation of the statement: 'Surely God is good to the upright, the pure in heart'. That much is evident when he/she sees the wicked prospering and the

---

[21] Buber, 'The Heart Determines', p. 113.

innocent faithful suffering. The question is where does the deception lie? If the wicked prosper (v.1) is the solution to question the God who is believed to make the promise? This is the conclusion to which the prosperous are themselves led in v. 11: 'How does God know? Is there awareness in Elyon?' But v. 17 suggests that this solution is flawed and that the psalmist realizes this flaw.

What is to be questioned by the contradiction to faith found in the context of the world is not the God who stands behind the statement but rather the understanding that interprets God's goodness simply in terms of material well-being in the present context. In other words, it may not be God, and God's goodness, which are deceptive in the light of circumstances, but the very trust that in the circumstances themselves the full truth of the situation is revealed. The deception in the usual understanding of v. 1 is not centred in faith itself but is, in fact, centred in the interpretation of the prosperous life. A shallow and false sense of *shalom* sees God being good and near when circumstances are comfortable. The psalmist asserts that there is a reality in relation to faith that goes beyond any superficial association of circumstance with faithfulness. There is truth to be seen in the sanctuary that questions the so-called 'reality' of the world outside. Not all truth is to be gleaned from our experience of the world.

But the psalmist discovers not only the deception in the usual understanding of the statement in v. 1 but also the truth that is there. In the end the psalmist wants to say once again that God is good to the upright. Discovering the deception that can be in one understanding of the statement means that a realisation of another truth within it is possible. The goodness of God for the psalmist is, in the end, not to be measured in terms of material well-being, but in terms of being near to God.

However, caution is also needed here lest we step out of one naive way of thinking into another. The psalmist's insight comes in the sanctuary. But while it is not just worldly experience that leads to insight, neither is it just spiritual experience. The psalmist has had to think hard and long about what he/she has observed in the world, and their experience in the sanctuary has come only after that effort. While we cannot be deceived into thinking that all truth is to be perceived from what we experience daily in the world, neither should we be foolish enough to think that our piety is all we need. What is revealed in worship and the hard thinking required to understand what we experience in the world supplement each other. Both have a part to play in our quest for truth and understanding as faith and experience come together.[22]

Having said this, what might we learn about preaching from this psalm? Wisdom teaching and reflection heavily influence psalm 73. It begins with a traditional declaration and then proceeds by means of personal observation, reflection, experience of the sanctuary, and prayer to a new understanding of faith. This psalm and other wisdom psalms model for us a way of seeking to understand our faith. It raises the possibility of examining faith at points where it comes in for hard questioning, by stating the accepted declarations of faith and then testing them out against both experience in the world and experience in the sanctuary. This could be a constructive exercise, and might even be reflected in the very

---

[22] Cf. Tate, *Psalms 51-100*, p. 238.

construction of the sermon. Sermons ought not always to be neat proclamations of the conclusions the preacher has reached privately in their study. They can also be exploratory and model the processes of reflection on the faith. And part of those processes is embracing both the doubts and questions raised in relation to faith through both our experience in the world and in the sanctuary. This is 'theological reflection' in the best sense: the confluence of experience and theological tradition. In the end both have their part to play. Experience leads to a refinement of theological expression and theological tradition provides the framework within which experience is examined.

But not only does Psalm 73 provide us with a good model of theological reflection, it models the bringing together of a respect for the traditional statements of the faith *and* an embracing of the harsh realities of the world, especially experiences of pain and suffering.[23] There is no shying away from that meeting. In fact, it is at that meeting place that faith can be deepened and new understandings of God's ways in the world emerges. And yet in the enclaves of Christianity in the western world, there are many subtle and not so subtle ways in which the comfortable and the powerful, and often those in government, deny pain and suffering both at home and abroad. Such denial is often in terms of necessary budget restrictions, or, especially in the early twenty-first century, a real fear of international terrorism. But the dividing line between any real concern or fear, and a selfish desire to preserve our own comfort or a lack of welcome for genuine refugees can easily become blurred.[24] Governments, even in my own country, have increasingly exploited such fears for political and social ends, with no little desire to keep the 'godless' at a distance. But who are the godless in these contexts? That is precisely the issue the psalmist addresses.

The subject matter of the psalm is not divorced from the message of the Gospel. The tension that can arise between traditional statements of faith and the experience of the world, especially of suffering, is one that Jesus faced constantly. Note especially the debates over what is lawful on the Sabbath in the Gospels (Matt 12:1-14//Mark 2:23-3:6//Luke 6:1-11; also Luke 1310-17; 14:1-6; John 5:1-16; 9) and even over who is welcome to receive the blessings of the gospel (Mark 7:24-30). Jesus himself embodies both the streams of tradition (see Luke 24:44 etc.) and the pain of the world in the cross.

Psalm 89 – Waiting for God's Faithfulness

Psalm 89 presents two issues in relation to preaching. The first has to do with genre. It is often classified as a Royal Psalm, that is, one that has to do specifically with the king of Judah and Jerusalem, a member of the Davidic dynasty. In a sense

---

[23] See also McCann, 'Psalm 73', p. 253 and the references to the work of Walter Brueggemann in this regard.

[24] Brueggemann and Miller see Psalm 73 speaking of a choice between responsibility and self-indulgence. See Brueggemann, W. and Miller, P.D. (1996), 'Psalm 73 as a Canonical Marker', *JSOT*, Vol. 72, pp. 45-56.

the problem of how to deal with the genre of a psalm or other reading arises whenever one is preaching. On the other hand, the peculiarities of royal psalms might raise new issues. The second issue has to do with the length of the psalm. It is clearly too long for a reading in worship (as are a number of other psalms) and the lectionary compilers have noted this in selecting only certain verses from the psalm. This raises quite a different set of matters that need to be addressed. I will take these up later.

However, the issue of genre needs some consideration as we begin. Royal Psalms generally focus on some aspect of the king's life or reign. It is often assumed that they are part of a liturgy celebrating an event in the life of the king. Such celebrations might include: enthronement (Pss 2, 21, 72, 101, 110); a royal wedding (Psalm 45); leading the nation in victorious battle (Pss 18, 20); the procession of the ark of the covenant (Psalm 132); or even lamenting some national or royal loss (Ps 144:1-11). These ten psalms were those initially identified by H. Gunkel, a pioneer in form criticism of Psalms.[25] Gunkel initially compared Ps 89:47-52 with this group. More recent scholarship would include the whole of Psalm 89 in this genre, and specifically as a royal lament. We have to deal with it, therefore, at the level of a Royal Psalm and as a lament.

In terms of its 'royal' nature, Psalm 89, like other Royal Psalms, celebrates human kingship as a reflection of divine kingship. This is particularly so in relation to the establishment of peace, power and justice in overtaking the forces of chaos in the world. In that context, the focus of the preacher in dealing with this or other Royal Psalms would be on the principles of leadership within the community and the exercise of that in conjunction with God's sovereignty over creation. The Royal Psalms with their ancient assumptions about kingship and rule might seem foreign to our present political circumstances. The issues of the exercise of justice, the use of power and the promotion of peace are certainly not.[26]

Psalm 89 has at its heart the Lord's promise of eternal faithfulness to the dynasty of David, which ruled over Jerusalem for about four and a quarter centuries. In the introductory section (vv. 1-4) the psalmist proclaims the eternal steadfast love and faithfulness of YHWH. He/she then quotes the promise made by YHWH to the house of David, that his covenant would be with that dynasty forever:

> [2] I declare that your steadfast love is established forever;
>   your faithfulness is as firm as the heavens.
> [3] You said, 'I have made a covenant with my chosen one,

---

[25] Gunkel, *Introduction to Psalms*, pp. 99-120.

[26] There is much more we could say about Royal Psalms, their relation to so-called Enthronement Psalms, which usually have much more to do with the kingship of the Lord than the human king, and the extent of the collection of Royal Psalms. For further thought and a brief history of the discussion see Mowinckel, S. (1962), *The Psalms in Israel's Worship*, 2 vols, Abingdon, Nashville, esp. vol. 1, chs 3 and 5; Eaton, J.H. (1986), *Kingship and the Psalms*, 2nd ed., JSOT, Sheffield, and Croft, S.J.L. (1987), *The Identity of the Individual in the Psalms*, JSOTSup 44, JSOT, Sheffield, esp. ch. 3.

I have sworn to my servant David:
⁴ 'I will establish your descendants forever,
    and build your throne for all generations.'

The remainder of the psalm breaks into 3 sections. Verses 5-18 speak of the sovereignty of the Lord over creation. Verses 19-37 speak about the Lord's ruler in Jerusalem, referred to by the name David, but meaning every king in the line of David. They focus on the importance of the Lord's promise for those monarchs. Finally, in vv. 38-51 there is a lament speaking about how things have gone wrong. Verse 52 is the benediction which concludes the third book within the larger Book of Psalms.

Since there is not the space to discuss the whole psalm in detail, we will focus on a few major points. First, the two sections vv. 5-18 and 19-37 are set up so that there is a point by point correspondence between the description of the Lord's kingship and the description of the promises to David as king. The main correspondences are as follows:

the Lord's hand/arm is strong (v. 13)
    the Lord's hand/arm will be with David and strengthen him (v. 21)

the Lord defeats his mythic enemies [Rahab] (vv. 9-10)
    the Lord promises to defeat David's foes (vv. 22-23)

steadfast love and faithfulness go before the Lord (v. 14)
    they shall be with David (v. 24)

the Lord rules/stills the raging sea (vv. 9-10)
    the Lord will set David's hand on sea/river (v. 25)

the Lord rules in heaven and is great above all around him (vv. 5-7)
    David rules on earth but will be the highest of kings (v. 27)

Israel's horn is exalted by the Lord's favour (v. 17)
    David's horn will be exalted in the Lord's name (v. 24)

The very end of the section on David's kingship, vv. 33-37, recalls the statements of vv. 1-4. There are in both places references to the eternal nature of the steadfast love and faithfulness of the Lord (v. 33; cf. vv. 1-2 where this is strongly emphasized), to the covenant with David's house and the Lord's oath (vv. 34-35 and v. 3), and to the continuation of David's line (v. 36 and v. 4). The references to the sun and moon in v. 37 could also recall the reference to the 'heavens' in v. 2 or v. 5ff.

In short, the psalmist sets up a reciprocal relationship between the Lord and the Davidic house. The promise of an eternal covenant with David is based on the sovereignty of the Lord over creation. In the theology behind this psalm the kingship of the Lord is inextricably bound with the Lord's creation of the cosmos.

The eternal nature of the Davidic throne is, therefore, founded on the eternal nature of creation and its creator. In turn, the Lord's chosen king exercises a rule which is an extension of the Lord's rule. The earthly king's authority is founded in the heavenly king, while the heavenly king's rule is continued and fulfilled in the earthly king's rule.

This reciprocal relationship is anticipated already in vv. 1-4. There the Lord's promise is said to be forever just as the psalmist promised to sing of the Lord's steadfast love forever. Moreover, the reciprocal covenant arrangement with David is permanent, *even if* David's descendants should sin (cf. 2 Sam 7:15-18). Both the Lord and the Davidic king are committed to mutual loyalty come what may.

But when we reach the end of the psalm we become aware that something is radically wrong with this arrangement. The psalm ends in vv. 38-45 with a description the Lord's rejection and spurning of his people. We read in part:

> [38] But now you have spurned and rejected him;
>   you are full of wrath against your anointed.
> [39] You have renounced the covenant with your servant;
>   you have defiled his crown in the dust.
> [40] You have broken through all his walls;
>   you have laid his strongholds in ruins.

We have little indication of context here. It sounds as though the nation could have been defeated in battle (v. 43) and the city could lie in ruins (v. 40). If the latter is indeed the case then the context could be the defeat of Jerusalem and subsequent exile at the hand of the Babylonians in 587 BCE. That is often assumed to be the context. But whatever the situation, contrary to the Lord's promise David's throne has been thrown to ground (v. 44, cf. v. 29), his enemies rejoice (v. 42, cf. vv. 23-23), the Lord has cut short his days (v. 45, cf. v. 29), and he has renounced the covenant (v. 39, cf. v. 34). The psalmist introduces a note of lament into the psalm:

> [46] How long, O LORD? Will you hide yourself forever?
>   How long will your wrath burn like fire?
> [47] Remember how short my time is—
>   for what vanity you have created all mortals!
> [48] Who can live and never see death?
>   Who can escape the power of Sheol?

The question 'how long?', which echoes other laments,[27] cuts to the heart of the issue. The promises of mutual loyalty were supposed to be forever. There is a breakdown in order. The Lord's fidelity is under question, as indeed is his kingship.

The psalmist seems to have a case against the Lord. It is little wonder that in vv. 46-48 a certain cynicism enters the psalmist's language: 'for what vanity

---

[27] Cf. Pss 6:3; 13:1-2; 35:17; 74:10; 79:5 etc.

(uselessness) you have created all mortals!'. This is the point at which the psalm ends. The psalmist does not resolve the question of whether the Lord will indeed fulfil his promise or not, but can only plead with the Lord to remember (v. 50). There is, as in other psalms, a raw confrontation with reality in this prayer, and a bold questioning of the Lord's faithfulness in light of that reality. It is very clear also that the psalmist wants to cling tenaciously to the possibility of the lord's faithfulness. That is the psalmist's only hope.

Finally let us return to a point raised earlier: the place of Psalm 89 in the lectionaries. In the *Revised Common Lectionary* portions of Psalm 89 are set in Year B for Advent 4 and one Sunday after Trinity. The verses set are respectively vv. 1-4, 19-26, and vv. 20-37. They come from the prologue and the section on the Davidic ruler in Jerusalem. In the second portion set the psalm is coupled with the Old Testament reading 2 Sam 7:1-14a. The promise to David and his house is therefore highlighted in both the Old Testament reading and the psalm.

In the selection of Ps 89:1-4, 19-26 for Advent 4, the lectionary writers would have us celebrate in Advent with Psalm 89 the faithfulness of God and unfailing support for his Messiah. However, this creates a problem. The psalmist certainly does speak about these things but would have us deal with much more. What happens when the Lord's promises fail to materialize? The psalmist would actually have us deal with the notion of what J.L. Mays calls a rejected Messiah.[28] He suggests that we would be more faithful to the psalm by reading it in Lent or on Good Friday. He says the scene painted in vv. 38-45 of the Davidic king rejected, with his crown in the dust, scorned, and in the power of his enemies 'has another counterpart in the passion narratives of the Gospels'. Reading the psalm on Maundy Thursday would be a more 'powerful witness that the very cosmic reign of God is involved in what is happening on that day; and it makes it very clear how much the outcome depends on and reveals the faithfulness of God.'[29]

Reading the psalm on that occasion might be appropriate, but the psalm is still appropriate for Advent, and more so if we consider the *whole* psalm. Firstly, it reminds us that what is hoped for in the Messiah, is in fact a thoroughgoing reflection of the work of God in creation. The paralleling of the reign of the Davidic king with that of the Lord underlines God's being and work as the foundation of all that is. Secondly, by considering the end of the psalm we are reminded that the one who comes to us in Advent is never, at least in this life, unambiguously present to us. The lectionary writers would have us proclaim the faithfulness of God and his unfailing support of his Messiah. That is to the good in Advent as we anticipate God's presence with us in Jesus, but it would be wrong to understand Advent too simply in these terms.

The work of the lectionary writers should not lead us into the enchantment of a domesticated reality, in which God comes to us in the form of a romanticized babe in arms, an incarnation of an unassailable Messiah. Psalm 89 paints a strong positive picture of the Davidic king as God's 'co-regent' and recipient of God's promise of eternal faithfulness. But it does not leave us there. The ending spells out

---

[28] Mays, *Psalms*, p. 288.
[29] *Ibid.*

the struggle of living under such divine promises. Should not our Advent hope embrace the jagged edges of God's coming to us, of absence in presence, and of unfulfilled promises as well? Should not our faith be a little disturbed in that season? That is the direction the psalmist would take us in if we take their work seriously and in its fullness. Maybe we should 'stretch' the lectionary reading of the psalm in Advent, not in terms of reading the whole 52 verses, but at least in the sermon by exploring the context in which the reading set is placed. Maybe then we can glimpse a little more clearly the true nature of the Lord's coming to us and his faithfulness.

Psalm 126 – Coming Home in Joy

Psalm 126 is a psalm of many guises. First, it is part of a collection of psalms (Psalms 120-134) known by scholars as the 'Psalms (or songs) of ascents'. Each of the psalms has a superscription 'a song of ascents (or steps)'. Many have tried to identify the reference to the ascents or steps, suggesting that the collection could be a series of songs for the exiles returning from Babylon, or a group of pilgrimage songs, or songs sung on the steps of the temple, or songs for a procession toward the temple.[30] Secondly, Psalm 126 is a communal lament, i.e. a lament sung by the whole community in response to some distress. The end of the psalm could suggest that the community's problem has something to do with crops and harvests. Thirdly, it has another life within modern lectionaries, being used in the *Revised Common Lectionary* in Advent and Lent.[31] I will consider the psalm in relation to preaching in its guises as a community lament and as a psalm of Advent.

Psalm 126 is a song about past joy and future joy.[32] The community remembers past deliverance and the joy associated with that and now petitions the Lord for further deliverance, basing the petition on remembrance of that past experience. The psalm breaks neatly into two parts: vv. 1-3 and vv. 4-6.

Verses 1-3 speak of a past time of restoration for Zion. The repetition of the Hebrew word *'az*, 'then' in v. 2 underlines the point. The opening words of the psalm, 'When the Lord restored the fortunes of Zion' echo those at the start of Psalm 85, another communal lament: 'LORD, you were favorable to your land; you restored the fortunes of Jacob.'(v. 1). The phrase 'restored the fortunes', employs the Hebrew root *šub*, 'to return', not only in the verb translated as 'restored' but also in the noun 'fortunes'. We are, thus, not looking at the remembrance of a time of excessive wealth or privilege. Rather, the psalmist contemplates the return to that which once had been, in other words what was normal for the life and wellbeing of the people. The root *šub* is also frequently found in the prophets with the sense of 'repent' (e.g. Amos 9:14; Joel 3:1; Jer

---

[30] See Crow, L.D. (1996), *The Songs of Ascents (Psalms 120-134): Their Place in Israelite History and Religion*, SBLDS 148, Scholars, Atlanta, pp. 1-27, 159-188 for detailed discussion.

[31] Advent 3, Year B, and Lent 5, Year C.

[32] Mays, *Psalms*, p. 399.

29:14; Zeph 2:7). It is, therefore, not only the language of restoration or return but also of repentance. I will return to the implication of this below. At least in v. 1 (and in v. 4) there is a clear acknowledgment that restoration is always at the initiation of the Lord. It is his 'return' that will make the restoration of his people possible.

Unlike Psalm 85, Psalm 126 has no mention of the people's iniquity or sin, nor is there any mention of the Lord's anger. In Psalm 126 the recollection of past restoration leads straight to remembrance of overwhelming and infectious laughter and joy. Even the nations are said to have recognized the great things the Lord had done (v. 2). However, the verbal connection between restoration and repentance, as well as the similarity and dissimilarity between Psalm 126 and Psalm 85 means that even as we are overtaken by joy in Psalm 126, we do not forget entirely about sin or repentance.

Verses 4-6, the second half of this brief psalm, speak of the future. The verb forms all speak of future action. The psalmist seeks further restoration from the Lord. That too will be filled with joy. Phrases on the 'restoring of fortunes', and 'shouts of joy', which are present in vv. 1-3, are repeated in this second section of the psalm and tie the psalm tightly together. The repetition further underlines the fact that joy in the community is to be seen as the work of the Lord.

In the latter part of the psalm, the language is concise, placing opposites together and linking elements that give a sense of sudden reversal. The poetry develops in such a way that we are lead into the fullness of this restoration joy. The words echo the message. Verse 5 says simply:

> May those who sow in tears,
> reap with shouts of joy.

The agricultural image is maintained in v. 6 giving rise to the suggestion that the psalm comes from a harvest context, used perhaps as a prayer for a successful harvest. The thoughts of v. 5 are extended in v. 6. 'May those who sow in tears' is expanded to 'Those who go out weeping, bearing the seed for sowing'. Sowing is an act of hope and expectation. The sower carries his/her future in their own hands. The seed must be cast abroad if anything is to come of it. At that point the sower's hope is taken out of their hands, and their future is dependent on the one who grants rain and warmth with which the seed might grow.

In this psalm the sower is said to sow in weeping. We do not know what the weeping is for. It could be that the act of sowing offers little prospect for the sower. The ground could seem dry and unreceptive. We have already noted that the language of restoration used in Psalm 126 is also found in Psalm 85, where it is connected to repentance. In that psalm there is reference to past sins and iniquities. It would not be too much to suggest that the language of weeping in Psalm 126 may be just as appropriate in the context of past sins and iniquities as in the context of dry, unreceptive ground. In ancient Israel, where some theological points of view associated various forms of hardship with sin,[33] the difference might have been slight. In any case, the use of the word *shub*, 'return, restore, or repent' invites us to play with all those ideas as we hear it. The psalm also suggests that an act of hope is not always one of high or joyous expectation. It also suggests that present distress or seeming hopelessness is not an argument for the denial of the Lord's power to effect change.[34]

Whatever the point of the weeping we soon see that deep despair can be turned into great celebration. 'Reap with shouts of joy' in v. 5 becomes 'shall come home with shouts of joy, carrying their sheaves' in v. 6. 'Going out' has become 'coming home', 'weeping' has turned into 'shouts of joy', and the seed that was just recently been carried out is now replaced by sheaves of grain.

In these last verses thoughts of 'coming home', of sheer joy, and of abundance fill the mind. They create a sense that what is a seemingly hopeless task is indeed a possibility. Moreover, its accomplishment can be sudden. This is the point of the reference to the 'watercourses of the Negeb' in v. 4. These dry wadis in a semi-arid region give little hint most of the time to the fact that they can overflow with water immediately after the rain comes. Finally, the seemingly hopeless task becomes one of overwhelming fruitfulness.

Psalm 126 possibly has an agricultural context. Even if this locates the psalm in a very different social context to those experienced by many readers today, it does, however, locate it in the midst of the day to day life of God's people. It fixes their hope in the coming of the Lord in the context of their struggles for security and subsistence. The great things of the Lord, for which the people hope, are not the miraculous events that transport them out of their daily existence into another world. The miraculous events they look for are in the transformation of the world they daily inhabit into that which God would have it be, a joyous and abundant place. While the psalmist seeks God's intervention so that the earth might yield a bountiful harvest for the benefit of God's people, there is nevertheless an intricate connection between God, people and 'nature' as we might call the world and its cycles of life. The proper restoration of the people requires the full yield of nature's bounty. The latter, in turn, is the proper concern of the people's prayer and worship as evidenced by the psalm. God relates to both people and nature, and the relationship between creatures is ultimately founded on their relationships with God. There is no presumption here of anthropocentrism, that is, a focus on humans as the be all and end all of creation. Nor is there any sense of nature as disconnected from human creatures. Rather, there is a three-way relationship focused around God.

Finally, we come back to v. 1 with its unusual and arresting expression:

> When the Lord restored the fortunes of Zion,
>   we were like those who dream.

---

[33] See for example Ps 37:28; Job 4:7-9; 8:20-22; and 11:13-20 etc. Cf. the associated view that obedience leads to well-being in e.g. Deut 7:12-15.

[34] Cf. Allen, *Psalms 101-150*, p. 175.

Commentators on the psalm have understood the reference to 'dreamers' in different ways. We could think of it in terms of those who are amazed at what has happened or who have not expected what did in fact happen.[35] But such understandings depend on a use of the word 'dream' in our modern world. When the Old Testament writers speak of 'dreaming' in a positive sense, as the psalmist does here, they are referring to real sleep-time dreams, not the sort of dreams we dream when awake, our 'day dreams'. They are speaking of a level of reality that was thought to be revealed by God in dreams. So in v. 1 the psalmist compares the people to those to whom God has revealed in dream, what God is about to do. W. Beyerlin argues this point in a short book on Psalm 126.[36] What is revealed in a dream is 'real' although it is still latent and hidden in the future from the perspective of human experience. In this context the present situation takes on a new dimension. He goes on to say that vv. 1-3 of the psalm refer both to the present and the future. He says: 'The dream like anticipating is in the present, the joy deriving from it is present, and the change of circumstances which God has already decided upon, still hidden in him but charismatically foreshadowed, is also present. But its manifestation in the ordinary world, and normal experience of it, is still in the future.'[37] While we would still want to stress that vv. 1-3 are about past experience, that past experience and the psalmist's hope for the future are both shaped by a reality perceived beyond present experience.

I have noted the similarity in opening statements between Psalm 126 and Psalm 85. The psalms are also similar in the way they juxtapose past deliverance and joy with present distress in the hope that there will be future joy. Both psalms have a sense of waiting and hoping for something that has in some way already been experienced. It is in this context that both have been set for Advent in the *Revised Common Lectionary*. Psalm 126 speaks of the hope that tears and weeping will be turned into joy and laughter through the restorative work of God. For that reason it is an appropriate psalm for preaching during Advent and Lent. It is in the context of tears and weeping for the world, and for our own brokenness, that we can look forward to the great thing God has done in Jesus Christ, both in his birth and in his death and resurrection.[38] In this context, the allusion to repentance in the word *šub* is far from out of place. The sense of waiting and expectation in the psalm also fits the times of Advent and Lent, as does the reference to being like dreamers. If we take Beyerlin's lead, we can see that what we await in Jesus Christ is a reality that has been revealed to us, and that we already experience the joy of his anticipated coming. Preaching from Psalm 126 would not only seek to give some sense of the unexpected yet real joy of what God seeks to do in the world. It would also need call the congregation to be like dreamers, whose lives are shaped not by the limits of their own experiences and visions but by the hidden reality of

---

[35] E.g. Westermann, C. (1989), *Living Psalms*, T. & T. Clark, Edinburgh, p. 48; Mays, *Psalms*, p. 399.

[36] Beyerlin, W. (1982), *We are Like Dreamers: Studies in Psalm 126*, T. & T. Clark, Edinburgh, pp. 15-23.

[37] *Ibid.*, pp. 22-23.

[38] Cf. Mays, *Psalms*, p. 400.

what God has already declared will be. It should also leave the congregation with a tremendous sense of joy in 'coming home' as the Lord comes to them in the midst of the tears of this earthly experience.

Psalm 139 – God Knowing Us

Life in the western world these days is a lot about the individual, their rights, and privacy. To some extent this is appropriate. We live in a world where many have been denied rights and privacy, and many an individual has suffered at the hands of powerful people, corporations, and countries. In general, however, the psalms and other Old Testament texts do not speak much about these matters. Issues of community or national concern are to the fore. Psalm 139 stands out as an exception, seeming to be the result of the self-reflection of an individual. But a note of caution is necessary because in its own way the psalm is about the invasion of our privacy – by God. While Psalm 139 is something of an exception in the Old Testament, it nevertheless still serves as a foil to the modern obsession with privacy and the individual. It does not deny the importance of the individual. In fact, it positively underlines it. But it also questions our rigorous pursuit of and desire for privacy, and whether it is ultimately in our best interest.

Psalm 139 is not an easy psalm with which to deal. For one thing it is not easy to determine what type of psalm we are working with, and hence where to start and what type of questions we should ask. It could be a complaint or protestation of innocence as some have suggested. Interpreters who take this line usually start with vv. 19-22 where we find a strident desire for God to kill the 'wicked'.[39] Therein lies another reason why this psalm is a difficult one; we have near its end one of the strongest expressions of vengeance we find in the whole book. We will return to this matter below. If vv. 19-22 are seen as the desperate wish of an innocent person, protesting the accusation of his or her accusers, then we could understand the place these verses have within the whole psalm.

The psalm is not easy to date either, but many would place it in the sixth century B.C.E., possibly just before the time of the exile. This is based on parallels with the books of Jeremiah and Job. The similarities between verses in the psalm and passages in Job especially could support the idea that the psalmist is suffering innocently.[40] However, we cannot tell if this is the case and there are a number of points that suggest we ought not to base our interpretation of the psalm on this assumption. Unlike psalms where the psalmist does vigorously defend his/her innocence (e.g. Pss 140-143), no specific threat to the psalmist is mentioned in Psalm 139, there is no reference to an accusation, nor is there a plea for God's help. On the contrary, the psalmist wants to flee from God (v. 7) and asks God to search him/her and root out any wicked way (vv. 23-24). This suggests that Psalm

---

[39] The strongest example of such an interpretation is that by Coote, R.B. (1991), 'Psalm 139' in D. Jobling et al., (eds), *The Bible and the Politics of Exegesis: Essays in Honor of Norman K. Gottwald on his Sixty-Fifth Birthday*, The Pilgrim Press, Cleveland, pp. 33-38.
[40] Cf. Ps 139:6 with Job 42:2-3; and vv. 13, 15 with Job 10:11.

139 is not a prayer by a person seeking help in the face of a particular crisis, but rather a more general prayer reflecting on the human situation. In other words, it is likely a wisdom psalm contemplating the relation of the individual to the transcendence and immanence of God. The connection with Job, especially chapter 10, would also fit here. Other passages that reflect on God's close scrutiny of the human life include Pss 11:4-5; 17:3; 26:2; Job 7:17-18; 13:9; and Jer 9:7; 17:10. There is also the possibility that the psalmist may have meditated on Psalm 8, with its view of humankind, 'just a little lower than the gods'. Finally, there is the difficulty that Psalm 139 poses problems for the translator in a number of verses.

The psalm breaks up into a number of sections. These are:

> vv. 1-6 The Lord's knowledge of the psalmist.
> vv. 7-14 The Lord's presence everywhere.[41]
> vv. 15-18 The Lord as the psalmist's creator.
> vv. 19-22 The psalmist's hatred of the Lord's enemies.
> vv. 23-24 The psalmist's desire to be known as righteous.

The psalm moves constantly forward with its on logic. The way the sections have been constructed helps this movement. Each of the first three sections ends with praise (vv. 6, 14, 17-18). Moreover, each of the first two strophes contains verses that foreshadow the next section: v. 5, 'You hem me in, behind and before, and lay your hand upon me' anticipates the psalmist's contemplation of flight from the Lord in vv. 7-13; and v. 13, 'For it was you who formed my inward parts; you knit me together in my mother's womb' foreshadows vv. 15-16. There is also an *inclusio* between vv. 1-3 and 23-24. It is focused around several words that appear at the beginning and end of the psalm: 'search', 'know', 'thoughts' (although a different word is used in each place), and 'way'. Also the Hebrew word *qûm* 'to rise up' is used in both v. 2 and v. 21, in the former in relation to the psalmist, and in the latter in regard to the wicked. So while the psalm moves us forward through the sections it also brings us to a conclusion that echoes the beginning. This is important for understanding what the psalm has to say to us.

Verses 19-22 stand out for their content as we have already noted. The repetition of the word for 'thoughts' in vv. 1 and 17 and also the note of praise struck in vv. 17-18, set vv. 19-22 off in other ways.[42] But that is not to say they are not part of the psalm as a whole. The *inclusio* between v. 1-2 and 23-24, as well as the repetition of 'to rise up' in vv. 2 and 21 as noted, signal that we have to read these startling verses in the context of the whole. They may rightly cause us some concern at first glance but the shape of the whole psalm will not allow us to excise them easily or just forget them. In terms of preaching from the psalm, the preacher is challenged to consider how these words might be understood and how the preacher might constructively deal with them in preaching.

---

[41] Many would break this section at v. 12, and have the next section as vv. 13-18, because of the reference to the Lord 'knitting the psalmist together' in v. 13.

[42] See also the work of Holman, J. (1971), 'The Structure of Psalm CXXXIX', *VT*, Vol. 21, pp. 298-310, for further thoughts on how vv. 19-24 function in the psalm.

The first two sections of the psalm have often been considered as clear statements of the Lord's omniscience and omnipresence. The Lord knows all about the psalmist (vv. 1-5), a knowledge that is 'wonderful' for the latter (v. 6), and wherever the psalmist goes, the Lord is there, which makes the psalmist proclaim his/her 'wonder' again (v. 14). But care must be taken here. The psalm does not want to make a statement about the Lord's omni-this or that. The psalm is not a philosophical or theological treatise on the nature of God.

What is essentially described in these verses is the complete knowledge the Lord has *of the psalmist* and the Lord's constant presence *with the psalmist*. It is talking about an extraordinarily intimate relationship, a deep sense of communion of one with another, of the 'I/me', the psalmist, with the 'thou', the Lord.[43] These pronouns pervade nearly every line of the psalm. This is not abstract knowledge of something, but rather knowledge of someone. The psalmist is speaking as much about his/her being known by the Lord as of the Lord knowing them. The Lord gains this knowledge by 'searching' it out, by exploring, investigating, or 'digging' it out.[44] It is not static knowledge, but rather knowledge gained through constant and thorough attention to the subject.

But how much intimacy, how much 'presence', can a relationship bear? Or more specifically, how much divine presence can the psalmist cope with? This is a major point of discussion among scholars. A number argue that the psalmist feels not only comfort and assurance as a result of the close scrutiny of the Lord, but also a good deal of intimidation, and resentment.[45] This may sound strange at first. The close presence and intimate knowledge that the Lord has of the psalmist would seem naturally to produce reassurance. On the other hand, to be open to constant scrutiny, especially by the one who judges all actions and thoughts, even the most private, could become unbearable.

The psalmist's inner feelings are expressed in two ways. The elements of praise in vv. 6, 14, 17-18, and the final petition for the Lord to search the psalmist out in vv. 23-24, express the comfort and assurance at the Lord's presence felt by the psalmist However, in v. 5 the psalmist also gives voice to a feeling of being 'hemmed in' and having the Lord's hand 'upon him'. The Hebrew word for 'to hem in' carries connotations of being confined, bound, or besieged. 'To lay a hand on' need not imply something negative, but it can (cf. Ps 38:2). At the very least v. 5 is an ambiguous statement, giving either a sense of security, or of being confined, and afflicted. Secondly, the psalmist asks in v. 7, 'Where can I go from your spirit? Or where can I flee from your presence?' While this could be a rhetorical question,

---

[43] See further Brown, W.P. (1996), 'Psalm 139', *Interpretation*, Vol. *50*/3, pp. 280-284, esp. p. 282; Terrien, S. (2003), *The Psalms: Strophic Structure and Theological Commentary*, Eerdmans, Grand Rapids, p. 879.

[44] The word *haqar* 'to search' can also carry the sense of exposing something, or even of mining, e.g. Ezek 39:14; Job 28:3.

[45] E.g. Broyles, C.C. (1999), *Psalms*, NIBC, Hendrickson, Peabody, MA, pp. 485-486; Terrien, *The Psalms*, pp. 876-877; and Mazor, Y. (1997), 'When Aesthetics is Harnessed to Psychological Characterization. "Ars Poetica" in Psalm 139', *ZAW*, Vol. 109, pp. 260-270, esp. pp. 260-262.

with the answer 'nowhere' understood without any negative connotation, that is not the only way in which the question can be heard. While the verb 'to go' would seem rather neutral, it is parallel to the verb 'to flee' which carries all the connotations of flight from danger. This same desire was evoked in Job at his plight (Job 7:17-21; 14:5-6). Moreover, going away from the Lord's spirit, and fleeing from the Lord's 'face', as it says in the Hebrew, are both the opposite of what might be expected. The spirit and face of the Lord both indicate acceptance and blessing when offered to a person.

In a sermon on Psalm 139, Paul Tillich captured this sense of the psalm extremely well.[46] He said that recognition of the fullness of the omnipresence of God or the omniscience of God leads to our desire to do away with God, to try to escape, and summarized: 'man cannot stand the God who is really God.'[47] He went on: 'Omniscience means that our mystery is manifest. Omnipresence means that our privacy is public.'[48]

There is a level of honesty in this psalm that touches the experience of many, and touches them deeply. We are reluctant to be known so well. There are things in our lives we keep hidden from others, even God. But if God is really the one we believe God to be then it follows that we are never out of the presence of God, or unknown to God. Nothing can separate from this God, nor can anything we do hide who we are from God. The psalmist talks about scaling the heavens, or descending to the depths of Sheol, of going to the farthest limits of the earth, or hiding in the darkest places, but none of these things will separate him/her from God. In our age we might speak about great acts of piety, or hiding in the very places where we least expect to encounter God in conversation or deed. But the psalmist would say that we cannot keep ourselves from the judging eye of God. To believe so is an act of hubris.

Such close scrutiny may well be fearful. But that is not all the psalmist has to say. There are also words in this psalm of great comfort and grace. After the psalmist contemplates possible escape from the Lord (vv. 7-9) he/she says that even in the remotest parts of the earth, the Lord will be there to lead them by the hand and to hold them fast. The presence of God, which is daunting to say the least, is also there for guidance and support. The same hand that is set upon the psalmist in v. 5, is there to guide and seize in a supportive way in v. 10.[49] The reason for this divine protection follows in vv. 13-16, for it was this same 'Hound of Heaven' who formed the psalmist in secret places, in the depths of the earth, and in the darkness of their mother's womb. The places of the psalmist's creation echo the places that will fail to hide the psalmist from the Lord in later life. Further, the verbs used to describe the creation of the psalmist, translated by 'knit' and 'weave' (vv. 13, 15), are verbs of manual dexterity. The hand that now seems oppressive (v.

---

[46] Tillich, P. (1949), 'The Escape from God', in *The Shaking of the Foundations*, SCM, London, pp. 38-51.

[47] *Ibid.*, p. 45.

[48] *Ibid.*, p. 46.

[49] See Mays, J.L. (1994), *Psalms*, John Knox, Louisville, who says on p. 429: 'The psalmist wants God to be his judge so that God can be his shepherd'.

5) not only leads but even once fashioned the psalmist. It does not catch the psalmist out in judgment, but creates and supports.[50] Alongside the fear of exposure that is felt before God, the psalmist also discovers God's graciousness.

Other points underline the reassurance associated with the Lord's presence and knowledge. I noted above that the word for 'thoughts' in v. 1, 'you discern my thoughts from far away', is repeated in v. 17, although there the psalmist says 'How weighty (precious) to me are your thoughts, O God!'. This sets up another *inclusio* within the psalm, this one around the first three sections. It contrasts the two sets of 'thoughts' – more correctly 'will' or 'plan'. The psalmist's own thoughts, intimately known by the Lord and, on the admission of the psalmist in v. 24, possibly even 'wicked', now give way to the precious nature of the Lord's thoughts in the psalmist's mind. The psalmist, so open and vulnerable before the Lord, is overwhelmed with praise and a desire for the one whose presence and knowledge also bring fear.

In addition, the verses of praise, which occur at the end of the first three sections, also balance the sense of dread in the psalmist. Verses 6 and 14 are joined together by the word 'wonderful' in reference to the Lord's works. The psalmist marvels at his own creation. That leads to praise and further wonder at all the Lord's work. The psalmist then declares 'Wonderful are your works; that I know very well'. The psalmist, who is known so well by the Lord, knows one thing himself or herself, namely, that the Lord's works are wonderful. That, of course, includes the psalmist who can even feel hemmed in by the Lord. Verse 18 presents problems of translation but is nevertheless important. Whether the psalmist 'comes to the end' or 'awakens', as is more likely the translation (probably from sleep), he/she knows that they are still with the Lord.[51] The order of the pronouns is important. We might expect that since it is the Lord who pursues the psalmist wherever the latter tries to go, the psalmist would say '*you* are still with *me*'. But no, it is '*I* am still with *you*'. The psalmist has realized that nothing will separate him/her from the Lord, not even the things the Lord will discover about the psalmist. We might wonder, from our modern perspective, whether the oppression and the desire for flight that the psalmist expresses, are not somehow bound up with a fear that openness before God will lead to an awareness of self that is too hard to bear. But even from this perspective, the psalmist would still stress the reassuring wonder of the Lord's creation and support.

The psalm speaks boldly about the Lord's presence with us, and knowledge of us. As one writer puts it the psalm 'is a celebration of God's invasion of our privacy'.[52] This invasion is, however, for the purpose of leading. If it is for judgment ('searching', 'digging' etc.) then that judgment is for the purpose of furthering communion and relationship. We are not created by God to be 'private'

---

[50] Cf. Brown, W.P. (2000), '*Creatio Corporis* and the Rhetoric of Defense in Job 10 and Psalm 139', in W.P. Brown and S. D McBride (eds), *God who Creates: Essays in Honor of W. Sibley Towner*, Eerdmans, Grand Rapids, pp. 107-124, esp. p. 111.

[51] Terrien, *The Psalms*, p. 881 notes that the Latin translation of 'When I awake' in v. 17 ('*Resurrexi*') led to the attribution of the verse to Christ at Easter.

[52] Brown, 'Psalm 139', p. 282.

individuals, seeking an end in self-autonomy. We are created for relationship with the Lord, and while that may be daunting on occasion, it is cause for wonder and praise. J.L. Mays has remarked that Psalm 139 'reflects an understanding of the human enclosed in divine reality. ... the Lord as the total environment of life.'[53] At times, when feeling totally isolated and abandoned even by God the psalmist may despise their life: 'But I am a worm, and not human; scorned by others, and despised by the people' (Ps 22:6). But such statements are made in times of isolation. In Psalm 139, wonder and praise at their own creation leads the psalmist to praise the Lord. In his sermon Paul Tillich, having underlined the desire of the psalmist to escape God, goes on to say that as the psalmist contemplates his/her own creation by God, admiration of the divine wisdom overcomes the horror of the divine presence and the psalmist reflects on the friendly presence of the infinite creative wisdom.[54]

I have noted that a source of consternation in the psalm is the sentiment expressed in vv. 19-22. It is understandable that many would want to shun thoughts of killing when they invade marvelous words of faith. A similar thing happens at the very end of Psalm 104 in v. 35. Reconciling these thoughts with a desire to be near God may not be possible for some, but the Bible is not a book that expects compliance at every turn. It provokes thought about God and seeks to promote faith and it does not always do it with 'positive' thoughts and cheerful statements. Nevertheless, we ought not to dismiss vv. 19-22 without thinking carefully about them.

First, we should note that the psalmist is not speaking primarily about his or her own enemies but about those who oppose God. They are the psalmist's enemies only because by their actions they first oppose, lie about, and promote themselves against God. Secondly, vv. 19-20 is not so much a firm petition as a wish.[55] Although, this does not lessen the sentiment as the psalmist's hatred of God's enemies is hardly qualified in vv 21-22. Thirdly, vv. 19-22 must be read in the context of what follows. Having made the harsh statement in vv. 19-22 the psalmist then wishes that God would search them again:

> [23] Search me, O God, and know my heart;
> test me and know my thoughts.
> [24] See if there is any wicked way in me,
> and lead me in the way everlasting.

Even this last wish of the psalmist is put under the scrutiny of God's searching presence and knowledge. This sentiment, no less than any other the psalmist might utter or think, is subject to the searching and testing of God. Not only does the psalmist desire the wicked to be removed, but he/she also desires that any wicked way in him/herself be removed. We could ask does the psalmist's desire for God to kill the wicked come into the category of a 'wicked way'? From

---

[53] Mays, *Psalms*, p. 425.
[54] Tillich, 'The Escape from God', p. 48.
[55] This is noted by a few scholars, e.g. Broyles, *The Psalms*, p. 486.

our Christian perspective it might very well. The psalmist, while honest before God in terms of the thoughts he/she has, is also open to having all those thoughts scrutinized by God.[56]

The palmist comes full circle in the psalm. From being searched by the Lord, and then seeking to escape, to desiring that very same scrutiny but with the recognition that the one who does the searching desires to lead the psalmist (v. 10). So the psalmist surrenders to God's presence and asks to be lead in the everlasting way. The psalmist seeks a furthering of the communion between them.

Psalm 139 presents a text for preaching which involves self-reflection. A sermon on the psalm should in some way model that process. It offers a chance to echo possibly unspoken thoughts about the inescapable presence and knowledge of God, especially as it relates to matters we keep deeply within ourselves. On the other hand, it offers the opportunity to affirm that such close scrutiny is for the purpose of a deeper communion. It affirms the wonder of the human form and nature and sees that not as an opportunity for self-aggrandisement or absorption, but rather as a source of praise of God. The inherent worth that the psalmist feels, in spite of the sense of close divine judgment, is not only something applicable for the psalmist. It raises the question of the inherent worth of all people of integrity, a worth based in God's presence with and knowledge of all peoples. At the moment in my own country the psalm challenges how the majority relates specifically to indigenous people, asylum seekers, and many other groups.

There is also an opportunity in preaching on this psalm to relate the communion about which the psalmist speaks to that we have with God in Jesus Christ. Paul expresses in christological terms a sentiment similar to that found in the psalm:

> For I am convinced that neither death, nor life, nor angels, nor rulers, nor things present, nor things to come, nor powers, nor height, nor depth, nor anything else in all creation, will be able to separate us from the love of God in Christ Jesus our Lord. (Rom 8:38-39)

The incarnation of God the Son in Jesus is itself a drawing close to humankind, and a deep searching out and knowing of humanity by God. The prayer that the psalmist prays at the end, that God might continue to search them out and see if there is any 'wicked way' in them has already been answered in Jesus Christ. In fact, in Jesus Christ not only does God search us out but he has even borne the 'wicked way' that we all share and provided the leading in the 'way everlasting' that is our salvation. In Christian terms, the deep communion between God and God's people about which Psalm 139 speaks, is fulfilled in the communion we have in Jesus Christ, and the leading toward which all the searching and knowing moves, is found in the bread and wine that are the food of our pilgrimage, and in the 'way' of Jesus which is our discipleship. The modern pursuit of and desire for privacy, which the psalm counters, is, in fact, counter to the work of God in the redemption of creation.

---

[56] Cf. Terrien, *The Psalms*, p. 879.

Appendix

Types of Psalms

Torah Psalms

    1, 19*, 119

Royal Psalms

    2, 18, 20, 21, 45, 72, 89, 101, 110, 132, 144

Individual Laments

    3, 4, 5, 7, 9-10, 11, 12, 13, 14, 17, 22, 25, 26, 27, 28, 31, 35, 39, 41, 42-43, 53, 54, 55, 56, 57, 59, 61, 64, 69, 70, 71, 77, 86, 88, 109, 120, 140, 141, 142

Community Laments

    44, 58, 60, 74, 79, 80, 83, 85, 90, 94, 123, 126, 129, 137

Hymns and Prayers of Praise

    8, 19*, 29, 33, 65, 66, 67, 76, 84, 95, 100, 103, 104, 111, 113, 114, 117, 134, 145, 146, 147, 148, 149, 150

Songs of the Lord's Kingship

    47, 93, 96, 97, 98, 99

Thanksgiving Psalms

    30, 32*, 34, 40, 75, 92, 107, 116, 118, 124, 138

Liturgies

    15, 24, 81

Psalms of Trust

    16, 23, 62, 63, 91, 115, 121, 125, 131

Penitential Psalms

     6, 32, 38, 51, 102, 130, 143

Songs of Zion

     46, 48, 87, 122

Psalms Telling of Israel's History

     78, 105, 106, 135, 136

Wisdom Psalms

     36, 37, 49, 52, 73, 112, 127, 128, 133, 139

Other Mixed Psalms

     50, 68, 82, 108

Psalms marked with (*) have sections belonging to more than one type.

Select Bibliography

Commentaries

Allen, L.C. (1983), *Psalms 100-150*, Word, Waco.
Broyles, C.C. (1999), *Psalms*, Hendrickson, Peabody.
Clifford, R.J. (2002), *Psalms 1-72*, Abingdon, Nashville.
Clifford, R.J. (2003), *Psalms 73-150*, Abingdon, Nashville.
Craigie, P.C. (1983), *Psalms 1-50*, Word, Waco.
Craigie, P.C. (2004), *Psalms 1-50*, 2nd ed. with supplement by M.E. Tate, Nelson Reference & Electronic, n.p.
Davidson, R. (1998), *The Vitality of Worship: A Commentary on the Book of Psalms*, Eerdmans, Grand Rapids.
Limburg, J. (2000), *Psalms*, Westminster John Knox, Louisville.
Mays, J.L. (1994), *Psalms*, John Knox, Louisville.
Schaefer, K. (2001), *Psalms*, Liturgical Press, Collegeville.
Tate, M.E. (1990), *Psalms 51-100*, Word, Waco.
Terrien, S.L. (2003), *The Psalms: Strophic Structure and Theological Commentary*, Eerdmans, Grand Rapids.

General Introductions

Allen, L.C. (1987), *Psalms*, Biblical Word Themes, Word, Waco.
Anderson, B.W. with Bishop, S. (2000), *Out of the Depths: The Psalms Speak for us Today*, 3rd. ed., rev'd and expanded, Westminster John Knox, Louisville.
Bellinger, W.H. (1990), *Psalms: Reading and Studying the Book of Praises*, Hendrickson, Peabody.
Brueggemann, W. (1984), *The Message of the Psalms*, Augsburg, Minneapolis.
Bullock, C.H. (2001), *Encountering the Book of Psalms: A Literary and Theological Introduction*, Baker Book House, Grand Rapids.
Craghan, J.F. (1988), *The Psalms: Prayers for the Ups, Downs and In-betweens of Life*, Glazier, Wilmington, IN.
Crenshaw, J.L. (2001), *The Psalms: An Introduction*, Eerdmans, Grand Rapids.
de-Claissé-Walford, N.L. (2004), *Introduction to the Psalms: A Song from Ancient Israel*, Chalice Press, St. Louis.
Hunter, A.G. (1999), *Psalms*, Routledge, London.
Jinkins, M. (1998), *In the House of the Lord: Inhabiting the Psalms of Lament*, The Liturgical Press, Collegeville, MN.
Lewis, C.S. (1958), *Reflections on the Psalms*, Geoffrey Bles, London.
Magonet, J. (1994), *A Rabbi Reads the Psalms*, SCM, London.
McCann, J.C. (1993), *A Theological Introduction to the Book of Psalms: The Psalms as Torah*, Abingdon, Nashville.
Miller, P.D. (1986), *Interpreting the Psalms*, Fortress, Philadelphia.
Parrish, V.S. (2004), *A Story of the Psalms: Conversation, Canon, and Congregation*, Liturgical Press, Collegeville.

Pleins, J.D. (1993), *The Psalms: Songs of Tragedy, Hope, and Justice*, Orbis, Maryknoll.

Psalms, Worship and Theology

Bonhoeffer, D. (1970), *The Psalms: The Prayer Book of the Bible*, Augsburg, Minneapolis.

Bradshaw, P.F. (1995), *Two Ways of Praying*, Abingdon, Nashville.

Brueggemann, W. (1988), *Israel's Praise: Doxology against Idolatry and Ideology*, Fortress, Philadelphia.

Brueggemann, W. (1982), *Praying the Psalms*, St. Mary's, Winona.

Brueggemann, W. (1995), *The Psalms and the Life of Faith*, P.D. Miller (ed.), Fortress, Minneapolis.

Brueggemann, W. (2001), *Spirituality of the Psalms*, Fortress, Philadelphia.

Capps, D. (1981), *Biblical Approaches to Pastoral Counselling*, Westminster, Philadelphia.

Collins, D.E. (1991), *Like Trees that Grow beside a Stream: Praying through the Psalms*, Upper Room Books, Nashville.

Craven, T. (1992), *The Book of Psalms*, Message of Biblical Spirituality 6, Liturgical Press, Collegeville, MN.

Goldingay, J. (1993), *Praying the Psalms*, Vol. 44, *Grove Spirituality Series*, Grove Books, Bramcote.

Green, B. (1994), *Like a Tree Planted: An Exploration of Psalms and Parables through Metaphor*, Liturgical Press, Collegeville, MN.

Guiver, G. (1988), *Company of Voices: Daily Prayer and the People of God*, SPCK, London.

Israel, M. (1990), *A Light on the Path: An Exploration of Integrity through the Psalms*, DLT, London.

Knight, J.C. and Sinclair, L.A. (eds) (1990), *The Psalms and Other Studies on the Old Testament Presented to Joseph I. Hunt*, Nashotah House Seminary, Nashotah.

Levine, H.J. (1995), *Sing unto God a New Song: A Contemporary Reading of the Psalms*, Indiana University, Bloomington.

Mays, J.L. (1994), *The Lord Reigns: A Theological Handbook to the Psalms*, Westminster John Knox, Louisville.

McCutchan, S.P. (2000), *Experiencing the Psalms: Weaving the Psalms into your Ministry and Faith*, Smyth & Helwys, Macon, GA.

Petersen, E.H. (1989), *Answering God: The Psalms as Tools for Prayer*, Harper & Row, San Francisco.

Reid, S.B. (2001), *Psalms and Practice: Worship, Virtue, and Authority*, Liturgical Press, Collegeville, MN.

Rienstra, M.V. (1992), *Swallows Nest: A Feminine Reading of the Psalms*, Eerdmans, Grand Rapids.

Shepherd, M.H. (1976), *The Psalms in Christian Worship: A Practical Guide*, Augsburg Minneapolis.

Zenger, E. (1996), *A God of Vengeance? Understanding the Psalms of Divine Wrath*, trans. L.M. Maloney, Westminster John Knox, Louisville.

General Index

Index of Authors

Index of Scriptures